T0311528

Frugal Innovation

In light of growing discourse on 'frugal innovation', this book offers novel approaches to innovation based on extensive empirical research. The study complements a decade of scholarly attention on frugal innovation by taking a research-based approach to innovation in resource-scarce and complex institutional contexts. The findings suggest that concepts such as frugal, reverse, *jugaad*, social, grass-roots and inclusive innovation in fact represent heterogeneous assemblies of innovation for social, environmental and economic value. The conceptual framework invites attention to more plural sources and elements in the study of models of innovation to inspire further research in the fields of strategy, innovation, entrepreneurship, economic sociology and development studies. The design framework offers models, metrics and competencies for practitioners and policy-makers to identify, evaluate and design frugal innovations. The comprehensive view of frugal innovation demonstrates how firms can implement globally competitive strategies by pursuing innovation for humanity to improve lives for everyone, everywhere.

YASSER BHATTI completed his graduate studies in strategy, innovation and entrepreneurship at the University of Oxford, jointly at the Saïd Business School and Green Templeton College. His research interests in the fields of innovation, entrepreneurship and strategy focus on innovation under constraints, the localisation and globalisation of innovation, and the role of emerging market economies and situated actors (such as social entrepreneurs) in emerging trends in innovation, particularly frugal and reverse innovation. He has served on the scientific advisory board of the European Commission Project on Frugal Innovation and holds research and teaching affiliations with the University of Oxford, Imperial College London, Warwick University and Queen Mary University of London.

RADHA RAMASWAMI BASU has over forty years of experience in technology innovation and management. She is widely recognised as a leading female entrepreneur in hi-tech companies and as a pioneer in the Indian software business. Radha is founder and CEO of iMerit Inc., a technology services company (www.iMerit.net) that pioneers the 'smart sourcing model', working on latest AI, machine learning and ecommerce services for global clients. Radha was Founder and Director of the Frugal Innovation Lab at Santa Clara University and sits on the boards of NetHope, Santa Clara University Miller Center for Social Entrepreneurship and Jhumki Basu Foundation. She has won numerous awards including the first UN Women GEMTECH award, Excelsior Leadership, Top25 Women of the Web, CEO of the Year 2000 and Leader of the Millennium.

DAVID BARRON is a Rhodes Trust Associate Professor in Organisational Sociology at the Saïd Business School, University of Oxford, as well as the Vice Principal and a Fellow and Tutor in Management Studies at Jesus College, Oxford. After graduating from Cambridge in 1979 with a degree in natural sciences, he worked for several years as a social worker in Scotland and London, before completing his MA and PhD in sociology at Cornell University. David Barron's research is concerned with the sociology of organisations, quantitative research methods and social networks.

MARC J. VENTRESCA is an Associate Professor of Strategic Management, Saïd Business School, University of Oxford, and a Governing Body Fellow of Wolfson College. He is also Senior Research Fellow at the Technology and Management Centre for Development at Queen Elizabeth House. His research and teaching focuses on innovation, institutions and infrastructure, with empirical work on emerging technologies and nascent markets. He earned degrees at Stanford University, is an economic and organisational sociologist and a specialist on innovation strategy and entrepreneurial ecosystems. Ventresca joined Oxford in 2004, after serving on the faculty at the University of Illinois, Northwestern University and the University of California.

Policymakers around the world and especially in emerging markets can leverage frugal innovations to better promote human welfare. The models and tools in this book should support leaders in their efforts to foster equitable growth and sustainable development.

– Shaukat Aziz, Chairman of the Oxford Emerging Markets Symposium Steering Committee and former Prime Minister of Pakistan

This book should give tremendous impetus for serious and rigorous academic research on innovation under severe constraints.

– Vijay Govindarajan, Coxe Distinguished Professor at Tuck, Dartmouth and author of the New York Times *best seller,* Reverse Innovation

This book complements previous books in helping to establish frugal innovation as a field that merits serious attention in the diverse worlds of academia, practice and policy. It extends prior work by developing models, frameworks and tools to help scholars, innovators and managers to deliver meaningful and much needed innovation for all of humanity.

– Jaideep Prabhu, Professor of Marketing at Judge Business School, Cambridge and co-author of best sellers Jugaad Innovation *and* Frugal Innovation

To solve the wicked problems confronting humanity and the planet, we need frugal innovators –wise problems solvers who operate with a business mind, social heart, and ecological soul. Building on earlier works on frugal innovation, this scholarly book offers a rigorous theoretical framework to understand, teach, and practice the art and science of designing and delivering frugal solutions that integrate six key elements: affordability, accessibility, simplicity, sustainability, quality, and purpose.

– Navi Radjou, Fellow at Judge Business School, University of Cambridge and co-author of best sellers Jugaad Innovation *and* Frugal Innovation

Frugal innovation is a topic of considerable interest to companies, policy makers and researchers. It offers both innovation to connect the poorest and most disadvantaged citizens to the benefits of new products and services and opportunities for firms to identify new and potentially lucrative markets. This important book offers important new conceptual and practical insights into frugal innovation and should be seen as essential reading for anyone engaging with this topic.

– *Alex Nicholls, Professor of Social Entrepreneurship, Saïd Business School and Fellow in Management, Harris Manchester College, University of Oxford*

Targeted to scholars and providing a solid foundation for future research, *Frugal Innovation* also offers keen insights on how social entrepreneurs conceive of innovation in multiple dimensions. Practitioners will find experience-based frameworks that help them synthesize and communicate the integrative nature of innovations that benefit the underserved. Like social entrepreneurship, 'frugal innovation' is a term with many meanings. Integrative, synthetic, and clear, the authors examine multiple dimensions of innovation and distill frugal innovation as a hybrid approach tuned to environments with extreme resource constraints and resource voids. Both researchers and practitioners will benefit from learning how social entrepreneurs themselves perceive innovation.

– *Thane Kreiner, Howard and Alida Charney University Professor and Executive Director, Miller Center for Social Entrepreneurship, Santa Clara University*

New models of innovation are desperately needed in global health systems which are being squeezed by increasing demand, declining budgets and rising complexity of disease. This book shows how frugal innovations can play a vital role in containing soaring healthcare costs while upholding quality standards, which simply cannot be compromised in healthcare.

– *Ara Darzi, Professor of Surgery at Imperial College London, member of the United Kingdom's House of Lords and former Parliamentary Under-Secretary of State at the Department of Health*

Frugal Innovation: Models, Means, Methods is a must-read for academics, entrepreneurs, corporates and investors. It will advance how to get to inclusive solutions not merely based on cost effectiveness and financial returns but combining them with purpose and impact. This book shows that frugal innovation is not just another innovation term, but that empirically based models and theories that the authors have proposed will help enable creating and scaling solutions under resource constraints both by social entrepreneurs and traditional businesses.

– Venkata Gandikota, President and Co-Founder, The Nordic Frugal Innovation Society

This book is needed! The marrying of social value and business value has gained steam in many circles with a focus on value – both human and economic. Frugal Innovation widens the path for intrepid innovators by grounding insightful conceptual frameworks upon an extensive base of empirical evidence.

– Kristian Olson, Director of the Consortium for Affordable Medical Technologies and Associate Professor, Harvard University Medical School

Frugal Innovation
Models, Means, Methods

YASSER BHATTI
University of Oxford

RADHA RAMASWAMI BASU
iMerit Technology Services

DAVID BARRON
University of Oxford

MARC J. VENTRESCA
University of Oxford

CAMBRIDGE
UNIVERSITY PRESS

CAMBRIDGE
UNIVERSITY PRESS

University Printing House, Cambridge CB2 8BS, United Kingdom

One Liberty Plaza, 20th Floor, New York, NY 10006, USA

477 Williamstown Road, Port Melbourne, VIC 3207, Australia

314-321, 3rd Floor, Plot 3, Splendor Forum, Jasola District Centre, New Delhi - 110025, India

103 Penang Road, #05-06/07, Visioncrest Commercial, Singapore 238467

Cambridge University Press is part of the University of Cambridge.

It furthers the University's mission by disseminating knowledge in the pursuit of education, learning and research at the highest international levels of excellence.

www.cambridge.org
Information on this title: www.cambridge.org/9781316638644
DOI: 10.1017/9781316986783

First published 2018
First paperback edition 2022

A catalogue record for this publication is available from the British Library

Library of Congress Cataloging in Publication data
Names: Bhatti, Yasser Ahmad, 1975- author. | Basu, Radha, author.
Title: Frugal innovation : Models, Means, Methods / Yasser Bhatti,
    University of Oxford, Radha Basu, iMerit Inc., California, David Barron,
    University of Oxford, Marc Ventresca, University of Oxford.
Description: New York : Cambridge University Press, 2018. | Includes
    bibliographical references and index.
Identifiers: LCCN 2017055914 | ISBN 9781107188976 (hardback)
Subjects: LCSH: Creative ability in business. | Thriftiness.
Classification: LCC HD53 .B518 2018 | DDC 658.4/063–dc23
LC record available at https://lccn.loc.gov/2017055914

ISBN 978-1-107-18897-6 Hardback
ISBN 978-1-316-63864-4 Paperback

We dedicate this book to the late Pamela Hartigan, who spread her optimism far and wide to help make a better world, served by better business.

Entrepreneurs, whether primarily commercial or social in orientation, are cut from the same cloth: resourceful, pragmatic, innovative and opportunity-oriented. All entrepreneurs need to keep in mind social and financial goals. Social entrepreneurs prioritise social gain and pursue financial gain to sustain and expand their social mission and its growth.

– Dr Pamela Hartigan, 1948–2016
Director, Skoll Centre for Social Entrepreneurship at the
Saïd Business School, University of Oxford

Contents

Figures

Tables

Foreword

You are holding in your hands one of the most extensive studies of what has come to be called 'frugal innovation'. Rooted in several years of sustained empirical work, this volume deals comprehensively with the various constructs associated with low-cost innovation in resource scarce and institutionally complex contexts. The authors reveal the many facets of frugal innovation through a process of discovery grounded in practices of social entrepreneurs, and in prior studies by academics. The result is real progress: understanding what frugal innovation means and why it is important – and why it should be important – to innovation scholars, practitioners and policymakers.

Doctoral students and scholars will find the surveys of the literature and theory to be essential resources for understanding frugal innovation and related constructs. For those seeking to advance knowledge about frugal innovation, primary and secondary case studies offer fascinating opportunities to understand how this idea is implemented in practice. The authors draw on the literature and experiences of actual innovators to build a theoretical framework for scholars who seek to increase the body of knowledge about this concept. In addition to identifying what frugal innovation is and means, the authors test the boundaries of the idea, and then offer a series of tools for practitioners seeking to implement frugal innovation as a process.

The ideas that permeate this book reflect that low-cost innovation is fundamentally about change that does not drive more luxury but focuses on equitability. In the end, the phenomenon raises fundamental questions about the purpose of the systems of innovation that dominate the landscape of change in most established contexts. Innovation under principles of frugality leads to foundational questions about the purpose of the system that we customarily rely upon to generate change. At its heart, frugal innovation challenges orthodoxy.

Anita McGahan
Rotman Chair in Management and Professor of Strategic Management at Rotman School of Management, University of Toronto

Preface

Almost a decade has passed since the idea of frugal innovation began to be globally recognised. With so much already achieved, this is an opportune time to further help to authenticate the growing but occasionally confusing frugal innovation agenda for researchers, practitioners and policymakers. This book complements other books on frugal innovation by breaking critical ground in drawing from the perspectives of social entrepreneurs as a focal lens to base pluralistic arguments for frugal innovation underpinned by empirical research and theory development. It builds on and extends original doctoral thesis by Dr Yasser Bhatti, successfully defended at the Saïd Business School, University of Oxford in the summer of 2014.

Social entrepreneurs, as well as multinational firms, are creating the market for frugal innovations – potentially profitable and socially valuable solutions that are affordable, adaptable and accessible. Often, frugal innovations are the result of efforts to tackle local problems of global concern in the fields of education, healthcare and housing. By starting our analysis with social entrepreneurs and building on the assumption that they carry out social innovation, we transition to frugal innovation as a concept that helps to capture the plural sources and elements of innovation, beyond just social innovation, that they actually see as important in their work, context and indeed as occurring around them. As a unique source transcending private and public sectors, they provide fresh insights on broader issues of equitable and sustainable growth through innovation which is becoming increasingly important for markets, civil society and governments.

Our research shows how the emerging trend in frugal innovation deals with, makes use of and overcomes resource constraints and institutional voids to create social value and generate profit, the former improving lives and the latter making solutions sustainable. We discuss how the concept of frugal innovation (defined through the findings of this study) compares with the nuanced meanings found in the existing literature and argue that frugal innovation is best construed as 'means and ends to do more with less for the many', thereby moving beyond the view that frugal is mainly about cost, affordability or simply constraint.

With conceptual frameworks and theoretical models, the primary audience for this book consists of strategic management researchers and organisational theorists studying: (i) strategy and innovation; (ii) social entrepreneurship; (iii) development studies; (iv) sustainability and (v) design and engineering. The presentation style, arguments and analyses are tailored for academic researchers and policymakers, as well as for postgraduate MSc and PhD candidates writing research-based dissertations.

In addition, with design frameworks and practical models, this book also provides tools to help practitioners and policymakers to identify, measure and evaluate frugal innovations. It aims to create awareness among entrepreneurs and firms of ways to improve lives by providing greater social value. Given increasing competition from low-cost global competitors, this study should help businesses and social entrepreneurs, as well as large firms, to learn about core competencies associated with frugal innovation to become more globally competitive. The findings can benefit practitioners and policymakers in the following ways:

- Entrepreneurs of all kinds, whether primarily social, such as Jacqueline Novogratz of the Acumen Fund, or commercial, such as Elon Musk of Tesla Motors, who seek to maximise the triple bottom-line benefit to profits, people and the planet by doing more with less for many;
- Firms and organisations that support and promote frugal innovation, including TATA (India), General Electric (USA), Haier (China), Danfoss (Denmark), Nissan (Japan) and many others, as well as those adopting frugal innovation strategies to discover new markets and applications abroad or at home;

- Policymakers and think tanks, such as the European Commission Directorate-General of Research and Innovation (Belgium), NESTA (UK), Social Innovation Generation (Canada), the Rockefeller Foundation (USA), the SERCO Institute (UK), the Schwab Foundation for Social Entrepreneurship (Switzerland) and the Grameen Foundation (Bangladesh and global) that seek to promote inclusive growth and development through business.

We hope that this book will advance the academic research agenda in innovation studies and raise awareness in both the practice and policymaking communities. There is still much work to be done and we invite readers to share their views with us so that we can collectively advance knowledge about innovation and for humanity.

Acknowledgements

We are grateful to Paula Parish, Valerie Appleby and their team at Cambridge University Press for encouraging us to publish this work and to Zoe Swenson-Wright and Wendy Nardi for editorial proofreading and indexing. We also thank faculty colleagues who have offered critical insight and inspiration at various points: Pamela Hartigan, Guillermo Casasnovas, Silvia Dorado, Sue Dopson, Tim Morris, Ray Loveridge, Afua Osei, Ara Darzi, Greg Parston, Matthew Harris, James Barlow, Matthew Prime, Mokter Hossain, Jacqueline del Castillo and Abrar Chaudhry. We acknowledge support from Xiaolan Fu, Shaista Khilji, Preeta Banerjee, Peter Hesseldahl, Sanjay Jain, Rajnish Tiwari, Cornelius Herstatt, Shahzad Ansari, Anita McGahan and William Oliver who helped us to organize a symposium on frugal innovation at the 2013 Academy of Management annual meeting. We are grateful to colleagues Jonathan Levie, Mark Hart, Eric Carlson, Godfrey Mungal, Thane Kreiner, James Koch, Geoffrey Desa, Elizabeth Sweeny, Cassandra Staff, Katrina Jazayeri, Woody Powell, Jim Patell, Johanna Mair, Ignasi Marti, Paolo Quattrone, Ingrid Lunt, Chris Sauer and Marc Thompson, who worked with us in conference settings and other contexts, and to Jaideep Prabhu, Alex Nicholls, Rafael Ramirez, Barbara Harrell-Bond, Ian Scott and especially Louise Ventresca and Muhammad Sharif Bhatti, as well as all those, including the research respondents and the Ednamary crowd, who supported the original research and development of this book. We also acknowledge funding from the Higher Education Commission of Pakistan, Green Templeton College, Skoll Centre for Social Entrepreneurship, Saïd Business School Research Assistance Fund and Miller Center for Social Entrepreneurship at Santa Clara University that helped to support the research underpinning this book.

Abbreviations

BOP	Base of the Pyramid
EDEA	Entrepreneurial Design for Extreme Affordability
FIL	Frugal Innovation Lab
GSBI	Global Social Business Incubator
RBV	Resource-Based View
SCU	Santa Clara University
SE	Social Entrepreneur/ship
TCA	Thematic Content Analysis

Introduction

In this book, we reveal the multitude of models, means, methods, as well as measures that make innovation meaningful for the masses. We advance a view of frugal innovation that reconnects this idea both with social theory and with practical action, and that challenges the often accepted view that associates 'frugal' mostly with cost – perhaps frugal innovation is much more complex than that. This is why we took a more grounded approach and included the context of the innovation in our conceptual model, rather than focusing on the innovation per se. We view frugal innovation as innovation for humanity comprised of multidimensional innovations in technology, social, institutional and business model. We come to this finding by investigating how social entrepreneurs conceptualise innovation, both broadly and specifically, under extreme contexts marked by institutional voids and resource scarcity. We explore these issues by using qualitative, descriptive and analytical methods to study globally networked and formally recognised social entrepreneurs. Our analysis focuses on the meso level of innovation and value chains, incorporating micro-level observations through document analysis, interviews and observations. To extend our understanding of purposeful innovation carried out in challenging contexts, we connect the theoretical framing of innovation in extreme contexts with research on social and purposeful innovation.

The approach we have taken in this study moves away from a traditional focus on Taylorian efficiency or multinational companies (MNC) towards an examination of purposeful and social impact in constraint-based contexts that market-based approaches would consider extreme. Frugal innovation entails a process of problem solving in which the needs and contexts of developing world or marginalised consumers are put first. The frugal innovator develops accessible, adaptable, affordable and appropriate technologies, products and solutions to address human needs in emerging markets as well as developed markets. The efficiency approach has often been under-contextual; the social approach is analytically useful because it prompts researchers to be more explicit about contingencies, process and local variation. The case of innovation by social entrepreneurs working in developing or emerging markets is one such useful context for studying the social approach. The focus on learning from social entrepreneurs provides a different, useful and extensive empirical base. Therefore, this work is novel in that it (1) starts from different theoretical premises; (2) engages more directly with the constraint and void aspects of context for a 'process' rethink; and (3) proposes fresh and integrative dimensions for frugal innovation.

Since its debut in 2010, literature about frugal innovation has relied on anecdotal examples or conceptual studies, often lacking strong theoretical foundations and generally reducing frugal innovation to cost or affordablility. Much work cites examples of frugal innovation without providing a clear basis for the choice of cases or labels and often cite many of the same examples. Perhaps for these reasons, while the rate of publication on this topic is increasing, frugal innovation has not yet found much exposure in top journals (such as the chartered Association of Business Schools list of four-star journals, or the Financial Times list of fifty journals used to rank business schools). We are hopeful that this book will contribute to changing the situation, by providing an extensive empirical account derived from innovators, building a theoretical foundation from those insights to pave the way for further empirical work which can help to bring a higher level of exposure to the field. Our approach to understanding frugal innovation is based on the assumption that this type of innovation is multidimensional and obliquitous. Obliquity is characteristic of systems that are complex, imperfectly understood, and that change their nature as we engage with them.

It is most challenging in extreme contexts shaped by the simultaneous challenges of resource constraints and institutional voids. Despite some discussion of innovation in extreme contexts in the

development literature, organisation theory and strategic management researchers rarely touch on this aspect of innovation. Although
social entrepreneurs are credited with creating social innovation,
we know little about their views. Our analysis supports claims that
actors are devising new innovation processes (means) and outcomes
(ends) to generate business and social wealth. Social entrepreneurs, as
well as multinational firms, grassroots organisations and networks of
innovators, are creating the market for frugal innovations – potentially profitable and socially valuable solutions that are affordable,
adaptable and accessible. And they are supported by a growing cadre
of funders characterised as impact investors or social venture capitalists. This form of socially responsible investing spurs and supports
frugal innovations that often result from tackling local problems of
global concern in diverse fields such as education, healthcare,
housing and transportation.

This study contributes to developing models of innovation
in contexts shaped by institutional voids or complexities and resource
scarcity. It reveals how social entrepreneurs perceive the conceptual
drivers, determinants and features of innovation. Social entrepreneurs
are involved in more than social innovation. They assemble offerings
and ventures that may combine varied innovation approaches,
are often more concerned about institutional and social innovation
than about technology innovation per se, and often pack combinations of innovations into emerging concepts that resemble frugal
innovation. Furthermore, we find that social entrepreneurs are more
focused on resource challenges and investors on institutional challenges. The findings suggest that innovation among social entrepreneurs can be conceptualised as a multidimensional construct with
three innovative process components – social, institutional and technological – that help to achieve three outcome components:
affordability, accessibility and adaptability, all designed to address
three main challenges, namely institutional voids, resource scarcity
and affordability constraints.

One of the main goals of this study is to help researchers in
organisational theory, strategy and the management sciences specify

better models of innovation by revealing how social entrepreneurs in extreme conditions perceive innovation. Two models of innovation are used to present these findings. The first model shows 'why' social entrepreneurs hold a range of different views on innovation, reflecting various motivations, means and outcomes related to social, user, efficiency and challenge concerns. The second model shows 'how' social entrepreneurs turn to a mix of technological, social and institutional innovations to deal with, make use of, and overcome constraints. We use the models and propositions developed through qualitative insights to propose a theory of frugal innovation as an emerging 'market', championed and generated by the activities of both social and mainstream entrepreneurs, corporates and policy actors.

The concept of frugal innovation is a useful way to conceptualise the process of integrating existing innovation approaches in extreme contexts with more familiar processes of product innovation or business model innovation. Unlike organisations involved in high-profile innovation, such as NASA, the 'mission' undertaken by social entrepreneurs is often more focused on pioneering new solutions to current challenges common peoples face: i.e. to create offerings for people who live and work at the less privileged interfaces of the modern world. Notwithstanding the mundane problems, novel offerings can have a profound impact on the lives of many millions or even billions of people. This is the 'why' of frugal innovation: a broadly shared desire to provide consumer value and amenities that offer extreme affordability. In this research report, for example, we demonstrate with data and models that the motivations for attempting frugal innovation are diverse and range from philanthropy, social issues, challenges and markets to the search for efficiency, but are seldom reducible to cost alone.

In our research, we use mainly qualitative methods, with a particular focus on retroduction, sometimes called abduction, as opposed to a pure grounded theory inductive approach. This approach offers an iterative deductive–inductive process that helps make the research transparent and rigorous. There is no shortage of studies that purport to use a purely grounded theory approach, in which researchers often continue to work within preconceived goals, assumptions and expectations. We tried initially to pursue a grounded theory approach, but our efforts encountered difficulties to implement in practice. The retroduction approach seemed more consistent with and reflective of the iterative sense-making process of research design, defence and implementation. Furthermore, this methodological approach helped us avoid treating perceptions as merely socially constructed.

Content analysis and thematic coding revealed intriguing results and two models of innovation. Innovation Model 1, on the views of social entrepreneurs, is introduced in Chapter 2, while Innovation Model 2, on innovation under constraints as viewed by social entrepreneurs, is revealed in Chapter 3. Chapter 4 integrates lessons from these two models of innovation to propose a theory of frugal innovation. In Chapter 5, we test the models and the proposed theory to popularly recognised published accounts of innovation, beyond those from which our findings were empirically drawn. In Chapter 6, we review emerging concepts in innovation and suggest how our findings inform specifically the literature on frugal innovation. Finally, in Chapter 7, we discuss implications that could be useful for scholars, practitioners and policymakers.

For theory, this research demonstrates that a peculiar kind of constrained innovation, captured as a concept, idea, framework or process, is being articulated by social entrepreneurs in the form of frugal innovation. Its impact and use are diffusing: bringing priorities for purposeful and social outcomes closer to mainstream entrepreneurs and large corporations. Frugal innovation offers opportunities to disrupt some prevalent assumptions about innovation, relating to its sources, lead users, patterns of diffusion and outcomes. Innovation is always subject to constraints. But in the context of frugal innovation, we find that the most significant constraints are institutional voids, a lack of resources and the need to make products affordable to low-income customers. Interestingly, these constraints or challenges are not unique to innovation in developing or emerging markets, but also increasingly exist in pockets of developed markets. This work is instrumental in developing a theory of frugal innovation by postulating propositions based on empirical data. The theory, models and constructs explored here will be valuable for future research.

When it comes to practice, the strength of social-value-enhancing strategies and frugal innovations that are adaptable, accessible and affordable means that firms can discover new applications and for previously overlooked market segments. The fact that social innovation in a broad sense and frugal innovation more specifically have caught the attention of policymakers suggests that this work is part of an evolving field of innovation studies and can engage a wider-impact community, offering scope for timely and relevant policy-making.These detailed constructs and relationships can help to identify various stakeholders involved in the market for frugal innovations; the toolkit offered here enables practitioners to identify and categorise the lifecycle stages of frugal innovations. However, policymakers may want to focus more on encouraging practitioners to experiment and evolve, rather than on trying to benchmark elusive and ever-changing 'ideal' innovations. For the practitioner, we characterise the ten core competencies that have proven to be successful in scaling innovations for low-resourced environments and which often emerge as solutions for broader use in both emerging and developed markets.

Our contribution to developing models of innovation in contextual conditions marked by institutional voids or complexities and resource scarcity will support future work in innovation in challenging and extreme contexts. Although we use the increasingly popular term, frugal innovation, to describe our findings, others may prefer the following modifiers: reverse, inclusive, grassroots, bottom of the pyramid, extreme affordability or *jugaad*. All of these constructs have synergies with the contextual characteristics or principles of innovation we present, characterised here as means and ends to do more with less for many.

PART I

Models of Frugal Innovation

I Outline of the Context, Literature and Methodology

This book was inspired by substantial interest in social innovation and social entrepreneurship outside of the developed Global North and the popular use of various terms and constructs that describe forms of innovation related to social enterprises. The objective of this book is to stimulate research and policy debates about the how and why of innovation that addresses the means and ends of value creation for the many, with less. We motivate this by engaging the literature of innovation studies with basic social science questions about institutional constraint and opportunity, in the context of diverse, empirically-informed contexts to understand 'frugal innovation', an important emerging concept for innovation research, policy and practice. Our research captures the views of social entrepreneurs, who innovate under constraints. We argue for and provide new models, methods and the beginnings of a theory of frugal innovation.

Such innovation is described using a wide range of constructs, including social, frugal, inclusive, catalytic, grassroots, *jugaad* and Ghandian innovation. We do not wish to be embroiled in the debate over broad 'umbrella constructs' or to act as 'validity police' in narrowly defining issues (Hirsch and Levin, 1999). Instead, we recognise Hirsch and Levin's life cycle of scholarly constructs, which progresses from excitement to validity checks and then to an understanding of typologies, before either becoming stable constructs or disappearing from the literature. Our research instead builds on findings from the experiences of social entrepreneurs, to contribute to models of innovation that start from different assumptions about resources, process and purpose. This empirical move both connects different kinds of

9

evidence to the discussion and also reframes some conventional assumptions in the mainstream innovation literatures (Bamberger and Pratt, 2010; Chandy and Prabhu, 2011). We present this work as an invitation for research colleagues to experiment and decide how best to further develop frugal innovation concepts, models and theories.

In this chapter, we cite the main literature, though not exhaustively as one would typically do in a literature review chapter (for detailed literature review see Bhatti, 2014), outline the questions that arise, summarise our methodology for investigating these questions and share our main findings.

1.2 THEORETICAL FRAMING FROM THE LITERATURE

Jan Fagerberg (2005) reviews the broad area of innovation studies and identifies four emphases in the research literature: 'innovation in the making', 'the systemic nature of innovation', 'how innovation differs' and 'innovation and performance'. Our work builds out from the question of 'how innovation differs'. We know how innovation differs across sectors, types of organisations and geographical locations and among entrepreneurs, managers and other individuals. However, we know very little about the ways in which social entrepreneurs (Elkington and Hartigan, 2008; Mair and Martí, 2006; 2007; 2009), rather than commercial entrepreneurs (Austin, Stevenson and Skillern, 2006; Sarasvathy, 2001; 2006), conceptualise models of innovation (Desa, 2009a; Guillén, 1994; Mair, Battilana and Cardenas, 2013; Marinova and Phillimore, 2003; Sarasvathy, 2001). Focusing on models of innovation and specifically on social entrepreneurs and the way they understand innovation provides an opportunity to study innovation outside the status quo and in unique contexts.

Our review picks up on this point: to begin to situate innovation in a broader view of institutional opportunity and constraint. We find that some research in development studies examines the way in which innovation occurs despite the simultaneous challenges of institutional voids and resource scarcity. We found little or no work in the fields of organisation theory or strategic management that attends to these issues. We connect this finding with research on broadly social and purposeful innovation (distinct from a conventional focus on technology innovation). Nicholls and many others propose social entrepreneurial activity as market-based innovation focused on societal change (Nicholls, 2006a; 2006b; Nicholls and Murdock, 2011). Much of the research on social entrepreneurship asks who social entrepreneurs are and what they do. This population is especially relevant to our study. In our review of the literature, we show how little is known about how social entrepreneurs conceptualise innovation in extreme contexts shaped by resource constraints and institutional voids.

Research by organisational institutionalists on social entrepreneurial ventures has only thinly been concerned with the origins of innovation (Lounsbury and Crumley, 2007). Although some studies have explored how social entrepreneurs face the challenges of institutional voids and resource scarcity (cf. Austin, Stevenson and Skillern, 2006; Dart, 2004a; 2004b; Desa, 2009a; 2009b; Grimes et al., 2012; Haugh, 2005; Mair and Martí, 2009; Mair, Martí and Ventresca, 2012; Mulgan et al., 2007a; 2007b; Seelos and Mair, 2005), few analyse how innovation is perceived or understood by social entrepreneurs.

To explore scholarly and practical examples, we connect two main streams in the literature: innovation studies and social entrepreneurship (as shown in Figure 1.1). The literature on innovation (stream 1) looks at innovation faced with a single constraint: either institutional voids or resource scarcity. Few if any studies of innovation explore more complex cases, where innovation must simultaneously grapple with institutional voids and resource scarcity. The social entrepreneurship literature (stream 2) argues that social entrepreneurs often have to function and innovate in extreme conditions shaped by both institutional voids and resource scarcity.

This study seeks to advance the models and theories of innovation by bridging a gap in the literature between studies of innovation

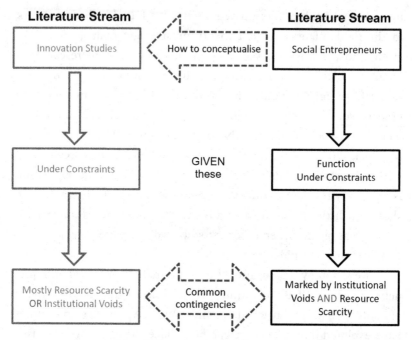

FIGURE I.I Identifying gaps in the literature

in relation to social entrepreneurship and studies that relate to institutions and resources. Posing the question of how social entrepreneurs and similar actors conceptualise and approach innovation reveals new insights into different ways of innovating (Fagerberg, 2005).

1.2.1 Why Focus on Innovation?

Studies of strategy in contexts that include institutional voids, resource constraints or scarcity have focused on multinational companies (MNCs) and large business groups (Khanna and Palepu, 1997; 2006), entrepreneurship (Puffer, McCarthy and Boisot, 2010; Tracey and Jarvis, 2007; Tracey and Phillips, 2011), social entrepreneurship (Mair and Martí, 2009) and market building (Mair, Martí and Ventresca, 2012). Analyses of actors facing constraints in innovation value chains (cf. Hansen and Birkinshaw, 2007; Roper, Du and

Love, 2008) link studies that assess the strategic responses of entrepreneurs and large businesses to institutional voids or resource constraints.

By focusing on innovation, we aim to show how social entrepreneurs perceive the interplay between these two different types of challenges. Using innovation as the unit of analysis creates a bridge between the different perspectives of entrepreneurs and large businesses when responding to institutional voids and resource constraints. We contend that a focus on innovation in context provides a more specified understanding of these challenges and can better provide insights to address them.

1.2.2 Why Focus on Institutional Voids and Resource Scarcity?

Much work on innovation has explored 'innovation under constraint'. Although such constraints take many forms, the literature has typically focused on resource constraints (Nohria and Gulati, 1996; Rao and Drazin, 2002) in the absence of formal institutional contexts (Altenburg, 2009; North, 1990). While some studies have explored the enabling effect of resource constraints on innovation outcomes, most have argued that resource constraints inhibit innovation, while slack resources support creativity and innovation (Weiss, Hoegl and Gibbert, 2011). Yet, research in creative cognition psychology has found that actors are most innovative when given fewer rather than more resources, supporting the hypothesis that 'less is more' (Gibbert, Hoegl and Välikangas, 2007, p. 16). Other work has provided evidence, albeit largely anecdotal, that remarkable (and even disruptive) innovation outcomes can be achieved with limited financial resources and a dearth of formal institutions (cf. Bold, 2011; Christensen et al., 2006; Govindarajan and Ramamurti, 2013; Hart and Christensen, 2002).

Some emerging work on innovation in the face of dual constraints points to new analytic issues, including the rising popularity of innovation in developing and emerging markets (Bhatti, Khilji and Basu, 2013) and the more general concern with markets at the base of the pyramid (Prahalad, 2005).

The idea that resource scarcity can be an impediment to innovation as well as an enabler that identifies new opportunities and enforces efficiency makes it useful to identify perceptual norms among entrepreneurs facing resource constraints: how 'objective' conditions are mediated by entrepreneurial perceptions (Dorado and Ventresca, 2013). The idea that institutions can be formal as well as informal allows us to identify perceptual norms among entrepreneurs seeking to fill structural voids or deal with complexities in their operating environment (Mair, Martí and Ventresca, 2012).

1.2.3 Why Study Social Entrepreneurs to Inform Models of Innovation?

Much research attributes social innovation to social entrepreneurs (cf. Minks, 2011; Phills, Deiglmeier and Miller, 2008; Pol and Ville, 2009; Seelos and Mair, 2005; 2007). This work is important, though to some large degree it asserts rather than explores key steps in this process. Our reading points to one critical issue: We do not fully understand how social entrepreneurs conceptualise social or even general innovation. In addition to studying practice, it is also important to understand how social entrepreneurs conceptualise innovation, providing insights into the models of innovation favoured by social entrepreneurs (Mair, Battilana and Cardenas, 2012) to add to the list of commercial models of innovation built up by scholars over many years (cf. Chandy and Prabhu, 2011; Guillén, 1994; Marinova and Phillimore, 2003; Sarasvathy, 2001). We make use of the fact that the vocabularies used by social entrepreneurs can reveal their ways of conceptualising innovation.

Social entrepreneurs are specifically relevant as a study population because they face double-edged challenges that we want to understand. First, they function in a field that lacks complex, informal institutions. Second, they lack resources specifically allocated to social enterprise and innovation (Mulgan et al., 2007b). In addition, they innovate in environments marked by institutional voids and complexities, where their beneficiaries reside (Mair, Martí and Ventresca, 2012), also without adequate resources (Hart and Prahalad, 2002; Prahalad, 2005; Prahalad and Hammond, 2002). This purposeful choice of informants gives us an important contrast for analysis. In the course of our literature search and review before we commenced the research, we had found almost no research on innovation as interpreted by social entrepreneurs facing both institutional voids and resource scarcity.

1.2.4 Under-Researched Assumptions about Social Innovation and Social Entrepreneurship

The ideas of social entrepreneurship and social innovation in much research are often so intertwined that it can be difficult to distinguish them. Paul Tracey and Owen Jarvis (2007) argue that social entrepreneurship is innovation that leads to positive social change. For them, the notion of trading for a social purpose is at the core of social entrepreneurship. Another prevalent view is that the primary objective of social entrepreneurs is to create social value, while a secondary but necessary objective is to create economic value to ensure financial viability (Mair and Martí, 2006).

The terms 'socially entrepreneurial ventures', 'socially innovative entrepreneurs' and 'innovative social purpose business enterprises' are used interchangeably (Perrini and Vurro, 2006). Francesco Perrini and Clodia Vurro (2006) posit that the three key constructs are entrepreneurship, innovation and social concerns. We argue that this approach has led scholars to label the activities and outcomes of social enterprises as social innovations and their agents as social innovators. Like mainstream entrepreneurship, social entrepreneurship has often been defined as innovation-based. The traditional approach of social entrepreneurs generally emphasises social innovation, entrepreneurial activism and frame-breaking approaches to non-profit management (Dart, 2004a). Other definitions of social entrepreneurship include 'innovative, social value creating' (Austin,

Stevenson and Wei-Skillern, 2006, p. 2) and the view that 'social entrepreneurs are change promoters in society; they pioneer innovation within the social sector' (Perrini and Vurro, 2006, p. 69). Perrini and Vurro argue that social enterprises 'are characterized by altered and mixed behaviour, a strong entrepreneurial orientation and above all, an unquestionable accent on social innovation' (p. 59). Others 'define social entrepreneurship as the innovative use of resource combinations to pursue opportunities ... that yield and sustain social benefits' (Mair and Noboa, 2006, p. 122).

Many researchers have investigated the sources of creativity among social entrepreneurs and the factors and processes that enable innovation. Yet few, if any, empirical investigations have explored how social entrepreneurs perceive or think about innovation. In a compendium of works on social innovation, for example, editors Alex Nicholls and Alex Murdock (2011, p. 3) link social innovation to social entrepreneurship in a framework of intersecting institutional logics across civil, private and public sectors by 'drawing on the cognate social entrepreneurship literature [to] suggest a further important insight into the nature of social innovation'. By studying social enterprises in four countries, contributor Janelle A. Kerlin (2011) argues that different forms of social innovation become institutionalised over time in different contexts. However, she and other contributors to the volume do not question the assumptions that social enterprises create social innovation or that the entrepreneurs who run them are social innovators.

Contributor Heather Cameron (2011) carried out an empirical study using forty-one semi-structured interviews to learn how social entrepreneurs analyse risk and position themselves within the social innovation ecosystem defined by the Skoll World Forum on Social Entrepreneurship – largely within universities. Although Cameron's study is informative, given the Focauldian style of analysis she adopts, her interviews about social entrepreneurs focus on Foucault's intellectually derived key themes: the function of the social entrepreneur, risks, measuring impact, the role of the university and the role of the Forum. Cameron's approach does not reveal social entrepreneurs' core perceptions, conceptualisations or thoughts about innovation. Also by studying social enterprises, contributor Fergus Lyon (2011) investigates how inter-organisational relationships operate in cases of social innovation. This empirical analysis likewise assumes that social enterprises are in the business of creating social innovation; it investigates how these organisations deal with issues of trust and power when building and maintaining collaborations, implying that its findings can be extended to include social innovation. More recent work by Paul Tracey and Neil Stott (2017) posits that many things labelled as social innovation may actually have relatively little in common and that this may be overcome by better categorising different types of social innovation that have to do with social entrepreneurship, social intrapreneurship and social extrapreneurship.

What is common in these and similar studies is how many scholars assert rather than test how and under what conditions social enterprises produce social innovation and that social entrepreneurs are social innovators. We take a step back and start from the perceptions of social entrepreneurs to investigate the concept of innovation. We achieve this not by asking them about the types of innovation most often associated with social entrepreneurs. We simply ask them about innovation.

1.3 WHAT DO WE KNOW ABOUT SOCIAL INNOVATION?

Many observers argue that social entrepreneurs provide innovative leadership in social enterprises (Dees, 1996; 2011), while socially entrepreneurial organisations emphasise the role of innovation (Borins, 2000). However, like the term 'social entrepreneurship', social innovation has poorly defined boundaries, meanings and definitions (Caulier-Grice et al., 2012; Murray et al., 2010). Julie Caulier-Grice and co-authors (2010) suggest that social innovation is far broader than social entrepreneurship, and that there are both opportunities and challenges through the discovery and use of new knowledge. And in the literature, social innovation is even more elusive than social entrepreneurship, for which concepts, definitions and analyses have been relatively well defined (cf. Mair and Martí, 2009; Nicholls and Murdock, 2011). Robin Murray, Julie Caulier-Grice and Geoff Mulgan (2010) co-authored the 'The Open Book of Social Innovation' as a result of major collaboration between NESTA (the National Endowment for Science, Technology and the Arts) and the Young Foundation, two organisations which have long espoused the role that social innovation can play in solving major concerns of our time. They define 'social innovations as new ideas (products, services and models) that simultaneously meet social needs and create new social relationships or collaborations' (p. 3). They further contend that social innovation does not have fixed boundaries – it occurs in all sectors, public, non-profit and private, and a lot of the creativity is taking place at sectoral boundaries. According to Timo J. Hamalainen and Risto Heiskala (2007) there are five types of innovation (techno-logical, economic, regulative, normative and cultural) that together form the sphere of social innovations.

This book builds on a stream of social innovation literature that describes social innovation as the work of social entrepreneurs, emphasising the role of individuals in developing innovative solu-tions for difficult social challenges (Bornstein, 2004; Bornstein and Davis, 2010; Dees and Anderson, 2006; Goldsmith, 2010; Hartigan and Elkington, 2008; Hoogendoorn, Pennings and Thurik, 2010). Nicholls and Murdock's (2011, p.2) literature review shows that social innovation research focuses on 'systems and processes of change in social relations' at one extreme and on 'innovation around the conceptualization, design and production of goods and services that address social and environmental needs and market failures' at the other. Moreover, social innovation is a practice-led, contextually based field (Murray et al., 2010) and most texts have analysed suc-cessful case studies rather than the patterns and stages of social innovation (Caulier-Grice et al., 2012). Similarly, most of the litera-ture on social innovation has focused on the process perspective and practical concerns relating to the development and implementation of successful programmes and strategies.

For example, Sandra M. Bates (2011) in, *The Social Innovation Imperative*, claims to present the first detailed, structured methodology for social innovation derived from academic models and practical experience. It offers a 'how-to' guide addressing acute or 'wicked problems' such as healthcare, education, poverty, disaster response, neglected elderly people and environmental destruction. Wicked problems are complex issues that are particularly hard to resolve, in part because they involve several different constituencies, with conflicting or competing objectives (Bates, 2011). However, this book does not explore how social entrepreneurs themselves perceive social or any other kind of innovation. Although practice is important, our working hypothesis is that understanding how social entrepreneurs think about and perceive the work of 'innovation', builds additional layers of knowledge about how innovation under constraint and scarcity may occur.

1.4 INNOVATION UNDER CONSTRAINT

When we first set out on this study, a search of the literature revealed few scholarly papers on innovation in institutional voids or with resource constraints, let alone with both constraints simultaneously. A search on *Business Source Complete* and *Proquest* revealed only two peer-reviewed papers using the search criteria [innovation AND ('institutional void' OR 'institutional voids')]. Neither paper offered empirical insight into innovation under these conditions. A similar search through both databases using the search criteria [innovation AND ('resource scarcity' OR 'resource constraint'] revealed 48 and 227 results respectively. Many of these papers were in the fields of environmental or development studies; few were in organisational or management studies. When we added the term 'social entrepreneur' or 'social entrepreneurship' to the search criteria, the search returned no papers.

Like Desa (2008), who found little research on whether entrepreneurship in resource-constrained environments was different from conventional business entrepreneurship, we found little or no literature discussing whether innovation in resource-constrained environments was different from mainstream innovation. There was some acknowledgement in the development literature of the double-edged problem of institutional voids and resource scarcity, but no in-depth studies of innovation facing both challenges simultaneously. This is surprising, given the likelihood these two constraints are both present in developing market economies or in other contexts where social entrepreneurs are active. Looking at the situations in which both factors co-occur offers a fascinating opportunity for innovation scholars to study interesting and 'extreme' contexts.

Most researchers have looked at the effects of financial resource constraints on innovation team performance (cf. Paananen, 2012; Rao and Drazin, 2002; Weiss et al., 2011). This suggests that there is potential to meta-theorise and study resources (beyond financial resources) to move the level of analysis from teams to firms. By using a combination of resource-related and institutional theories, we can take a further step and link a firm's innovation activities to its institutional environment and available resources. This pointed us to social entrepreneurship as a useful starting point for the study of innovation in a context of institutional voids and resource scarcity.

However, despite the now substantial and rich body of research published about social entrepreneurs and their relationship with innovation, we don't know how they think or talk about innovation. Indeed, there is not much knowledge about social innovation, the activity routinely attributed to social entrepreneurs (cf. Minks, 2011; Phills et al., 2008; Pol and Ville, 2009). It is important not only to observe what social entrepreneurs do, but also to understand how they talk about what they do, as this can provide insights into why and how social entrepreneurs innovate in the ways that they do.

1.5 THE QUESTION OF FRUGAL INNOVATION

Although we were motivated by the growing discourse around frugal innovation, and the role of social entrepreneurs in creating such innovation, we wanted the social entrepreneurs themselves to provide us with fundamental information about innovation models and practices. Our approach differs from most work on frugal innovation because it does not begin by asking 'what is frugal innovation?', or even assuming that such a thing exists. Instead, we go directly to the innovators and those involved with them, to ask what innovation means to them, without introducing the concepts of social or frugal innovation or other related terms.

Our approach does not lead respondents towards a particular notion or conceptualisation of innovation. For this reason, it provides a more 'grounded' (not to be construed as a purely grounded methodological approach in the sense of Barney Glaser and Anselm Strauss) and reliable understanding of innovation, where the construct does not mask the nature of innovation, as revealed by social entrepreneurs. We have merged established streams of literature from social entrepreneurship and innovation to explore an interesting research opportunity. Other relevant, emerging concepts found in the literature, such as frugal innovation, reverse innovation, grassroots innovation, inclusive innovation and *jugaad* innovation are introduced into the discussion only after our respondents have alluded to them.

The term 'frugal innovation' was coined in the late 2000s through activities by large corporations such as Tata and Nissan-Renault and through activities in large emerging markets such as in China (Gupta and Wang, 2009). The term and the idea was propagated popularly by *The Economist* in 2010 and then picked up by public policy experts and academics in the early 2010s. Two early policy reports by NESTA and the SERCO Institute in the UK attributed frugal innovation largely to social entrepreneurs (Bound and Thornton, 2012; Singh et al., 2012). Alongside, highly acclaimed work by Navi Radjou, Jaideep Prabhu and Simone Ahuja brought awareness of this different type of innovation to global competitiveness in terms of *jugaad* (2012) and by Vijay Govindarajan and Chris Trimble to international business in terms of reverse innovation (2012). Almost ten years on, definitions abound for frugal innovation (see Pisoni, Michelini and Martignoni, 2018 for latest review). But there is still scope to contribute to clear and crisp conceptual, theoretical and operational definitions and frameworks at various micro–meso–macro levels of analysis, such as among individual innovators, organisational forms and sectoral domains. Without having the benefit of an integrative theoretical foundation, many practitioners and some scholarly publications on frugal innovation have had to rely on conceptual studies or on anecdotal evidence. Such papers have sought to promote specific objectives, such as corporate marketing of new product offerings, strategic approaches for international business or public sector reform. A recent systematic literature review in progress of published examples of frugal innovations (Hossain, 2016; 2017) reveals that most of these come from Western MNCs, with only a small amount generated locally or in developing countries. Yet, much of frugal innovation activity is associated to activities in developing or emerging market countries (Petrick and Juntiwasarakij, 2011; Zeschky, Widenmayer and Gassmann, 2011). This may well be the case because much local innovation is not recognised or made widely visible, which makes it challenging to link conceptual understanding with evidence.

We believe that our approach arguably presents one of the most in-depth, extensive studies of the topic, using established academic theories and research methods from the domain of social entrepreneurship and innovation to frame and build models of innovation from the perspectives of social entrepreneurs from around the world working closely with their local communities. And we seek to understand this activity in the unique features of the contexts in which they operate, often marked by challenges and constraints. We build up on and support previous work that frames these constraints as resource scarcity and institutional voids, weaknesses or complexities (Bhatti, 2012; Bhatti and Ventresca, 2013; Prabhu, Tracey and Hassan,

2017; Soni and Krishnan, 2014). Whether social entrepreneurs adhere to or associate themselves with certain constructs around innovation, we leave it to the respondents to divulge.

1.6 HOW DOES THIS BOOK APPROACH INNOVATION DIFFERENTLY?

We use an empirical approach to connect the little we know about social entrepreneurs' views of innovation with social and purposeful innovation, rather than adopting the status quo's focus on technology innovation. The received wisdom is that social entrepreneurial activity is market-based innovation focused on societal change (Nicholls, 2006a; Nicholls and Murdock, 2011). Fundamentally, social entrepreneurship is challenging because it attempts to merge two ostensibly contradictory organisational goals – social value creation and profit generation – in environments where even a basic institutional infrastructure may not exist (Grimes et al., 2012).

Much has been achieved in social entrepreneurship research since Perrini and Vurro (2006) argued that the main difficulty impeding systematic empirical studies in social entrepreneurship was the lack of a general framework for comparing very diverse experiences. Given that social enterprises by nature can be rather diverse, we maintain that it is premature for scholars to generalise that all of them engage in social innovation. Consequently, when researching social innovation among social entrepreneurs, we discovered a continuing shortage of empirically informed frameworks through which to compare innovations across diverse social enterprises.

Before grappling with practical concerns or defining good or bad strategies for social innovation, social scientists must pay more attention to the way social entrepreneurs conceptualise and perceive innovation as a construct, phenomenon or concept. This book moves away from practice towards a more conceptual approach, which can generate models and concepts of innovation that transcend what social entrepreneurs actually do on the ground. Some of the unaddressed questions in social innovation research include the following: *Is social innovation collectively perceived as one construct or a varied group? To what extent do academic conceptualisations of social innovation match or differ from those of social entrepreneurs?*

Setting out to address these issues, we take a step back to explore the fundamental question: *How do social entrepreneurs conceptualise innovation broadly and specifically under constraints or in extreme conditions marked by institutional voids and resource scarcity?* The gaps in the literature suggest that this work will be a seminal study in delineating innovation into models of understanding based on the empirically gathered perceptions of social entrepreneurs. As this study aims to understand patterns and concepts of innovation, it does not seek out successful cases but rather looks at early stage social entrepreneurs, who may not yet be considered 'successful'. Furthermore, the geographical and sectoral diversity of informants in this study allows a broader perspective on innovation carried out by social entrepreneurs.

The preceding subsections have outlined the research opportunity that lies at the intersection of the innovation studies and social entrepreneurship literatures, specifically by merging institutional and resource-related theories. Note that this work does not specifically seek to address how social entrepreneurs actually innovate. Instead, it aims mainly to understand how social entrepreneurs perceive and present innovation under constraints, which may at times allude to how they actually innovate.

1.7 THE CONCEPTUAL FRAMEWORK

We have established the importance of understanding social entrepreneurship and innovation in the context of institutional voids and resource scarcity. Social entrepreneurs and innovators must devise low-cost strategies, either tapping into or circumventing institutional voids and resource limitations to innovate, develop and deliver products and services to low-income users with little purchasing power, often on a mass scale. We develop in this section an initial conceptual framework that incorporates elements from two classic theoretical perspectives to identify and motivate our object of study: innovation, as perceived by social entrepreneurs within extreme contexts.

Miles and Huberman long ago styled a conceptual framework as a written or visual presentation that 'explains either graphically, or in narrative form, the main things to be studied – the key factors, concepts or variables – and the presumed relationship among them' (Miles and Huberman, 1994, p. 18). We envisage a conceptual framework that takes into consideration the contingency perspective from the study of organisation–environment relations to specify the context in which social entrepreneurs operate, including resources and institutions both upstream and downstream from their innovation activities. We also use a value chain innovation perspective to analyse innovation inputs and outputs both upstream and downstream of the innovation process, with attention to both institutional voids and resource scarcity.

We examine perceptions of innovation among social entrepreneurs from a contingency perspective (Lawrence and Lorsch, 1967; Woodward, 1965) because contingency theory postulates that decision-making depends on various internal and external constraints or situational factors.[1] Contingency theory is a form of foundational logic used by management scholars, which underpins many organisation and strategic management theories. Its roots can be found in works by Joan Woodward (1965) and Paul R. Lawrence and Jay W. Lorsch (1967), who argued that the variations they observed in organisational designs associated with high performance (based on various contextual factors) implied that there was not 'one best way' to organise. The contingency approach has underpinned

---

[1] However, we share a word of caution here on the use of contingency theory and resource dependency theory. In the original cited works by Woodward, Lawrence and Lorsch, and their modern inheritors, the contingencies and resources were objectively measurable qualities shared by all concerned. Given the nature of research questions focusing on perceptions of social entrepreneurs, these contingencies and resources are to be seen as 'perceived contingencies' and 'perceived resources' by our informants.

institutional theories on design and change (cf. Greenwood et al., 2008; Hargrave and Van de Ven, 2006; Hinings and Reay, 2009; Thornton, Ocasio and Lounsbury, 2012). Through the contingent lens, we analyse the boundary conditions within which processes and structures of innovation pan out among social entrepreneurs. This research seeks to understand not only broader concepts of innovation, but also how relevant actors conceptualise innovation under the dual external constraints. These literature streams highlight that social entrepreneurs hold interpretive assumption about two main external constraints: resources and institutional conditions.

Another way to examine perceptions of innovation among social entrepreneurs is to visualise the innovation process in terms of the value chain. Value chain analysis has been used to study a range of innovation questions (cf. Dedrick, Kraemer and Linden, 2010; Hansen and Birkinshaw, 2007; Kaplinsky and Morris, 2001; Roper, Du and Love, 2008;). Morten T. Hansen and Julian Birkinshaw (2007) advise, 'To improve innovation, executives need to view the process of transforming ideas into commercial outputs as an integrated flow rather like Michael Porter's value chain for transforming raw materials into finished goods' (p. 3). The innovation value chain is basically comprised of a recursive process of knowledge sourcing, transformation and exploitation (Roper, Du and Love, 2008), thereby incorporating everything from inputs to outputs.

Value chain analysis is a useful tool for identifying mixed constraints that are either supply- or demand-driven and occur either upstream or downstream of the value chain. Elco van Burg et al. (2012) explore a new approach to reconciling inconsistencies in the literature regarding how resource constraints affect opportunity identification by entrepreneurs. Previous studies show that resource constraints have mixed effects on how entrepreneurs identify innovation and entrepreneurial opportunity. Sometimes, resource constraints lead to identifying more opportunities; at other times, entrepreneurs see fewer opportunities. Burg et al. (2012) distinguish between supply and demand constraints and their relationship with supply and demand opportunities. Based on a quantitative study of 219 small and medium-sized enterprises (SMEs), they find that resource constraints direct the entrepreneur's attention towards opportunities inside rather than outside the constrained domain. What is specifically relevant for this study is Burg et al.'s (2012) suggestion that researchers should simultaneously consider different types of resource constraints and sources of opportunities. We do so in this study by considering mixed resource constraints, which can represent either an opportunity or an impediment to innovation. And we extend the work of Burg et al. (2012) with this focus on perception of constraints (Gioia and Thomas, 1996).

Social entrepreneurs can encounter constraints both upstream and downstream of the innovation process. Upstream, social entrepreneurs have to deal with institutional voids (Khanna and Palepu, 1997) and complex institutional contexts (Mair, Martí and Ventresca, 2012), as well as limited resources. Downstream, social entrepreneurs have to create outputs to address the needs of the base of the pyramid (BoP), that is, the largest and poorest socio-economic segment of the population (Prahalad, 2005). They must find the means to provide access to these outputs through various institutional structures and mechanisms. Resource scarcity can mean the inability of vast populations to afford the means to address not only wants but also needs (Seelos and Mair, 2007). Some of these constraints might be viewed as threats, others as opportunities, depending on various environmental and behavioural factors.

In the 'extreme resource constrained' contexts (Mair and Martí, 2009) that social entrepreneurs often function in, resources may be scarce at all points along the value chain – meaning that affordability affects not only the end market consumer but also any firm wishing to use another firm's outcome in its own process. And that affordability itself has a negotiated character. The challenge for companies doing business, designing products and managing costs for the BoP market is that customers are willing (London and Hart, 2004; Prahalad, 2005) but often unable to pay due to income constraints (Seelos and Mair, 2007), which are another form of resource constraint facing service providers in these environments. We depict this as a downstream resource constraint in the value chain framework. The unique social, cultural and institutional characteristics of the BoP markets mean that traditional industrial-scale products, services and management processes will not work for them (Prahalad, 2005). Affordability is not just a concern at the end point or outcome of innovation; it is a cumulative of the value creation transversal across the entire process. For this reason, we examine how all users face resource constraints upstream and downstream at every point of the value chain, in a context that includes institutional complexities or voids.

DiMaggio and Powell (1983; 1991) developed institutional theory arguments in the context of organisations and industries to account for how context models shape the form and focus of change. Extending this to the societal level, institutions are 'the humanly devised constraints that structure human interaction' through informal cultural norms as well as formal legal rules (North, 1990, p. 3). Douglass C. North's formal and informal institutions are classified by W. Richard Scott (1995; 2008) into three analytic categories: regulative, normative and cultural-cognitive. The regulative pillar includes society's state-enforced laws; the normative pillar involves the roles and expectations set for specific groups by professional societies; the cultural-cognitive pillar includes generally accepted beliefs and values shared among individuals. Each of these pillars provides a summary of relevant social sciences literatures (Hoffman and Ventresca, 2002). Together, they comprise a conceptual framework and toolkit through which to evaluate and to understand institutional architectures and action processes. We view these as general institutions.

For our analysis of contextual resource scarcity and institutional voids, we extend this institutional theory perspective with a further material consideration. The pillars approach provides us important tools to understand how cognitive models and perspectives combine to generate conventional, socially-stable understandings of the world in practice. This approach under-specifies a focus on material infrastructure – the complex, durable institutions that enable markets to function, such as ports, roads, energy distribution systems, schools and hospitals. Rahul Tongia and Eswaran Subramanian (2006) discuss directly the analysis of such durable, material institutions, suggesting that the developing world is particularly lacking in institution rule systems, including infrastructure and capital market mechanisms. They compare commercial information and communications technology (ICT) solutions in the United States to those in the developing world; in the former, infrastructure and market mechanisms are available, while in the latter, the same institutional facilities are rare or non-existent. Ray et al. (2004) find that resources and capabilities including technical IT skills, knowledge and infrastructure flexibility can affect operational processes. However, they view infrastructure from a resource-based perspective (Arikan and Barney, 2001; Barney, 1991; Peteraf, 1993), whereby the infrastructure is held or controlled by the firm. Other tangible, material elements of infrastructure, such as ports, roads and training universities, are often provided as public infrastructure for the public good, rather than being controlled by firms. We differentiate between such infrastructure assets controlled by firms and viewed through the resource-based view (RBV) lens and infrastructure assets that are not controlled by firms but instead by governments and other authoritative professional bodies, in accordance with the institutional theory lens.

By using the contingency and value chain perspectives coupled with insights from the analysis of institutional rules, we propose the following conceptual framework for innovation in contexts shaped by institutional voids and resource scarcity, as shown in Figure 1.2. In Figure 1.3, we summarise the three main constraints that innovators have to overcome in underserved markets.

We see this interpretation of value chain analysis as a conventional analytical tool well-grounded in management practice may help to increase cases of innovation by social entrepreneurs from

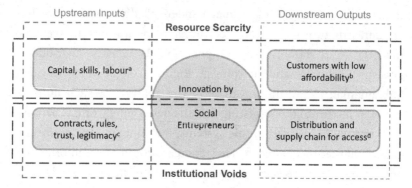

FIGURE 1.2 Conceptual framework

a Upstream, social entrepreneurs lack capital, skills and labour resources;
b Downstream, clients or customers are resource-deficient with low purchasing power;
c Upstream activities take place in environments in which institutional complexities or voids affect conventions about contracts, rules, trust and legitimacy;
d Downstream, there is not much institutional supply-chain and distribution infrastructure, such as roads, ports or transportation capacity.

the odd example here or there to standard practice. Although the unit of observation is the entrepreneur, the unit of analysis is the value chain through which the social entrepreneur seeks to innovate. And the framework we propose introduces perceptions of the actor at each point in the process. The above conceptual framework is a starting point to access this extensive work, which seeks to build models of innovation by empirically revealing the perceptions and views of social entrepreneurs.

Models as abstract conceptualisations have been used widely to make sense of how things are or will be. Examples include economic, policy, business, geographic and biological models. However, lessons learnt from over-reliance on econometric modelling suggest that pure reductionism does not do justice to the complexity and plurality of

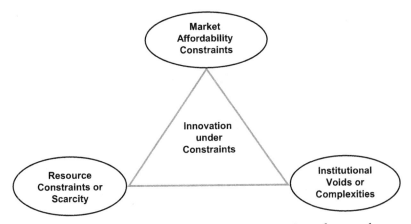

FIGURE 1.3 Main constraints on innovation in underserved markets

realities (Sen, 1986; Stiglitz, 2015; Toole, 1990). To avoid such risks, we refrain from using purely economic models and focus more on conceptual models of innovation to better understand the wide range of perspectives that social entrepreneurs bring to innovation.

1.8 RESEARCH QUESTIONS

We use this framing to take up the question of how actors conceptualise innovation generally and specifically in unique, extreme contexts marked by resource scarcity and institutional voids. The main question is: *How do social entrepreneurs conceptualise innovation generally and specifically under constraints or extreme conditions marked by institutional voids and resource scarcity?*

We develop the following three sub-questions to motivate the research:

1. How do social entrepreneurs conceptualise innovation?

Objective: To investigate through exploratory and descriptive analysis how social entrepreneurs think about innovation and claim to do, as opposed to what they 'really' do on the ground.

Significance: Contributes to and broadens key features of innovation models relevant to management theory and policy by specifying actor perceptions.

2. How do social entrepreneurs conceptualise innovation within institutional voids?

Objective: To include actor perceptions of institutional voids, or related ideas about institutions, in available models of innovation

Significance: Contributes to the literature and options for policy, showing how contextual conditions based on institutional rules and conventions shape models of innovation.

3. How do social entrepreneurs conceptualise innovation in a context of resource scarcity?

Objective: To include actor perspectives shaped by resource scarcity or constraints in available models of innovation.

Significance: Contributes to the literature on how contextual conditions based on resources-based arguments shape models of innovation.

Questions 2 and 3 together provide the substantive advance for a theory of innovation under constraints by creating a bridge between existing innovation models and methods and the insights for institution- and resource-related theories.

1.9 APPROACH AND METHOD

This study uses qualitative methods to study two communities of social entrepreneurs, many of whom are motivated by the potential for social impact to build technology- and science-based ventures. These informants are globally networked and formally recognised social entrepreneurs, identified through a process where they have applied to a prestige global 'boot camp' programme. These sample are not random, but rather represent highly stylised sets of social entrepreneurs, articulate about what they do and why.

We analyse innovation and value chains at the meso level, while micro-level observations incorporate business plan summaries, interviews with entrepreneurs, investors and academics and observations made at an annual, intensive social entrepreneurship and innovation 'boot-camp'. The lead author conducted two international fieldwork trips spanning four months, collecting 81 interviews and 163 archival documents. We have used thematic content analysis (TCA), in particular the technique of template analysis, in order to assemble and digest evidence from these data sources.

The suitability of a qualitative research methodology derives from the nature of the social phenomenon studied (Morgan and Smircich, 1980), namely, how social entrepreneurs talk about innovation. According to Louis Cohen and Lawrence Manion (1980, p. 27), 'the purpose of social science is to understand social reality as different people see it and to demonstrate how their views shape the action which they take within that reality'. Our research objective calls for an in-depth, detailed study that explores the ways in which social entrepreneurs perceive innovation in context.

We developed a descriptive, qualitative research design to collect data that describes how social entrepreneurs think about innovation. This design suits the relatively limited knowledge available about actor conceptualisations of innovation. Acknowledging the risks and limitations of building theory based on innovation as socially constructed, we chose not to pursue a purely inductive, field-based, grounded theory approach (Glaser and Strauss, 1967). Instead, we adopted the methodological approach of retroduction (Ragin, 1994; Ragin and Amoroso, 2010), which supports the iterative use of deduction based on current knowledge and of induction based on emerging evidence. Retroduction is gaining use in management and entrepreneurship research, with the growth in interest of pragmatist philosophy of management and organisations sciences research (Farjoun, Ansell and Boin, 2015).

We identified two social entrepreneurship programmes convened in Silicon Valley, California as our source of social entrepreneurs. The Global Social Benefit Institute (GSBI®), which is part of Miller Center for Social Entrepreneurship at Santa Clara University and the Design for Extreme Affordability (DEA) programme, which is part of d.school (Hasso Plattner Institute of Design) at Stanford University. The former is a professional programme that seeks to accelerate growth for existing social entrepreneurs from around the world, while the latter is a university degree module that serves as an incubator for enrolled students. The focus on participants and alumni of these programmes gave us access to a globally and sector diverse group of social entrepreneurs and textual sources (business plans), as well as the opportunity to carry out in-depth interviews and observations.

We were drawn to these two programmes because they have both produced widely recognised examples of social entrepreneurship and impact, including ventures such as Kiva, Whirlwind Wheelchair, Anudip, Toughstuff, Thrive, MIT OpenCourseWare, Vision Spring, Jaipur/ReMotion Knee, Embrace and D-Light. Our initial reasons for choosing these California-based programmes were logistical – both programmes were ongoing, with high credibility and with well-documented activities and participants. They offered access to historical documents in the form of business plan summaries from multiple social entrepreneurs, whom we could also meet in person. Both programmes have extensive networks that span global networks in social entrepreneurship community; their members originate all over the world and focus on diverse markets – mainly in emerging and developing economies but also developed. The well-networked programmes offered a concentrated, accessible opportunity to collect extensive and diverse data during the span of time an early career research project allows. The international profile of these universities solved one set of logistics: how to speak to social entrepreneurs from many countries where social enterprises were being established. This choice presented a different challenge: how to interpret the findings from this 'select' set of social entrepreneurs, a topic we return to in the discussion of findings.

At the start of this chapter, we identified our object of study as the conceptualisation of innovation, and specifically the models of innovation held by and animating the actions of social entrepreneurs. The subjects of study were individual social entrepreneurs and the experts who worked with them, including academics, mentors and investors. These informants, who represent diverse geographical locations and sectors, provided direct and indirect data sources (interviews, business plans and other commentary) for this analysis of how social entrepreneurs perceive innovation. Because the respondents come from many geographical and market sectoral categories, there is much variation in the data. We used this variance to develop greater understanding of innovation that takes into account complex constraints.

This is a brief overview of the research methodology, its strengths and weaknesses. We provide a more detailed version of the design, data and methods in Appendix C. After exploratory fieldwork, negotiating access and collecting data, we drew most heavily on the GSBI programme data analysis and findings. We also made use of rich but more limited data from the edea site to perform an external validity and limited generalisability test, also summarised in Appendix C.

I.IO CONTRIBUTION TO ORGANISATION THEORY AND STRATEGIC MANAGEMENT

Despite growing interest, the current scholarly understanding of innovation among social entrepreneurs is based largely on the assumption that social innovation is produced by social entrepreneurs. This assumption, while common, has so far not been empirically tested. It lacks a unified and coherent framework that captures the unique constraining environment in which social entrepreneurs innovate. Our work investigates empirically how social entrepreneurs conceptualise innovation. We use these empirical insights to propose a theoretical model useful for further research on frugal innovation, as carried out in or for challenging contexts.

Models of innovation derived from the perceptions of social entrepreneurs add directly to wider efforts to specify how such actor perceptions shape innovation process and outcomes. Our contribution progresses such models, challenging and extending current assumptions about social innovation and other emerging concepts, including frugal, grassroots and reverse innovation, all frequently associated with social entrepreneurship. This study foregrounds the perceptions of entrepreneurs and the 'models' of innovation in complex content, in the specific ways shown in Table 1.1.

Table 1.1 *Summary of main findings*

On innovation:	1. Social entrepreneurs are involved in more than social innovation.
	2. Social entrepreneurs use a combination of existing models of innovations.
	3. Social entrepreneurs are more likely to be concerned about institutional and social innovation than about technology innovation.
	4. Social entrepreneurs pack combinations of innovations into new emerging concepts, such as frugal innovation.
On constraints to innovation:	5. Social entrepreneurs and their customers and complementors face a combination of constraints to innovation – institutional voids and resource and affordability constraints.
	6. Social entrepreneurs are more focused on resource challenges, while investors are more focused on institutional challenges.
On methods:	7. Extreme contexts marked by constraints are not unique to developing or emerging markets but also exist in developed markets though differently distributed or recognised.
	8. This is one of a few qualitative studies to use and acknowledge the value of retroduction (or abduction), as opposed to a purely inductive or deductive approach.

Overall, this study reveals the ways social entrepreneurs perceive conceptual drivers and determinants and key features of innovation. To describe our findings, we structure and report on the insights of our respondents as frugal innovation in more complex contexts. This grounded approach starts with the basics: how social entrepreneurs conceptualise innovation. It provides a major large-scale, evidence-based set of results showing what frugality is in innovation, what is innovative about frugal innovation, what motivates social entrepreneurs and other frugal innovators to adopt this approach to innovation and what strategies they use to achieve such purposeful innovation.

In the next two chapters, we report on the results from content analyses and thematic coding. We propose two models of innovation based on these findings. Model 1 (views of innovation among social entrepreneurs) is the focus of Chapter 2; Model 2 (innovation under constraints; the views of social entrepreneurs) is the focus of Chapter 3. In Chapter 4 we integrate lessons from these two models of innovation to propose a theory of frugal innovation. In Chapter 5, we assess the models and the proposed theory and its applicability by reviewing ten published examples of innovation popularly cited in support of emerging innovation concepts. In Chapter 6, we review some of these emerging concepts in innovation and discuss how the findings from this study mainly contribute to the literature on frugal innovation. In Chapter 7, we outline some implications and relevant lessons from this empirical project for theory, practice, policy and future research.

2 Conceptualising Innovation

Model 1

The purpose of this chapter is to help organisational theorists and strategic management scholars develop theoretical models to understand perceptions of innovation among social entrepreneurs. We explore what social entrepreneurs think about innovation and what they say they do, this is distinct from what they do in practice. Explaining what they think about what they do, social entrepreneurs present a narrative of perceptions and features of models of innovation that are relevant for innovation management theory, practice and policy.

The findings and discussion in this chapter suggest that social entrepreneurs vary in how they view and justify innovation. We use evidence on the various ways of understanding the logic, motivations and approaches of innovation to define new concepts such as frugal innovation in empirically grounded ways. We show that innovation among social entrepreneurs is not limited to social innovation. This finding will be valuable for future researchers who associate innovation with social entrepreneurs or question the focus in much current research on the sources and intent of social innovation.

2.1 INTRODUCTION

Much of the research on social entrepreneurship focuses on social entrepreneurs as individuals and what they do. This project opens a different direction for study by asking how social entrepreneurs perceive innovation, both broadly and also under extreme conditions shaped by institutional voids and resource scarcity. To motivate this inquiry, we organised the study to answer three component questions. Here, we report on the first one: *How do social entrepreneurs conceptualise innovation?* This chapter reveals our findings in response to this question, derived from a thematic content analysis of the data.

We gathered data on the thoughts and actions of entrepreneurs. Our findings rely on their narratives instead of focusing on what entrepreneurs in practice. The practise of innovation often involves change brought about by an iterative approach requiring experimentation and strategy reformulation. Our methodological approach uses documents, interviews and observations to tease out perceptions of innovation among social entrepreneurs by encouraging them to be introspective. In other words, this qualitative methodology provides social entrepreneurs with an opportunity to think about and be mindful of what they and others have done or are doing in relation to innovation. Although we acknowledge the limitations of claims based on perceptual data, we believe that the narratives of social entrepreneurs can explain useful perceptions and features of innovation.

While some literature on innovation presents innovation as a coherent, well-defined concept, social entrepreneurs understand the process and the outcomes in very different ways, depending on their motivations, means and outcomes. These concepts (described by new vocabularies) serve as boundary objects, through which many different actors interact to build a community of shared interests and values. We find in these shared concepts evidence of values held in common and which provide bases for action across the seemingly disparate notions of innovation among social entrepreneurs.

2.2 ANALYSIS AND CODING

The analysis of data comprising texts from business plans and other sources, interviews with entrepreneurs and other field intermediaries, and field notes proceeded in four main stages. This was not a purely sequential process, but entailed moving back and forth in an iterative, systematic way. The use of archival data from 163 entrepreneurs and interview and field notes from observing seventy respondents allowed us to triangulate our findings. In this section, we show how the work proceeded from data to the findings reported in this chapter. The four main stages of analysis are summarised in Table 2.1.

Table 2.1 *Stages of analysis: How social entrepreneurs conceptualise innovation*

Stages	Tasks	Outcomes
1. Collate data and develop descriptions.	1. Collate documents, scan handwritten notes and transcribe interviews. 2. Identify responses to questions.	Responses to application form questions. Responses to questions. Handwritten notes with first pass on analysis.
2. Categorise data.	3. Identify first-order codes.	Twenty-five codes: *By grass root individuals; By large firms; By entrepreneurial actors; By designers; For the underserved; For meeting needs; For cost leadership and competitive advantage; For social improvement; For challenge; Non-profit motive; For high profits; For profit/non-profit; Reasonable profits; Making do; Good enough solutions; Surpassing expectations; Radically improving some performance metrics; No attainable solution; Staying ahead of competition; Rectifying inequity; Design breakthroughs; Little scaling; High scalability; Ambition to scale; Proof of concept.*
3. Identify patterns and connections among first-order codes.	4. Integrate first-order codes into second-order codes or themes.	Figure 2.1. Coding sequence. Eight second-order codes or themes are identified. *By whom, for whom, for what, economic orientation, nature of solution, necessity based, ideational based and scalability.* Table 2.3.

	Intermediate table summarising all codes and themes. Table 2.4.
	Breakdown of the number of passages that support data triangulation findings.
4. Aggregate the theoretical dimensions of perceptions of innovation.	Four theoretical dimensions identified: *User-based, Efficiency-based, Challenge-based and Social.*
5. Label dimensions based on emergent concepts or existing ones found in the literature.	Archival document data support different conceptions of innovation (user, efficiency, social and challenge).
	Tables 2.5a, b, c and d. Interview data support different conceptions of innovation.
6. Identify descriptions; exemplify findings for display.	Two axes for aggregating four dimensions into model: *Need-based versus Ideational* and *Proof of Concept versus Scalability.*
	Figure 2.2. Matrix model of perceptions of innovation.
	Figure 2.4. Interpretative theoretical perspectives on perceptions of innovation.

Literature uses various labels interchangeably such as codes, concepts, constructs, categories, themes and dimensions (Vaismoradi et al., 2013). To avoid some of this confusion in describing our findings, we refer to first-order codes as codes, second-order codes as themes and third-order codes as dimensions. Generally, the first-order codes should reflect directly the data (Hsieh and Shannon, 2005) and second-order codes or themes are aggregate codes which coherently reflect the data into higher level abstractions (Sandelowski and Leeman, 2012). At the minimum, a theme may describe the data at the manifest level such that it is directly observable or at the maximum, a theme may describe the data at the latent level such that it interprets the underlying phenomenon (Boyatzis, 1998). Therefore, it needs to balance representing meaning within the data set and also capturing response in relation to the research question (Braun and Clarke, 2006). Although the third-level abstraction can also be called aggregate themes, we call them here theoretical dimensions to reflect the fact that these themes resonate with those found in existing literature.

In the first stage, the data came from the GSBI application forms (which contained business plans and innovation summaries), transcribed interviews and digitised and scanned handwritten field notes. Descriptions in the application forms were already categorised using the following questions:

1. How is your approach innovative (better than alternatives)?
2. Describe the key innovation(s) of your organisation (e.g. business models, products or services, processes, value chain enhancements).
3. Explain the potential for these innovations to be deployed or replicated elsewhere.
4. Explain the potential for licensing these innovations.
5. What were the challenges and obstacles faced?

Although the full application forms exceeded 400 pages, the researcher concentrated on the section on innovation, as outlined in the preceding questions. These innovation summaries together amounted to 158 pages or around 65,000 words, which were used for thematic analysis. A total of 281 passages were coded from these documents, which contributed to developing the first-order codes detailed in this chapter.

Then, descriptions from the interviews and observation notes were categorised in accordance with the four main questions solicited in interviews, which were asked of all respondents and used for analytical purposes.

1. In what ways have you encountered innovation?
2. What is your perception of innovation? Can you provide examples?
3. How could this activity be useful to you or others?
4. What lessons have you learned from your activities to date?

In all, 242 passages from interviews and observation notes were used in the coding. The lead researcher carried out a thematic content analysis, using a template analysis technique recommended by Nigel King (2004a; 2004b). King's template analysis technique combines the approach outlined by Ellen Taylor-Powell and Marcus Renner (2003), using preset and emergent categories. The analyst begins with initial categories after a first read-through of the data and then adds emergent categories as they became apparent from iterative reviews of different sources of triangulated data (documents, interviews and observations). Colour codes and outline shapes were applied to analyse the first read-through of material. These colour codes and shapes were used to group notes into the four main investigative concerns mentioned above. The documents were read thoroughly at least three times before passages were chosen for coding. Passages addressing a common idea or thought were labelled using first-order codes. Double-coded passages were cross-indexed to help identify linkages and relationships that were used to identify second-order codes.

During the second stage, passages were categorised by identifying the first-order codes into themes. These were labelled and grouped to reflect the actual words of participants and texts in as far as possible, i.e. at the manifest level. While thematic content analysis themes were being developed, interpretation was kept to a minimum. Although the epistemological stance of this study is interpretivist or subjective, when conducting a thematic content analysis, the researcher's epistemological stance is objective or objectivistic (Anderson, 2007).

Using *in vivo* first-order codes, i.e. words taken from the text, we came up with twenty-five first-order codes, as shown in Table 2.2.

In understanding that these findings could be affected by the theoretical knowledge the researcher had accumulated and moderated during the data collection process, we adopted Charles C. Ragin and Lisa M. Amoroso's (2010) methodological approach of retroduction in place of pure induction. Instead of making an orthodox dichotomous choice between purely deductive or inductive

Table 2.2 *First-order codes: Conceptualise innovation*

Question	Texts and interviews were coded into	
How do social entrepreneurs view innovation?	1. By grass root individuals	14. Make do
	2. By large firms	15. Good enough solutions
	3. By entrepreneurial actors	16. Surpass expectations
	4. By designers	17. Radically improve some performance metrics
	5. For the underserved	
	6. For solving needs	18. No attainable solution
	7. For cost leadership and competitive advantage	19. Stay ahead of the competition
	8. For social improvement	20. Rectify inequity
	9. For a challenge	21. Design breakthroughs
	10. Non-profit motive	22. Little scaling
	11. For high profits	23. High scalability
	12. For profit/non-profit	24. Ambition to scale
	13. For reasonable profits	25. Proof of concept

research, we made use of an alternative approach: Retroduction, defined as an iterative combination of induction and deduction (Ragin and Amoroso, 2010), and sometimes referred to as abduction (Suddaby, 2006). In a retroductive coding scheme (Ragin 1994), one alternates between a priori and inductive codes. The categories are based on relevant theoretical frameworks and generated prior to the analysis (Ghaziani and Ventresca, 2005). Thus, the initial list of categories changed over the course of coding to accommodate data that did not fit the existing categories during each iteration. This process of revision continues up to the point at which mutual exclusivity and exhaustiveness are maximised (Weber, 1990). According to Ghaziani and Ventresca (2005), this type of coding strategy improves reliability (Stemler, 2001). It can also avert the two most common difficulties researchers encounterwhen using theory to generate a conceptual framework – the overuse and underuse of existing theory (Maxwell, 2005).

In the third stage, probably the trickiest part of the analysis, the task is to understand patterns and connections among the first-order codes so as to integrate them into second-order codes. This work involved repeatedly reviewing the first-order codes and identifying common themes that explained the variation and similarities across codes. These eight analytical themes were, probing who was the innovator, for what purpose and economic motive (orientation) were and for whom, what type of problem it aimed to solve (i.e. was it driven by necessity or ideation) and to what degree of scalability (scalability). These cross-cutting second-order codes amounted to themes. Table 2.3 shows how the first-order codes addressed each of these eight themes

In stage four, the analysis aggregated perceptions of innovation, grouping them by second-order codes into higher-level abstractions. The summary in Table 2.3, which illustrates how the first-, second- and third-level codes came together in both horizontal and vertical groups, provide the data matrix to make these judgments. In principle, the higher-level abstractions should be

Table 2.3 *Summary of codes and themes*

	User-based	Efficiency-based	Social	Challenge-based
By whom	Grassroots individuals	Large firms	Entrepreneurial actors	Designers
For whom	The underserved	The underserved	The underserved	The underserved
For what	To meet needs	Cost leadership and competitive advantage	Social improvement	The challenge
Economic orientation	No profit motive	High profits	Profit/non-profit	Reasonable profits
Nature of solution	Made do	Good enough	Surpassed expectations	Radically improved some performance dimension, or lowered cost
Necessity-based	No attainable solution	Stayed ahead of competition	No data	No data
Ideational	No data	No data	Rectifying inequity	Design breakthroughs
Scalability	Little scaling	High scalability	Ambition to scale	Proof of concept

consonant with existing concepts found in the literature (deduction). The four column headers shown in Table 2.3 were the outcomes, using themes associated with innovation in the literature, which served as third-level codes or theoretical dimensions: user-based, efficiency-based, social, and challenge-based.

The twenty-five first-order codes coalesced into eight themes and finally into four aggregate theoretical dimensions. The archival data from the 163 entrepreneurs interviewed and the field note data from observing 70 respondents triangulated the coding template and helped to validate this analysis. In summary, Figure 2.1 shows the first-order codes and third-level dimensions, while Table 2.3 shows the mediating role played by intermediate second-order codes or themes.

Table 2.4 shows a summary distribution of the 523 passages supporting the data triangulation of findings presented in this chapter. Most of the data supported social innovation, followed by challenge-based, user-based and efficiency-based innovation. Not surprisingly, the least represented category was efficiency, which is usually associated with a different logic of innovation and with

Table 2.4 *Distribution of passages that support data triangulation findings*

	Archival documents (163)	Interviews (70)	Total (%)
Social	100	75	175 (33)
Challenge-based	74	59	133 (25)
User-based	58	54	112 (21)
Efficiency-based	49	54	103 (20)
Total	**281**	**242**	**523 (100)**

FIGURE 2.1 Coding sequence for 'conceptualise innovation'

established scale associated with big business. Most of our informants represented early stage start-ups. The archival document we coded too support all four conceptions of innovation (user, efficiency, social and challenge). Tables 2.5 a, b, c and d each list representative data from interviews supporting these four broad conceptions of innovation.

Table 2.5a *Interview data: Social innovation n = 75 passages*

By whom	Entrepreneurial actors:
	• I don't agree with handout models like [name removed for anonymity] selling expensive solutions to NGOs and donors because it isn't sustainable. We instead believe in the market and sell directly to the consumer.
	• The World Bank and such international organisations aren't doing enough, in fact they put strings such as privatisation to basic human rights such as water, which isn't right. Entrepreneurship for such challenges is the path for charity and grants cannot be sustainable.
	• Frugal innovation is a nice effort to partner technology with entrepreneurship to come up with novel solutions for social problems that are chronic and very serious.
For whom	The underserved:
	• Bonergie aims to terminate poverty in BoP countries.
	• A lot of students now realise that they need to design solutions for the rest of the world – not just for the USA, because (i) markets are there for both MNCs and entrepreneurs; (ii) the Jesuit mission to help the underserved poor.
For what	Social improvement:
	• We are no solar light vendor. We are developer of BoP markets in order to improve the life of people in poverty.
	• My feeling is that innovation is an outcome that occurs after you've engaged with the society you wish to serve in developing countries.
	• I focus on innovating products mainly for social causes. One such project I am working on is an ATM dispenser for medicines that ensures the authenticity of the medicines and 24/7 availability.

Table 2.5a (*cont.*)

Economic orientation	Profit/non-profit: • A major difference between Salauno and Aravind is that we are for profit. But we believe we can make enough surplus to offer free eye care for low-end users and still make profits for our founders and investors. • I use a hybrid model of investing because the rate of return in social enterprises is very low and takes a long time. So, I make up for the delay in financial return through regular investing.
Nature of solution	Surpassing expectations: • So the self-imposed constraints have to be at a higher level than the norm, otherwise your solutions will be the same as everyone else's. • At Aravind, we are talking about design – not for the 1 per cent or the 99 per cent, but for the 100 per cent. • Frugal innovation is about jumping or leapfrogging alternative solutions to use high tech and high quality but at affordable levels.
Necessity	No data
Ideational based	Rectifying inequity: • Services for the poor are not marginalised in a separate unit. Rather, they are integrated to the extent that if the poor are not served, then the Aravind system breaks down for all. • Several of our Senior Design projects involve a social justice component which we implement through engineering solutions. • Aurolab was initiated because we wanted the poor to have the same high-end lenses, so it was a major contribution but not alone.
Scalability	Ambition to scale: • In a mature developed market, you can use retailers like Walmart and Amazon to sell multiple

Table 2.5a (*cont.*)

products to many customers. However, in
developing economies you need to partner with
intermediaries to focus on a use case, gain a large
'shadow effect' and then replicate it to scale in
those markets.

- Cost per outcome is an attempt by social ventures
  to be more financially relevant to investors.
  Reducing the cost per outcome also involves scaling
  up potential, since one can do more with little.
- Learning from us – we do 300K surgeries a year
  and have enabled others to do another 1 million
  a year.
- The innovations were meant to be replicable right
  from the start. If an innovation cannot be
  economically replicated, we discard it.

Table 2.5b *Interview data: Challenge-based innovation n = 59 passages*

By whom	Designers:
	• As a product designer, I am motivated by the outcome, but driven more by the challenge to innovate for demanding customer needs in demanding environments.
	• It is particularly hard for designers in the West to accomplish this for the developing world because of cost-reduction impediments and the inability to understand fully the needs of those communities.
	• I take up frugal innovation from Radha's perspective as being low-cost, rugged, user-friendly and simple. As an engineer, I recognise that these are very challenging design criteria.

Table 2.5b (*cont.*)

For whom	The underserved:
	• I perceive that innovation offers appropriate technologies for the Base of Pyramid in global markets. Pre-built solutions ingrained in engineers' minds are not successful.
	• Frugal innovation seems to solve the problems of the poor by designing solutions for them. This means understanding their needs in those particular contexts.
For what	Challenge:
	• As an engineer, achieving a 10 per cent cost reduction is difficult, with next 10 per cent even more so and 10 per cent after that even worse.
	• For the 'techie' students, frugal contexts present interesting challenges with different performance dimensions, as well as an understanding of the whole ecosystem that embodies engineering for humanity, as opposed to just the role of technology.
	• So, the self-imposed constraints have to be at a higher level than the norm, otherwise your solutions will be the same as everyone else's.
Economic orientation	Reasonable profits:
	• A challenge is how we move away from maximum margins to reasonable margins for all in the value chain.
Nature of solution	Radically improve some performance dimension or lower costs:
	• I told GE that the 10–15 per cent cost reduction being talked about means that they are not serious about addressing the BoP. Instead, they need a tenfold decrease.
	• BoP customers are actually pretty demanding and rather sophisticated in recognising more high quality and aesthetically expensive-looking

Table 2.5b (*cont.*)

	products in their choices. This is part of the challenge for designers in the North innovating for the BoP in the South.
Necessity based	No data
Ideational based	Design breakthroughs: • Most people try to carry out disruptive innovation through standard constraints, as opposed to self-imposed constraints. But recall Einstein's comment that the same level of thinking cannot solve the problems it created in the first place. • Here they rely on Moore's law to increase performance and lower prices. However, in the areas where I function, you need to do more than just that. • And we believe that careful attention to design can create innovative – and extremely affordable – solutions to the problems of the other 90 per cent. In other words: treat the poor as customers, not charity recipients.
Scalability	Proof of concept: • As an investor, I would look for a focused reference-ability model that achieves scale in developing economies. • I use design thinking to setup new micro-franchise businesses such as ideation and prototyping, microlight marketing and quick and dirty proofs of concepts. • The aim of our activity is to demonstrate that it is possible to make profits from waste and hence attract private sector participants into the industry.

Table 2.5c *Interview data: User-based innovation n = 54 passages*

By whom	Grassroot individuals:
	• I came up with the N100 light as a technology concept myself and then went out looking for a market. Based on feedback and learning, it changed to a better N200 model, but that doesn't mean that an invention without an application or market doesn't succeed. Take the examples of 3M post it notes and photovoltaic bulbs which both came out of serendipity.
	• [Our mission is] providing microfinance, training and virtual marketplace to grassroots youth entrepreneurs and women.
	• In India, innovation is at the grassroots level, as in the case of *jugaad*, a term that means making do with whatever resources are on hand. One common practice is to reuse a water pump engine for another unintended purpose, like powering a rural van. Or like the clay fridge. So people are creative, but in an unstructured way.
For whom	The underserved:
	• Over 15 years [we] have been investing to provide educational content and skills to underserved communities through the use of radio.
	• Fundamentally, we see extreme poverty as the ultimate source of vulnerability that must be shattered to ensure that opportunity and freedom flourish.
For what	Solving problems and meeting needs:
	• I took them (students) to Housesafe near Santa Clara, a community programme for battered women, and tried to have my students solve some of their needs. And the women surprisingly contributed to creating the solutions. So inequities lie everywhere and, relatively speaking, the differentials are worse in Silicon Valley where the rich-poor divide is huge.

Table 2.5c (*cont.*)

	• The breadth of exposure and ability to ground a Santa Clara education in immersion serving the world's neediest peoples are invaluable. Our objective, and the objective of the capstone projects, should thus not be defined narrowly in terms of training students to work in conventional US jobs.
Economic orientation	No profit motive:
	• There are now reports that warn innovators not to expect to become rich by serving the BoP.
	• As we are a fair trade business working out of an African economy we cannot afford high Western marketing costs. To achieve such costs would mean we would have to add unethical profit margins.
	• Mineral water and safe water retail prices are artificially inflated with un-necessary quality labels and standards
Nature of solution	Making do:
	• The family carried out all kinds of financial and technological improvisation to ensure that the device was sustained and maintained. They initiated advance service agreements and used spare parts not orginally designed for it.
	• Frugal innovation is about overcoming constraints, such as [limited] resources – and making do with what one currently controls.
	• The flying villagers in Peru are an example of *jugaad*. That kind of practice would never be allowed here in the USA.
Necessity-based	No attainable solution:
	• It isn't that easy to do, perhaps because the solutions are not suitable or appropriate to where the problems are.
	• Grassroots level entrepreneurs are still [a long way] away to [be able to] take the advantage of modern technology.

Table 2.5c *(cont.)*

	• We do not compete against anybody. It is a BOP high education market not attended to by any public or private university.
Ideational	No data
Scalability	Little scaling:
	• Like a lot of 'grassroots' organisations, we grew out of passion, not out of a rational plan to create an organisation that will last. But, obviously, passion can only carry you so far. So, we must now focus on sustainability and organisational stability. • … an institutional process will be emerged for scaling up grassroots entrepreneurs [by] adopting ICT. • *Jugaad* is limited to grassroots innovators with little [...] ambition for scaling. • *Jugaad* is not acceptable in India among corporations or even among villagers. If you say 'this is a *jugaad* water filtration device', the villagers will not use it. • *Jugaad* and frugal innovation cannot work in the USA because those sorts of cars and tractors would not be allowed to run on the roads here. In addition, used cars are so affordable here no one seems to need a Tata Nano.

Table 2.5d *Interview data: Efficiency-based innovation n = 54 passages*

By whom	Large firms:
	• As CEO of the (large) company I ran, I would now go back and have a project team working on, for instance, cookstove combustion, not just to fulfil a need or opportunity for profit, but to learn from new contexts and constraints.

Table 2.5d (cont.)

	• Japanese techniques borrowed from Demming's belief that quality is free, because if it weren't then you'd pay much more for it in after-sales service and loss. In the 70s and 80s, the Japanese showed that low cost and high quality were not mutually exclusive. • Frugal innovation may serve as a measure of success for a firm functioning in developing or emerging markets.
For whom	The underserved: • If there is one thing I would do, it is to make executives of large organisations aware of the opportunity in large BoP population markets. • GE's Healthy Imagination Initiative has not succeeded in reaching rural areas – it has reached middle-income towns but not the BoP.
For what	Cost leadership and competitive advantage: • To me it (innovation) is about solving a problem in the most efficient manner possible. • Competitive advantage emanates from increasing sustainability, lower costs, most useful functions, market access, best value quality and products easiest to buy through financing options. A lower cost or price is the easiest thing to achieve but it does not allow for a sustainable competitive advantage. The deeper you go in your business model to achieve other strategies, the more sustainable your competitive advantage becomes. • One side of frugal innovation comes from GE's pitch on a public relations campaign for CSR or other issues on emerging markets.

Table 2.5d (*cont.*)

Economic orientation	High profits: • Cost reduction has been about greater profit margins for the company. • I do not limit my endeavours to social products or ventures, but rather to a wide range of sectors like healthcare, energy and cosmetics – as long as they are deemed profitable. That is crucial to help sustain the business model in that particular context.
Nature of solution	Good enough: • What we (at Intel) learned from impending competition from OLPC was to redesign the processor for low-cost netbooks with good-enough performance. So yes, the West can learn from technology applications in developing countries. • It (frugal innovation) is all about common sense and de-sophistication. Recall the NASA ball point pen for $5 million versus a $1 pencil. • However, large firms do not use *jugaad* much, as it denotes unsophistication and an unstructured process of innovation. They do more of the formal R&D-led innovation.
Necessity-based	Stay ahead of the competition: • I used to work for Intel in the USA. There, it is about exceeding requirements with a focus on sophistication. Here, we outpace many of the technological features used by consumers. However, the Intel Atom processor was a change of mind-set brought about by competition from the OLPC. We redesigned the processor for low-cost and good-enough performance for netbooks.
Ideational-based	No data

Table 2.5d (*cont.*)

Scalability	High scalability:
	• I think social entrepreneurs are the same as entrepreneurs. Social entrepreneurs are good at experimenting and exhibiting proofs of concepts. However large organisations are good at scaling. This is no different from regular Silicon Valley entrepreneurial models, where small firms are sold to large ones. What is different, though, is the IRR from these ventures.
	• Soon you will see companies like eHealth and Husk Power being acquired by MNCs. This would help achieve scalability goals, as MNCs are good at replicating what works well.

2.3 AGGREGATING INTO THIRD-LEVEL THEORETICAL CONCEPTS

Our analysis identified several first-order codes around second-order themes; these have helped to define the various perceptions of innovation revealed in this study. In the fourth and final stage of coding and analysis, our objective was to take the first- and second-order codes and supporting data quotations and label them with theoretical dimensions based on emergent or existing concepts. We did so by comparing the second-order themes across the first-order codes shown in Table 2.3. Second-order themes were placed in rows and analysed for third-level theoretical dimensions across the columns.

By using cross indexing and building relationships across passages and first-order codes, iteratively reconfiguring the codes from one column to the other, we arrived at the final version shown in Table 2.3. First-order codes coalesced into second-order themes which further coalesced into third-level theoretical dimensions. Based on the existing literature; these aggregate dimensions are user-based innovations (Von Hippel, 1986; 1988; 2005), efficiency-based innovations (Govindarajan, Immelt and Trimble, 2009), social innovations (Nicholls and Murdock, 2011) and challenge-based innovations (Diamandis and Kotler, 2012).

2.4 GENERATING A MODEL AND TOWARDS THEORY

One objective for this research is to generate a typology of innovation based on insights from social entrepreneurs. Table 2.3 is directly useful for this work. All four categories share a common element: the innovations of social entrepreneurs target 'underserved' consumers. In some cases, consumers were underserved because existing market participants had failed to develop affordable products. Other consumers were underserved as a result of technology failure; technology, while appropriate for relatively wealthy consumers, is not designed well for such users. We also identified two dimensions where 'no data' existed in half the categories. These observations support a further distinction between two groups among the four third-level theoretical dimensions. The necessity-based and ideational categories were grouped together, as were proof of concept and high scalability. We used these dimensions 'need' and 'scalability' – to generate a fresh typology of innovation. Figure 2.2 presents this 2×2 matrix, which relates the four third-level codes.

2.5 DISCUSSION

The findings outlined in this chapter underscore how social entrepreneurs view varieties of innovation, beyond the talismanic social innovation. The view from social entrepreneurs suggests several distinctions which are not present in existing theory or empirical research about social entrepreneurs. Furthermore, this perceptual approach enriches broader conceptions of innovation. In this section, we digest these initial findings and consider the implications of these data. We develop these ideas further in later chapters, after providing further evidence from the study about context and constraints.

Efficiency-Driven Innovation FIRM LEVEL Efficiency and financial bottom line focused, large firm and MNCs centric, with ambitions for cost leadership based globally profitable competitive advantage e.g. 'Reverse' innovation strategies by GE, TATA, EasyPaisa, Haier (Govindarajan and Trimble, 2012)	Social-Driven Innovation COMMUNITY LEVEL Socially beneficial, entrepreneurial, with ambitions to scale but not necessarily profit from it e.g. Aravind, NHH, Grameen Microfinance, BRAC (Nicholls, 2006)
User-Driven Innovation INDIVIDUAL LEVEL Grassroots, need based, mostly individual based, little ambition for profit or scale e.g. Local jugaad applications, Honey Bee Network, Mumbai Dabbawallas (Von Hippel, 2005)	Challenge-Driven Innovation SECTORAL LEVEL Challenge focused for radical cost or performance improvements, entrepreneurial & network enabled; various social, economic, technological goals e.g. X-Prize, $300 House, OLPC, Tata Nano (Diamandis & Kotler 2011)

The left rows are labelled **Scalability** (top) and **Proof of Concept** (bottom). The bottom is labelled **Necessity based** (left) and **Ideational based** (right).

FIGURE 2.2 Model 1: Matrix model of perceptions of innovation

The argument that frames this discussion is the too frequently accepted and under-examined view that social entrepreneurs do social innovation. The findings in this study challenge this apparently simple claim. We do so first to understand in richer empirical terms how social entrepreneurs view innovation in general and then to investigate how they characterise the kinds of innovation they purpose. Our position is an effort to ground ideas like 'frugal innovation' in the context of varieties of innovation in practice.

Jay Weerawardena and Gillian Sullivan Mort (2006) developed a bounded multidimensional model of social entrepreneurship based on the grounded theory method and drawing on nine in-depth case studies. We extend this approach, to understand the models of innovation reported by social entrepreneurs as 'multidimensional constellations of conceptually distinct characteristics that commonly occur together' (Meyer, Tsui and Hinings, 1993, p. 1175). To identify these 'distinct characteristics', we consider how social entrepreneurs think about their own experience and practice of innovation. The literature on social entrepreneurship attributes social innovation to social entrepreneurs without direct attention to what is social innovation (cf. Deiglmeier et al., 2008; Minks, 2011; Mulgan et al., 2007a; 2007b; Nicholls and Murdock, 2011; Pol and Ville, 2009).[1] In our study, social entrepreneurs report on many types of innovation that they engage with, including social innovation, but also other types already found in the existing literature and practice. The social entrepreneurs agreed to disagree that they were purely or only social innovators. The question then arises: What are the implications for theory and policy of these 'varieties of innovation' in the practice of social entrepreneurs? In the data, social entrepreneurs reference emerging concepts such as inclusive, *jugaad* and frugal innovation, suggesting their willingness to blend innovation approaches.

Our findings suggest that social entrepreneurs use different models (including logic and justifications) when describing the innovation they do. For example, in our analysis, social innovation models are associated with civic concerns, user-based models with domestic concerns, efficiency-based models with market concerns and challenge-based models with fame and fortune concerns. The civic concern seeks to create value by addressing communal or society-wide issues. The domestic concern seeks to create value for localised problems by and for users. The market concern seeks to create value through competition, greater efficiency, improved productivity and enhanced operational effectiveness. And the fame and fortune concerns seek to create value by being among the first to solve challenging problems that others have not been able to resolve.

We used our finding about the four social entrepreneur-recognised innovations to create a typology of innovation models using two integrated dimensions: proof of concept or high scalability and necessity or ideational motives. The model suggests that innovations when framed as solutions are associated with

---

[1] We underscore here the wide range of views described, going beyond a single, shared conception of social innovation.

different concerns or motives and ways of judging value – solutions by and for users, solutions that increase efficiency for firms, solutions that surmount challenges and solutions that achieve a social goal for communities. These principles justify the pursuit of one or a range of different innovations to serve underserved or marginalised segments of the population. We can therefore formulate the following propositions from these findings:

Proposition 1: Innovation for underserved or marginalised communities ranges from needs-based to ideational.

Proposition 2: Innovation for underserved or marginalised communities is motivated by social opportunity at one end and economic opportunity on the other.

Given that social entrepreneurs have a range of different conceptions of innovation, beyond social innovation, we look for a further way to capture these differences. We develop in this work the idea of 'frugal innovation', which was mentioned sporadically in the workshops and discussions and is explicitly reflected in the adopted name of the Frugal Innovation Lab at Santa Clara University, the location of the GSBI. The potential for frugal innovation as a multi-dimenstional research concept may provide several benefits for research and for policy.

We propose that the concept of frugal innovation relates to theoretical concerns about intra- and inter-organisational divisions of labour, organisational design, networks and collaborations and the transcendence of organisational boundaries. These extend many policy efforts to treat frugal innovation as simply a leaner version of other innovations. For instance, when it comes to organisational boundaries, social entrepreneurs are seen mainly as social innovators and business entrepreneurs, while firms are perceived as technology innovators. Through a common focus on serving the underserved, whether for profit or social improvement, both are adopting the concept of frugal innovation (cf. Bhatti, Khilji and Basu, 2013; Govindarajan and Trimble, 2012; Radjou, Prabhu and Ahuja, 2012;

Proposition 3a: *Frugal innovation is an attempt by social entrepreneurs to bring social innovation to the for-profit sphere of the business environment (social-based).*

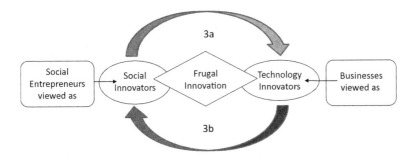

Proposition 3b: *Frugal innovation is an attempt by businesses to bring traditional Schumpeterian innovation to the non-profit sphere of the social environment (efficiency-based).*

FIGURE 2.3 Bridging the gap between social and business priorities through frugal innovation

see Bibliography for many others) as a common ground that transcends and reconciles the different motivations and approaches of social and commercial entrepreneurs and firms.

Similarly, understanding the emergence and development of cross-sector collaboration between social enterprises and corporations (Nicholls and Huybrechts, 2013) is still a contested activity, with few conventions or stable templates. While social innovation might seem to be at the opposite end of the profit-motive spectrum from business innovation, frugal innovation in the idiom of social entrepeneurs provides a bridge to integrate these activities in new combinations and to new purposes – bringing 'business' into the activities of social entrepreneurs and 'social' concerns into the activities of corporations (e.g. General Electric [GE] and Tata). This phenomenon is depicted in Figure 2.3.

We therefore propose the following:

Proposition 3: While social innovation and commercial innovation are conventionally located as the ends of a continuum, frugal innovation as a multi-dimensional concept and practice bridges these disparate notions of innovation together. It helps to bring business into the activities of social entrepreneurs and social concerns into the activities of corporations (e.g. GE and Tata).

Proposition 3a: Frugal innovation is an attempt by social entrepreneurs to bring social innovation to the for-profit sphere of the business environment (social-based).

Proposition 3b: Frugal innovation is an attempt by business to bring Schumpeterian innovation to the non-profit sphere of the social environment (efficiency-based).

Social entrepreneurs are pragmatists. In their business plans, vocabularies and activities, they reject pure forms. Instead, their work provides us evidence of experiments with different forms of innovation, in pursuit diverse means and ends. We see this directly in the model of innovation in Figure 2.2. In spite of the diversity of views among our sample of social entrepreneurs, we nevertheless found commonalities binding notions of innovation together. One such common theme that moved across and united different conceptions of innovation was a focus on addressing the needs and aspirations of disadvantaged, disenfranchised or marginalised segments of society – the underserved, who represent the base of the pyramid.

We use three standard theories as lenses to review these perceptual models: functional, process and institutional. This analytical step reveals the common concerns that bind together notions of innovation in the views of our informants. The abstractions revealed through the three lenses show that innovation is a set of ideas that can be collectively defined. We use the functional lens on each of the four types to show how they differ. We then use the process and institutional lenses to show, despite their differences, how the four recombine towards a common approach and objective.

We begin with the functional perspective. From a functional perspective, innovation (and specifically frugal innovation among social entrepreneurs), focuses on how outcomes are used and for what purpose. For instance, outcomes may satisfy unmet needs

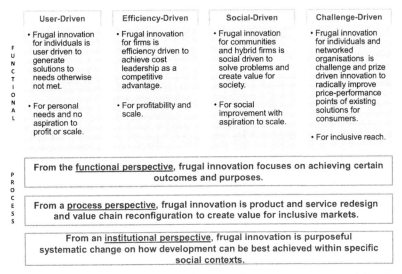

User-Driven	Efficiency-Driven	Social-Driven	Challenge-Driven
• Frugal innovation for individuals is user driven to generate solutions to needs otherwise not met. • For personal needs and no aspiration to profit or scale.	• Frugal innovation for firms is efficiency driven to achieve cost leadership as a competitive advantage. • For profitability and scale.	• Frugal innovation for communities and hybrid firms is social driven to solve problems and create value for society. • For social improvement with aspiration to scale.	• Frugal innovation for individuals and networked organisations is challenge and prize driven innovation to radically improve price-performance points of existing solutions for consumers. • For inclusive reach.

From the <u>functional perspective</u>, frugal innovation focuses on achieving certain outcomes and purposes.

From a <u>process perspective</u>, frugal innovation is product and service redesign and value chain reconfiguration to create value for inclusive markets.

From an <u>institutional perspective</u>, frugal innovation is purposeful systematic change on how development can be best achieved within specific social contexts.

FIGURE 2.4 Interpretative theoretical perspectives on models of (frugal) innovation

(user-based), become more efficient (efficiency-driven), solve social problems (social-driven), or solve difficult problems for underserved markets (challenge-driven).

Proposition 4: From the functional perspective, frugal innovation focuses on achieving certain outcomes and purposes.

2.5.1 Social Innovation

Nicholls and Murdock (2011, p. 2) define social innovation as 'the production of new ideas and new structures (Scott, 2008) and a process of recontextualisation within socially (re)constructed norms of the public good, justice and equity.' Our empirical findings show that this type of innovation is primarily focused on an ideational vision for social improvement that aspires to high scalability. This approach is generally used at the community level of analysis, although it is not limited to that level. From a social functional perspective, frugal innovation is social because it aims to solve problems and create value for society. In Chapter 5, we describe three case examples, the

Aravind Eye Hospital, the Narayana Hrudayalaya Cardiac Hospital and the Grameen Bank as reflecting this social approach to frugal innovation.

Proposition 4a: From the functional perspective, frugal innovation is ideational to achieve social improvement and scalability.

2.5.2 Challenge-Based Innovation

In *Abundance: The Future Is Better Than You Think,* authors Peter H. Diamandis and Steven Kotler (2012) describe how people come together to take on the challenge of solving seemingly unsolvable or critical problems. Luciano Kay (2011) studies the Ansari XPrize and the Northrop Grumman Lunar Lander Challenge in order to determine the effect of inducement and challenge prizes on innovation. Our empirical findings confirm that such innovators are motivated by the challenge of radically improving the cost performance of various social, economic and technological goals. As these goals span several areas, this approach can be best understood as occurring at the sectoral level of analysis. Seen from a challenge-based functional perspective, frugal innovation is motivated by the desire to meet a challenge and win a prize; its aim is to radically improve an offering for consumers, such as the price-performance points of existing solutions. The 'ideal' outcome of such a challenge is often to showcase a technical proof of concept that makes wide-scale inclusivity possible. Kay (2011) finds that the introduction of novel research and development (R&D) inducement approaches is associated with the participation of unconventional entrants. Our study supports earlier work in the field, since we find that challenge-based innovation attracts the interest of a wide range of actors, from investors and innovators to users. In Chapter 5, we describe three cases, the Tata Nano car, the Space X prize and One Laptop per Child, that exemplify this challenge-based approach to frugal innovation.

Proposition 4b: From the functional perspective of challenge-based innovation, frugal innovation is ideational – proving inclusive outreach by exhibiting proof of concept for a challenging concern.

2.5.3 User-Based Innovation

As defined by Eric von Hippel (2005), user-based innovation derives from user needs, with the users themselves as innovators. Our empirical findings confirm that such innovators are primarily focused on solving local needs (personal, family or community), with little or no interest in making a profit or scaling up their innovations. User-based innovation occurs at the individual level of analysis. From a functional perspective, frugal innovation is user-based insofar as it involves generating solutions to meet local needs not otherwise provided for by the market. In Chapter 5, we describe the Mumbai dabbawalas' case as an example of this user-based approach to frugal innovation.

Proposition 4c: From the functional perspective of user innovation, frugal innovation involves users innovating to meet local needs, with little or no aspiration to profit from or scale up their innovations.

2.5.4 Efficiency-Driven Innovation

We draw from the work of Porter (1998) to define efficiency-based innovation as being focused on attaining a competitive advantage through cost leadership. This approach to innovation aims to generate profits and achieve high scalability. It generally occurs at the firm level of analysis. From an efficiency-based functional perspective, frugal innovation is efficiency focused on achieving cost leadership as a competitive advantage. In Chapter 5, we describe two case examples, General Electric and EasyPaisa, as reflecting this efficiency-based approach to frugal innovation.

Proposition 4d: From the functional perspective of efficiency-based innovation, frugal innovation seeks to achieve cost leadership as a competitive advantage by generating high profits through low cost and high scalability.

2.5.5 Combining the Four Types to Define Frugal Innovation

We have shown how the four types of innovation differ and also share some commonalities. Serving the underserved is a common theme that is shared across all of the perceptions of innovation we report. However, varying perceptions of innovation show that social entrepreneurs are concerned about both technical and market uncertainty. By integrating these two understandings, we propose that social entrepreneurs conceive of innovation in ways that enrich available treatments in research and policy and that open up fresh directions to better specify research and to inform policy. Our informants broadly understand 'innovation' as a focus on the provision of solutions (products, services, distribution and business models) to underserved or marginalised consumers who face market or technology failure. The models they distinguish serve as boundary objects for practice. This more precise understanding can usefully inform new research.

If potential products and services target current markets, they face only technical uncertainty. If they aim beyond current markets, then they face both technical and market uncertainty. The former embodies capabilities, performance and interdependence with other parts of the system, while the latter involves building a new system that offers usage preferences and benefits to consumers. In summary, innovation among social entrepreneurs can be construed as an effort to overcome market or technology failures to create inclusive markets. The goal of creating inclusive markets and the challenge of creating value through the interdependence of technical and market uncertainty make it necessary to consider the whole value chain in the design and reconfiguration of solutions. Consequently, we argue that the functional perspective of frugal innovation outlined earlier can be made more dynamic, by engaging with a process perspective, whereby frugal innovation is viewed as a set of tasks or actions that can redesign products and services and reconfigure value chains to create value for inclusive markets.

Proposition 5: From the process perspective, frugal innovation is a set of activities undertaken to redesign products and services and reconfigure value chains, in order to create value for inclusive markets.

Our findings suggest that efficiency- and challenge-based innovation are characterised by producer, supply-side and push factors (Geroski, 2003). By contrast, user-based and social innovation are characterised by demand, consumer-side and pull factors. Social-based innovation can emerge from either the supply or the demand side. This challenges several stable boundaries in research on innovation and provokes further reflection. Over the last fifty years, the changing logics of development have shifted from supply-side handouts and technology transfer to more demand-side capability building and technology adaptation. The sources of change have also shifted from state and philanthropic development agencies to market-driven entrepreneurs, MNCs and community-led civic groups. Our findings suggest that the eclectic mix of need-driven individuals, challenge-driven networks of individuals, efficiency-driven corporations and socially driven individuals, organisations and communities are all working to overcome development shortcomings of the past.

From an institutional perspective, therefore, frugal innovation can be viewed as a purposeful, systematic change to ideas about how development can best be achieved within specific social contexts. This contributes to its development as a new field. The implication is that frugal innovation is less about innovation in products and technologies and more about a new concept of innovation and what it can strive to achieve.

Proposition 6: From an institutional perspective, frugal innovation is a purposeful systems change to ideas about how development can best be achieved within specific social contexts.

Figure 2.4 summarises the interpretation of frugal innovation outlined here. In Chapter 5, we discuss ways in which the emerging concept of frugal innovation relates to similar themes found in the literature, including reverse, grassroots, *jugaad* and inclusive innovation.

2.6 SUMMARY

We gathered data on how social entrepreneurs perceive and say that they carry out innovation. Our findings rely on this narrative of perception and implementation, rather than on what social entrepreneurs 'really' do on the ground. Since the objective of this research is to generate models of innovation from the perspective of social entrepreneurs rather than to benchmark practices or processes, it seemed appropriate to rely on perceptions and narratives to achieve this outcome.

The findings and discussion in this chapter suggest that social entrepreneurs view and justify innovation in different ways. We show that innovation among social entrepreneurs is not limited to social innovation. This is a valuable finding for future research, as it questions the conventional view that social entrepreneurs are always associated with social innovation. This study suggests that the literature's exclusive focus on one type of innovation is a suspect approach. Furthermore, there is evidence to suggest that a new field of innovation, frugal innovation, is emerging from the varying types of logic, motivation and approach described in this chapter and is becoming increasingly established as demonstrated in recent efforts to collate this literature (Agarwal et al., 2017; Hossain, 2017; Pisoni, Michelini and Martignoni, 2018).

In the next chapter, we outline the analysis and findings that address the next two sub-questions: How do social entrepreneurs conceptualise innovation under (1) institutional voids and (2) resource scarcity?

3 Conceptualising Innovation under Constraints

Model 2

The purpose of this chapter is to determine how the preceding perceptions and views of innovation are shaped by resource scarcity or constraints and by institutional voids or alternative forms of institutions. This exercise contributes to the literature on how contextual conditions based on resource dependency theory and institutional theory shape models of innovation.

The findings and discussion in this chapter show how social entrepreneurs view innovation under constraints and seek to deal with these constraints using existing innovation components. They report making use of social, technology and institutional innovation components. The mixed use of existing innovation approaches supported by data, analysis and interpretive findings suggests a hybrid approach to innovation. Sometimes contradictory assumptions stem from differences across the logics of justification that social entrepreneurs rely on when viewing innovation models. We take advantage of these contrasting logics to suggest a new theory that better explains innovation, as conceptualised by the respondents in this study. We draw out common themes across contrasting logics to develop an empirically derived concept of frugal innovation, then use this to develop an integrated view that provides common ground among varied perspectives.

3.1 INTRODUCTION

Remember that our main research question is: *How do social entrepreneurs perceive innovation broadly and under extreme conditions shaped by institutional voids and resource scarcity?* We posed this as three distinct sub-questions, of which the second and third are:

2. *How do they conceptualise innovation when dealing with institutional voids?*

3. *How do they conceptualise innovation in a context of resource scarcity?*

The objective of this chapter is to report findings from an exploratory and descriptive analysis of the second and third sub-questions. The literature review cited in Chapter 2 shows that there is scope to study innovation in a context of both institutional voids and resource scarcity. We seek to understand what the conceptual drivers and determinants of innovation look like in a context with both institutional voids and resource scarcity. To achieve this, we derived thirty-two first-order and nine second-order themes from data sources, which are then grouped into three theoretical dimensions (found in the existing literature) and transformed into a 'model of innovation under constraints'.

Any study of innovation by social entrepreneurs should consider how resource constraints are faced both upstream and downstream by users at all points along the value chain, who must also cope with institutional voids and resource scarcity. We follow the discussion in Section 1.7 and use a value chain conceptual framework to analyse data and determine how social entrepreneurs perceive innovation under constraints. The use of a value chain to analyse innovation activities is supported by established innovation studies (cf. Dedrick, Kraemer and Linden, 2010; Hansen and Birkinshaw, 2007; Kaplinsky and Morris, 2001; Roper, Du and Love, 2008). These constraints are reflected in the value chain conceptual framework as institutional voids and resource scarcity. In 'extreme resource constrained' contexts (Mair and Martí, 2009), resources may be scarce at all points along the value chain, meaning that affordability is a concern not just for the end market consumer, but also for any firm wishing to use another firm's outcome in its own processes. Affordability is not just a concern at the end point or outcome of innovation. We therefore analysed sub-questions 2 and 3 using a value chain innovation perspective to develop the conceptual framework for innovation activity under both institutional voids and resource scarcity.

From this value chain analytical perspective, we can hypothe-sise what innovation could mean to both the upstream supplier and the downstream consumer. From the social entrepreneur or supplier perspective, a solution has to be designed, produced, delivered and maintained to meet the needs of underserved consumers in con-strained environments. The entrepreneur may have to function in an environment marked by one or many constrained resources or institutions. From the consumer perspective, a solution may be low-cost and affordable. However, affordability extends beyond simply the cost of the solution to include operational and disposal costs. A product or service does not stand alone, but may need comple-mentary solutions, resources and infrastructure to perform to its full potential. This can mean not just lowering the cost of the product, but also rethinking how it can be designed to operate in the resource-constrained context in which it functions, using fewer resources among complex or thin institutional conditions.

3.2 ANALYSIS AND CODING

The sequence of coding from first- to second- to third-order codes and themes is depicted in Figure 3.1 based on 1,205 coded passages drawn from 163 documents and 70 interviews. Coding was carried out for three analytical concerns: institutional voids and resource scarcity, with the latter segmented into resource constraints and affordability constraints. The thirty-two first-order codes coalesced into nine second-order themes, of which three related to institutional voids: building structures, boundary issues and access provision. The next three second-order themes involved resource constraints: the scope of the solution, satisficing and improving performance or efficiency. The final second-order themes had to do with affordability con-straints: resolving needs or meeting aspirations, reaching out and developing capabilities. The second-order dimensions served to iden-tify the third-level theoretical abstractions discussed below.

Chapter 2 describes in detail the process of analysis of qualita-tive data comprising texts, interviews and field notes to arrive at the

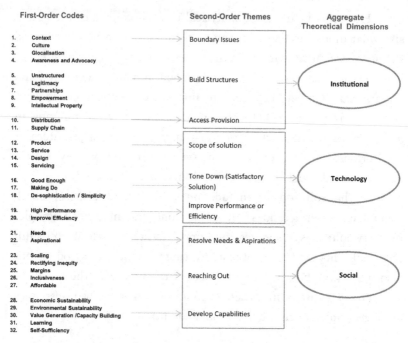

First-Order Codes | Second-Order Themes | Aggregate Theoretical Dimensions

1. Context
2. Culture
3. Glocalisation
4. Awareness and Advocacy

Boundary Issues

5. Unstructured
6. Legitimacy
7. Partnerships
8. Empowerment
9. Intellectual Property

Build Structures

Institutional

10. Distribution
11. Supply Chain

Access Provision

12. Product
13. Service
14. Design
15. Servicing

Scope of solution

16. Good Enough
17. Making Do
18. De-sophistication / Simplicity

Tone Down (Satisfactory Solution)

Technology

19. High Performance
20. Improve Efficiency

Improve Performance or Efficiency

21. Needs
22. Aspirational

Resolve Needs & Aspirations

23. Scaling
24. Rectifying Inequity
25. Margins
26. Inclusiveness
27. Affordable

Reaching Out

Social

28. Economic Sustainability
29. Environmental Sustainability
30. Value Generation /Capacity Building
31. Learning
32. Self-Sufficiency

Develop Capabilities

FIGURE 3.1 Coding sequence

findings outlined in this chapter. The four main stages of analysis are summarised in Table 3.1. Again, these stages were not linear; the analysis moved back and forth in an iterative process. This iterative process derived from the reasons described in Chapter 1 for using Ragin's (1994) and Ragin and Amoroso's (2010) retroductive approach, as well as a thematic content analysis using King's (2004a; 2004b) template analysis technique. We describe this process to show how we went from the data to the findings discussed in this chapter.

In the first stage, the lead researcher went through all the collated data, which included application forms, transcribed interviews and digitised and scanned handwritten field notes to identify passages that seemed to relate to either or both of the two investigative and analytical themes – institutional voids and resource scarcity. In the archival documents, 296 passages addressed institutional voids, as did 123 passages from the interviews and field notes.

Table 3.1 *Stages of analysis for research subquestions 2 and 3*

Stages	Tasks	Outcomes
Pre-step: Descriptions using interview questions previously analysed		Responses to the questions posed
1. Identify descriptions on A) institutional voids and B) resource scarcity	1. Emphasise text that corresponds to A) institutional voids and B) resource scarcity 2. Comparison across data sources 3. Comparison across types of respondents	Archival document data responses on institutional voids (bold and underlined) – 296 passages Interview data responses on institutional voids (bold and underlined) – 123 passages Archival document data responses on resource constraints (bold and italicised) – 398 passages Interview data responses on resource constraints (bold and italicised) – 131 passages Archival document responses on BOTH institutional voids (bold and underlined) and resource constraints (bold and italicised) – 50 passages Interview data responses on BOTH institutional voids (bold and underlined) and resource constraints (bold and italicised) – 41 passages Table 3.2. Number of passages coded from each data source Table 3.3.

Table 3.1 (cont.)

Stages	Tasks	Outcomes
		Comparison of types of respondents discussing institutional voids and resource scarcity Table 3.4. First-order codes for questions 2 and 3 Table 3.5. Number of passages that support third-level theoretical dimensions
2. Categorise information to generate main constructs on A) institutional voids and B) resource scarcity	4. Recode to generate constructs as first-order codes 5. Identify key descriptions as exemplary to the clusters	11 codes for institutional voids: *Unstructured; Partnerships; Legitimacy; Empowerment; Intellectual property; Context; Culture; Glocalisation; Awareness and Advocacy; Distribution; Supply Chain.* 21 constructs for resource scarcity: *Service; Product; Design; Servicing; Good enough; Making do; De-sophistication; HighPerformance; Improve Efficiency; Scaling; Rectifying Inequity; Margins; Inclusiveness; Affordability; Economic Sustainability; Environmental Sustainability; Value Generation/Capacity Building; Learning; Self-sufficiency; Aspirational; Needs*
3. Identify patterns and connections	6. Integrate first-order codes into second-order themes	Figure 3.1. Coding sequence Three second-order themes identified for institutional voids: *Build Structures; Boundary Issues; Access Provision*

Six second-order themes identified for resource scarcity:

Scope of solution; Satisfice; Improve performance or efficiency; Reaching out; Develop capabilities; Resolve needs and meet aspirations

Table 3.6.

Summarised intermediate table showing constructs and themes that address institutional voids and resource scarcity

Table 3.7.

Archival document data supporting the theoretical dimension of institutional innovation – 293 passages

Interview data supporting the theoretical dimension of institutional innovation – 188 passages

Table 3.8.

Archival document data supporting the theoretical dimension of technology innovation – 182 passages

Interview data supporting the theoretical dimension of technology innovation – 109 passages

Table 3.9.

Archival document data supporting the theoretical dimension of social innovation – 289 passages

Interview data supporting the theoretical dimension of social innovation – 144 passages

Table 3.1 (*cont.*)

Stages	Tasks	Outcomes
4. Aggregate theoretical dimensions on A) institutional voids and then on B) resource scarcity	7. Label dimensions based on emergent concepts or on existing ones found in the literature	Three dimensions for aggregating the above themes into: *Institutional innovation, Technology innovation and Social innovation* Figure 3.2. Theoretical dimensions and the overlap between resource constraints, institutional voids and affordability constraints

Table 3.2 *Number of passages coded from each data source (baseline)*

	Archival documents (163)	Interviews (70)	Total (%)
Institutional voids	296	123	419 (40)
Resource scarcity	398	131	529 (51)
Both resource scarcity and institutional voids	41	50	91 (9)
Total	**735**	**304**	**1,039 (100)**

Table 3.3 *Frequencies of themes by types of respondents discussing institutional voids and resource scarcity*

	Entrepreneurs	Investors	Faculty	Mentors
Institutional voids	23	22	39	39
Resource scarcity	53	11	36	31
Ratio IV/RC	**0.4**	**2**	**1.1**	**1.3**

The purpose of separating the two data sources was to provide transparency during triangulation. In the archival documents, 398 passages addressed resource scarcity, as did 131 passages from the interviews and field notes. Fifty passages addressed both institutional voids and resource scarcity, as did forty-one passages from the interviews and field notes. Table 3.2 provides a breakdown of passages drawn from different data sources for purposes of coding and triangulation. In total, 1,039 passages were coded; almost twice as many were drawn from the 163 archival documents as from the 70 interviews and respondent field notes.

Table 3.3 shows a comparison of the types of interview respondents who addressed the two analytical constraints. Almost twice as many entrepreneurs discussed resource scarcity issues as talked about institutional voids. The other respondents, mentors, investors and programme administrators and lecturers were more concerned about institutional voids than about resource scarcity. In particular, almost twice as many investors talked about institutional voids as discussed resource scarcity, while the opposite trend was seen among entrepreneurs. This suggests that the entrepreneurs focused more on resource challenges, while the investors focused on institutional challenges.

In the second stage, the researcher categorised the data by identifying first-order codes along institutional voids and then along resource scarcity. As in Chapter 2, the idea here was to use *in vivo* codes that reflected as closely as possible the actual narratives. New first-order codes were added to the template with each iterative round of analysis. Some codes were changed, merged or split as the data sources provided additional information that could not be accommodated within the existing template. Table 3.4 shows the settled thirty-two first-order codes, eleven of which addressed institutional voids and twenty-one resource scarcity.

In the third stage, the researcher sought to identify and understand patterns and connections among the first-order codes, so as to integrate them into second-order themes. He did this by repeatedly reviewing the first-order codes until he found common aspects that explained the variation across second-order themes. Table 3.6 shows the outcome of clustering first-order codes into second-order themes.

Finally, in stage four of the analysis, the researcher sought to aggregate the theoretical dimensions of institutional voids and then of resource scarcity. The theoretical dimensions were derived by grouping second-order codes into higher-level dimensions. The purpose here was to label dimensions based on emergent concepts or on existing ones found in the literature. Three dimensions were found that resembled those found in the existing literature: *technology innovation, social innovation and institutional innovation.*

Sample quotations from the data supporting the three aggregate theoretical findings, further broken down using second-order and first-order codes, are outlined in Tables 3.7, 3.8 and 3.9, which are

Table 3.4 *First-order codes for research subquestions 2 and 3*

Questions	Texts and interviews were coded into	
How do they perceive and deal with innovation under institutional voids?	1. Unstructured 2. Partnerships 3. Legitimacy 4. Empowerment 5. Intellectual Property	6. Context 7. Culture 8. Glocalisation 9. Awareness and Advocacy 10. Distribution 11. Supply Chain
How do they perceive and deal with innovation under resource scarcity?	12. Service 13. Product 14. Design 15. Servicing 16. Good Enough 17. Making Do 18. De-sophistication 19. High Performance 20. Improving Efficiency 21. Scaling	22. Rectifying Inequity 23. Margins 24. Inclusiveness 25. Affordability 26. Economic Sustainability 27. Environmental Sustainability 28. Value Generation/ Capacity Building 29. Learning 30. Self-sufficiency 31. Aspirational 32. Needs

all appended at the end of this chapter. Although the tables for each dimension were originally ordered by data source to provide transparency during triangulation, here they have been condensed for presentation. Table 3.5 summarises the number of passages from different data sources, coded to support the three aggregate theoretical dimensions. In total, 1,205 passages were coded: almost twice as many from archival documents as from interviews and field notes. While institutional and social innovations enjoyed almost equal support in the data, technology innovation received about a third less. This suggests that social entrepreneurs are more likely to be concerned with institutional and social innovation than with technology innovation. In

Table 3.5 *Number of passages that support third-level theoretical dimensions*

	Archival documents (163)	Interviews (70)	Total (%)
Institutional innovation	293	188	481 (40)
Technology innovation	182	109	291 (24)
Social innovation	289	144	433 (36)
Total	**764**	**441**	**1,205 (100)**

another finding, this table demonstrated that, as the baseline number of passages was 1,039, 166 passages were double-coded across social, institutional and technology dimensions. The overlap suggests intersecting spaces between the dimensions, with two or three innovation dimensions occurring alongside each other, which supports Model 2.

3.3 AGGREGATING INTO THIRD-LEVEL THEORETICAL CONCEPTS

In the fourth and last stage of the coding and analysis, the objective was to take the first- and second-order codes and to label the codes or dimensions based on emergent or existing concepts. Table 3.6 is an intermediate table which summarises first-order constructs grouped by second-order themes in the left column and groups them by relevance to institutional voids and resource scarcity in the top row. This table shows how the first order codes coalesce into the second order, and the second order codes coalesce into the third-level theoretical dimensions shown in the last row.

The third-level theoretical dimensions are based on the existing literature and represent technology innovation (Schumpeter, 1934a; 1934b), social innovation (Mulgan et al., 2007b) and institutional innovation (Hargrave and Van de Ven, 2006). In Chapter 4, we shall discuss these three innovations and their relationship to the

Table 3.6 *Intermediate table summarising constructs and themes*

Theme/ Context:	Institutional voids		Resource scarcity	
	Soft	Hard	Constraints	Affordability
Boundary Issues	Context Culture Glocalisation Awareness and Advocacy			
Build Structures	Unstructured Legitimacy Partnerships Empowerment Intellectual Property	A		
Access Provision		Distribution Supply Chain		
Scope of Solution		B	Product Service Design Servicing	
Satisfice (Provide Satisfactory Solution)			Good Enough Making Do De-sophistication	
Improve Performance or Efficiency			High Performance Improve Efficiency	C
Resolve Needs and Aspirations				Needs Aspirational
Reaching Out				Scaling Rectifying Inequity Margins Inclusiveness Affordability
Develop Capabilities				Economic Sustainability Environmental Sustainability Value Generation /Capacity Building Learning Self-sufficiency
Theoretical Dimension	Institutional Innovation		Technology Innovation	Social Innovation

Note: A, B, C and D indicate an overlap of concerns that affect the next theme(s) analytical concerns of institutional voids and resource scarcity in greater detail.

Note that the three theoretical dimensions of institutional, social and technology innovation are not mutually exclusive. The arrows labelled B, C and D in Table 3.6 indicate overlapping concerns from one type of innovation to the next. For instance, arrow B shows how constructs identified with institutional innovation overlap with constructs identified with technology innovation. Arrow C shows how constructs identified with technology innovation overlap with constructs identified with social innovation. Finally, the circular link shown as Arrow D shows how constructs identified with social innovation overlap with constructs identified with institutional innovation.

In the next section, we describe how this cross-thematic and circular overlapping phenomenon suggests the formulation of Model 2: innovation under constraints.

3.4 GENERATING THE THEORETICAL MODEL

One of the main objectives of this research was to create models of innovation, as perceived by social entrepreneurs coping with institutional voids and resource scarcity. The first model of innovation was outlined in Chapter 2. The second model of innovation under constraints is developed here. When we reviewed Table 3.6, we noticed that the first-order constructs related to and 'continued' into the next set of first-order constructs that made up the second-order themes. These are depicted by arrows in Table 3.7 to show how data from one type of constraint links to another constraint.

We find that the construct of partnerships relates to both the soft (norms and rules) and hard features (infrastructure) of institutional voids (Arrow A). Hard institutional voids link to resource constraints through common distribution concerns and the design and servicing of products and services (Arrow B). The resource constraints faced by an innovator or firm relate downstream to how the

Table 3.7 *Sample data supporting the theoretical dimension of institutional innovation – 293 (archives) + 188 (interviews) = 481 passages*

(Un)structured

- Besides financing, the biggest obstacle to future growth is organising and putting a plan and structure in place that can effectively meet growing demand.
- In relation to the formal processes in the first world, it is difficult to lay out the complexities of developing country contexts to investors. Even the processes of business models and business plans are too structured for developing context complexities and uncertainties.
- In India, innovation is at the grassroots level, as in the case of *jugaad*, a term that denotes making do with whatever resources are on hand. One common practice is to reuse a water pump engine for another, unintended purpose, like powering a rural van. Or like the clay fridge. So, people are creative, but in an unstructured way.
- I think frugal innovation is an attempt to formalise *jugaad* by instilling a more structured approach and building partnerships with engineers in the West.

Partnerships

- Over the years, Engineers w/o Borders and other initiatives have made us aware of projects around the world. For instance, in El Salvador and Nicaragua, we do projects where the SCU has Jesuit partnerships. These relationships and partnerships are crucial for our projects' implementation and success.
- Frugal innovation is a nice effort to partner technology with entrepreneurship to come up with novel solutions for social problems that are both chronic and acute problems.
- Partnerships with NGOs are very useful in creating awareness and developing distribution networks in remote areas that NGOs often have access to.
- Because we are a start-up, we can't afford to invest time and energy in collaborations with the frugal innovation lab here or others like the MIT lab. I'd rather do it myself or with local partners.

Build structures

Table 3.7 (*cont.*)

Legitimacy
- Re-branding the image of a maid's job to allow maids to continue doing the same work, but improve their perception of their job, promotes the feeling of dignity and helps them reap their benefits appropriately.
- We are focused on advocacy and training to raise awareness of taboo issues (women's sanitary pads). Once the awareness is created, individuals naturally seek out sanitary pads. We cannot even donate pads in an environment where they aren't culturally or socially accepted.
- It is not just about low prices, but many of the energy firms are investing in building their image.

Empowerment
- To empower the disabled and promote economy freedom/ participation in an international platform.
- By paying even a token sum of Rs 10, the child not only feels compelled to continue his studies, but also feels honoured to be a paying member of the school.

Intellectual property
- Our fair trade and development objectives are very important to us and any licensing or copyright issues would be looked at in the light of how they would benefit the artisans involved.
- We value free access to intellectual property and general public licensing. We have distributed our software and other resources freely via the Internet. Of course, this depends on specific client requirements.

Context
- Padma has faced challenges at different levels of the intervention. First of all, when communicating with local farmers, it found that they use some local terms (not pure Bengali) for their farming and the farmers of different villages use different local terms. It was very hard then to capture those local terms and convert them into English to communicate with international researchers and again to redeliver the feedback to the farmers in their local terms.

Table 3.7 (cont.)

Boundary issues

- Initially, we imported pads but found that the pads were clogging toilets and were not biodegrading, creating greater health risks. So we came up with a patent pending chemical-free process to manufacture biodegradable pads. And the localisation manufacturing policy in South Africa and India helps to establish local manufacturing capability.
- In Silicon Valley, more sophistication is done because we can do it. However, the best or most innovative technology is not the best solution in all contexts.

Culture

- Instead of advocating a new technology or material, Build Change makes low- or no-cost modifications to existing, common, culturally appropriate and preferred ways of building to create long-term change and reduce deaths, injuries and economic losses during earthquakes.
- We assume that a change in culture won't happen until the society has the opportunity to go through a learning process, having live experiences with disabled people. From these ideas, Unidos takes its mission.
- It becomes quite expensive to innovate for the Base of Pyramid because of rural access, cultural interpretation and language (e.g. tribal leaders have to give authorisation for access to village people).

Glocalisation

- This project facilitates communication from the global to the local and back to the global level via intermediary knowledge brokers.
- An important part of the program is local manufacturing, to keep the cost of the equipment as low as possible. It will be easy to establish local manufacturing because no high-tech fabrication techniques are required. Thus, replication to other countries and regions is very possible.
- Initially, we imported complete systems at high cost from Brazil to Indonesia. But then we found a supplier in India from whom we import parts at a low price and assemble them locally in Indonesia using other local parts like taps.
- I learned much from travelling as a grant assessor with the World Bank and saw different tools and techniques all over Africa.

Table 3.7 (*cont.*)

Awareness and advocacy

- We run regular Moringa awareness sessions for large-membership groups and students of public high schools. We also run regular advertisements on a popular radio station that reaches over 10 million listeners. There is therefore a very high level of awareness about the nutritional and other benefits of Moringa, thus creating a huge demand for our products and services. Scaling-up and expansion will therefore be easily facilitated.
- Promoting a social transformation movement for the integration of the disabled through a warm and interactive formula with young volunteers, resulting in a more sensitive society and reducing the social fear of disabled people.

Distribution

- Second, there is a problem of access. In the developing world, reading glasses are primarily available in local optical shops in urban centres. The poor who live in rural areas have little-to-no access to these stores.
- Our primary distribution is small and highly targeted, unlike most filmmakers who seek massive but often important audiences through TV or theatrical release. This challenges us to reshape the ecosystem where finance, culture, behaviour and values all matter.
- So, successful distribution is and will be the real source of my frugality.
- GE's Healthy Imagination Initiative has not succeeded in reaching rural areas – it has reached middle-income towns but not the BoP. (2M)

Supply chain

- Many failed economic development programs create long supply chains, resulting in spare parts and repair facilities that are either non-existent or unavailable where they are needed.
- Sometimes food security problems can be addressed by properly matching the supply and demand of goods. Easy access to information on where the commodities are available and where they are needed can provide a safety net for food security problems.
- To me, frugal innovation is the IDE and Paul Pollocks of this world who seek to cut out a lot of the steps in the supply chain by using local content, materials and local labour.

Access provision

Table 3.8 *Sample data supporting the theoretical dimension of technology innovation – 182 (archives) + 109 (interviews) = 291 passages*

Good enough

- We emphasise daily execution over more esoteric approaches. Lately, I have heard from many people who have had a similar idea but were never able to get it off the ground. Kiva was able to start because we chose a small village in Africa and we made a small website in America. Now, both the village and the website have been elevated to a higher level thanks to a 'just start' mentality.
- Even if the solution is 80 percent right, but with 100 percent focus and with a team fully on board, you can succeed.
- What we (at Intel) learned from impending competition from OLPC was to redesign the processor for low-cost net-books with good enough performance. So yes, the West can learn from technology applications in developing countries.
- However, the Intel Atom processor was a change of mindset brought about by competition from OLPC. We redesigned the processor for low-cost and good enough performance for netbooks.

Making do

- For example, on a visit to Zimbabwe, Whirlwind's chief engineer, Ralf Hotchkiss, saw a moulded wide rubber tire on a pushcart. Hotchkiss first redesigned the tire so it could be used on a wheelchair caster and then figured out how to make the entire wheel out of moulded rubber. The result is an inexpensive, solid rubber, puncture-proof wheel with a footprint that is 30–50 mm wider than the casters on most commercially available wheelchairs. . . . In most cases, however, it is less that the technology or even the basic idea itself is new than that the technology is applied creatively to a wide variety of environmental conditions.
- We do *jugaad* to the extent of making do with what we have, but not to the extent that we let *jugaad* hold us back on quality delivery.
- We are considering using older technologies like the voice modems of the 80s to allow our target schools to download data over the radio analog network.

Satisfice (provide satisfactory solution)

Table 3.8 (*cont.*)

De-sophistication

- The Solar Sister model strength is that it is very simple and this simplicity enables it to be scalable from tens to thousands of women entrepreneurs.
- Our product is pretty sophisticated inside using MCU (microcontroller units) but I do try to design it in a modular fashion which makes replacing parts easy for schools in rural areas.
- Non-frugal Silicon Valley is all about high tech sophistication.
- However even impact investors have a difficult time investing in developing market, low-sophistication and low-cost innovations.
- It (frugal innovation) is all about common sense and de-sophistication. Recall the NASA ball point pen for $5m versus a $1 pencil.

Product

- The highly improved stove design is becoming very popular throughout the country and internationally; as a result it is becoming an excellent example, inspiring a young generation to invent new ideas that change our world in a tangible way, including me – I have again invented an energy saving device operating in LPG.
- So, I see frugal innovation as better engineering products that social enterprises need to develop.
- Cost reduction innovation of existing products doesn't work. Take the example of OLPC. It hasn't achieved its target price and it is losing time to cell phones, the latter being more simple, yet powerful and ubiquitous. Simply reducing the cost of existing products won't work.

Service

- The innovation is in practical use of modern ICTs to provide appropriate information in rural and urban poor communities. ... Audiovisual technology is used for developing local content in local languages and disseminating it to overcome low literacy levels.
- Plus, the $60–$80 cost of the radio is only a portion of the total $250 cost of the package. The main chunk is the content or media.
- We need SMS apps to be very user friendly. If we send too many SMSs, then it could cost too much to the end user to reply to our queries.

Scope of solution

Table 3.8 (cont.)

Design

- Whirlwind's solution was to design a folding wheelchair frame that the rider could narrow him or herself (or with the help of an assistant) while sitting in the chair, by pulling a lever underneath the seat and between the legs.
- I use design thinking to setup new micro-franchise businesses such as ideation and prototyping, microlight marketing and quick and dirty proofs of concepts.
- I agree that we cannot design in isolation of the USA for developing country applications. Our cook stove was first developed by Engineers w/o Borders at Berkeley. But our engineers went back and forth to Sudan and worked with a local engineer. Through this back and forth our cook stove went through fourteen iterations and we reached the current price of $16. So I don't think we designed and developed it just in Berkeley and then just dumped the cook stove – rather we tweaked it over and over again as necessary.

Servicing

- Robust, simple and appropriate, they can be easily maintained at village level and repaired using locally available materials and skills.
- Our product is pretty sophisticated inside, using MCU (microcontroller units), but I do try to design it in a modular fashion that makes replacing parts easy for schools in rural areas.
- Even the USA, with its mass production systems, has built the local ecosystem capacity to achieve long term sustainability and servicing.
- A local person is trained to service the units and to liaise with the company on usage stats. The person is nominally paid and hired to serve in that role.

High Performance

- (Our) Initiative introduces a new concept in water manufacturing based on Artisan in Mineral Water. This is a HUGE step towards making a difference, with the water industry proposing product conformity and standardisation.

Table 3.8 (*cont.*)

<table>
<tr><td rowspan="2">Improve performance or efficiency</td><td>

- Create a brand which will be nationally recognised for its high quality, fair prices and excellent service. ... Ability to compete with the technology of imported products.
- Here they rely on Moore's law to increase performance and lower prices. However, in the areas where I function, you need to do more than just that.
- Frugal innovation is about jumping or leapfrogging alternative solutions to use high tech and high quality but at affordable levels.

Efficiency

- Communities for setting up new RECs are chosen where there is an established NGO or MFI, which is efficient and economical.
- We are researching management information (MI) systems to improve efficiency by creating a streamlined data collection process that is easy to use and aggregates data.
- Cost per outcomes are an attempt by social ventures to be more financially relevant to investors. Reducing the cost per outcome also scales up potential, since one can do more with little.
- To me, it (innovation) is about solving a problem in the most efficient manner possible.

</td></tr>
</table>

needs of affordability-constrained consumers are met (Arrow C). In a circular fashion, the affordability constraint links back to the first constraint of soft institutional voids (Arrow D). The development of capabilities economically, environmentally or through learning is contingent on boundary issues of context, culture and globalisation or localisation. These linkages provide a basis for modelling these features using three intersecting circles. The cross thematic and circular linkages suggest the formulation of the second model of innovation under constraints, as depicted in Figure 3.2.

Figure 3.2 illustrates the theoretical model, showing the three theoretical dimensions – institutional innovation, technology innovation and social innovation – and how they coincide respectively with institutional voids, resource constraints and affordability constraints. As in Chapter 2, the social entrepreneurs we report on in this study

Table 3.9 *Data supporting the theoretical dimension of social innovation – 289 (archives) + 144 (interviews) = 433 passages*

Meet needs and create aspirations

Aspirational

- [We] use a unique model of non-profit incubation characterised by long term collaborations with our partners that permit them to diversify their skills, grow their management capacity, pursue their aspirations and actively test assumptions around regionally appropriate sustainable technologies.
- The company creates an ecosystem which connects technology, finance and grassroots organisations – to manage the energy needs, aspirations and resources of rural BoP beneficiaries.
- My colleagues here agree that a lot of customers are looking to go with high-end products perhaps to be aspirational and high status.

Needs

- The reason that these products have failed to take off is that they do not address the full range of East African BoP customers' need for electricity at a price they can afford.
- As a marketing person, I think it is understanding needs and not just making it cheaper or affordable.
- The user needs in developing markets are very different from those in Western nations, so we must place utmost relevance on defining user needs.
- Frugal innovation is about designing for social problems, needs and contexts, such as supply chain and lack of infrastructure concerns.

Reach out

Scaling

- This becomes an issue in scaling to cover that market segment, even though they probably need our software most.
- Currently, the field staff needs to be closely monitored; this could be a roadblock for expansion and increasing scale.
- Reducing the cost per outcome chart also scales up potential, since one can do more with little.
- Our whole model rests on training in-house and in large volumes. If a private hospital does two surgeries per day per doctor, then we have to do ten.

Table 3.9 (*cont.*)

Rectifying Inequity

- The world's marginalised groups – women, poor, ethnic, caste and tribal groups, disabled, elderly and people of colour – have the greatest need for information … The lack of access to these channels of information is partly what keeps them in poverty.
- The hospital values dignity as well as quantity. Poor consumers don't have the liberty to take economic risks, so they have to make a final choice or none at all, which one has to realise is a choice too!
- The development of GSMA standards helped to lower the cost of technology for all to be able to afford. And mobile is probably the only sector through which MNCs have innovated widely for the BoP.

Margins

- The elimination of information middlemen will allow farmers and fisherfolk to financially benefit from their produce and thus have more money in their pockets.
- At present, reading glasses are sold exclusively by eye doctors and optical shops at significant margins, making them too expensive for the average person.
- Our margins are calculated based on (i) the affordability for the BoP, (ii) offers from competition and (iii) enough to make money for women entrepreneurs.
- A challenge is how we move away from maximum margins to reasonable margins for all in the value chain.

Affordable

- It has been independently tested at the University of British Columbia's mining school, which showed that [we] outperformed the industries' state of the art centrifuge which costs 100 to 1,000 times more.
- The introduction of hand-drilled wells in Niger has benefited over 1,500 farmers and villages, providing access to water at an affordable cost in a country where water is absolutely crucial and surface sources are rare.
- I told GE that the 10–15 per cent cost reduction being talked about means that they are not serious in addressing the BoP. Instead they need a tenfold decrease.

Table 3.9 *(cont.)*

- Sometimes, the cost reduction may not always be great. It may be good for the enterprise but not for the farmer who serves as a seller.

Inclusiveness

- To make it possible for every person who needs a wheelchair in a developing country to obtain one that will lead to maximum personal independence and integration into society.
- [We are] an action research organisation aiming to develop, showcase and implement technologies and processes of comprehensive development of the rural and underdeveloped communities in the areas of education, health, communication, rural lighting and water lifting.
- If you put in enough money, you could create twenty hospitals, but they probably would not have the same ethos: providing vision to all and seeing all as one.
- We have a more humble approach as we focus on helping the underserved.

Economic sustainability

- Our equipment is really working (unlike charity) and is sustainable in many ways, as it gives employment to the poorest in the society.
- Our staff members should be oriented to take on the task of creating profitable income generation activities for women.
- (N)ow the challenge for us is to provide sustainable entrepreneurship for these families.
- Entrepreneurship for such challenges is the path for charity and grants cannot be sustainable.

Environmental sustainability

- To offer state of the art and own technology to solve frost damage problems worldwide. This environmentally friendly technology incorporates the necessary knowledge and know-how to study each orchard.
- To make future customers understand the social and environmental impact they would have if they 'bet' on our company.

Develop capabilities

Table 3.9 (*cont.*)

Value generation/capacity building

- The [company's] approach to producing monthly (video) magazines as a basic form of participatory media is our primary example of a base model of capacity building and technology that is then shaped for local demands towards specific goals.
- The approach begins with an active stakeholder dialogue to refine technology development and dissemination strategies; it ends with technical assistance and capacity building to enable local businesses and organisations to implement [our] solutions long after we have left.
- So, a key lesson is that you always focus on the long-term value you create for the client, not just the product you sell. ... Some cases, like [company], show that you can't just take a product-centric or service-centric view; you have to do both within the value created through your business model.

Learning

- We assume that a change in culture won't happen until the society has the opportunity to go through a learning process, having live experiences with disabled people.
- As CEO of the company I ran, I would now go back and have a project team working on, for instance, cook stove combustion, not just to fulfil the need or opportunity for profit, but to learn from new contexts and constraints.
- Although these lessons are from social enterprise, the lessons could be useful for all firms wishing to lower costs.
- On learning from us, we do 300K surgeries a year and have enabled others to do another 1 million a year.

Self-sufficiency

- We create a network of schools and educational leaders interested in self-sufficiency and the application of innovative solutions for the common good.
- Ensure the self-reliance of the rural landless by technology-mediated training and credit – now they have better access to land-water bodies and are able to carry the educational expenses of their children at higher educational institutions.

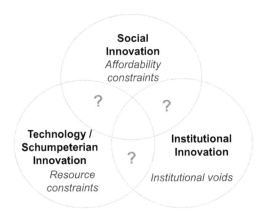

FIGURE 3.2 Model 2: Theoretical dimensions and the overlap between resource constraints, institutional voids and affordability constraints

agree to disagree that they are purely social innovators. The question again arises: What innovation is it that *their solutions* coalesce around? In Figure 3.2, we label the interstices where innovations overlap with question marks, in order to depict this unknown category of innovation. We next discuss how the concept of frugal innovation can help to fill this void. Discussions of frugal innovation suggest that efforts are being made to transform this blend of existing innovation approaches into a new field of professional and scholarly activity.

3.5 DISCUSSION

It is clear that social entrepreneurs perceive innovation as a combination of various existing types of innovation under constraints, as depicted in Figure 3.2. The third-level theoretical dimensions are based on the existing literature and represent technology innovation (Schumpeter, 1934a; 1934b), social innovation (Mulgan et al., 2007b) and institutional innovation (Hargrave and Van de Ven, 2006). Technology innovation helps us to understand how innovators cope with resource constraints. Institutional innovation helps us to understand how they seek to address institutional voids, and social innovation reveals the ways in which they manage affordability constraints.

The literature tells us that technology innovation is about creating the tools we need to achieve our goals. Social innovation creates novel solutions to social problems and allows the value created to accrue primarily to society as a whole, rather than to private individuals. Institutional innovation creatively defines who we are and why we do what we do, in the process changing 'foundational' societal rules and norms. However, taken separately, none of these three types of innovation can deal with the challenge of innovating in a context shaped by both resource scarcity and institutional voids. As in Chapter 2, this model shows that social entrepreneurs work beyond the prevailing notion of social innovation. The empirical data revealed myriad ways in which multiple constraints are taken into consideration or addressed. The following quotations illustrate these situations, which support the hybridisation conceptualised in the proposed model:

> We also need to learn how to systematise better the methodology used so that it can be replicated. To finally systematise the prototype of the radio telecenter model based on an integrated approach to sustainability in the long run, looking into economic, technological and social and their interfaces.
>
> The Fundacion Paraguaya's mission to pursue sustainable development through the promotion of entrepreneurship is founded on the belief that economic, social and environmental issues are intrinsically interrelated and can and should be tackled simultaneously.

The following quote exemplifys the bridging of social innovation (through learning and economic sustainability), technology innovation (through concerns for servicing) and institutional innovation (through distribution):

In order to expand efficiently, we employ a 'hub and spoke' model as a means of sales and distribution. The REC acts as the 'hub' from which the 'spokes' are used to distribute our products and services and expand our reach. The spokes consist of: direct retail sales, rural entrepreneurs, other NGOs, banks and other local organisations such as community groups or farmers' clubs. We train rural entrepreneurs to act as distributors and agents who branch out to the smaller local villages conducting promotions and sales. They become knowledgeable of our product range as well as technically proficient so that they can respond to clients' service and repair calls. This approach is innovative and mutually beneficial as it allows us keep our overhead and payroll down, while providing direct jobs to locals who are able to earn their own income and commissions.

Social entrepreneurs make use of a combination or hybridisation of existing innovation elements. One way this recombination can be identified, labelled and conceptualised through the emergent concepts proposed by some of these social entrepreneurs is through the introduction of the concept of frugal innovation into the model. In the next chapter, we analyse intersections among the three existing innovation streams as fertile spaces where frugal innovation can best be understood.

3.6 SUMMARY

The objective of this study is to reveal models of innovation under constraints, as perceived by social entrepreneurs. The model we propose here, based on the data, provides valuable insights into how social entrepreneurs view innovation under constraints and deal with such constraints using existing innovation components – overlapping concerns for *social innovation, technology and institutional innovations*. Our proposed model of innovation under constraints – supported by data, analysis and interpretive findings – is presented in Model 2 (Figure 3.2). The mixed use of existing innovation approaches suggests that the emerging concept of frugal innovation can be used to define this hybrid approach to innovation.

In the next chapter, we integrate findings and lessons from Chapters 2 and 3 to argue that developing a theory of frugal innovation is a potential project worthy of independent investigation within innovation studies.

PART II

Towards a Theory of Frugal Innovation

4 Integrative Results and Theory Development

In this integrative chapter, we suggest steps towards theory development using the two models of innovation generated in the previous two chapters, which are based on the perspectives of social entrepreneurs. In Chapter 2, we brought to the surface some important nuances in the way social entrepreneurs view innovation differently in relation to motivation and approaches beyond social innovation. Innovation Model 1 captured a hybridisation of social, efficiency-based, user-based and challenge-based types of innovation, suggesting that innovation from the perspective of social entrepreneurs can be thought of as a collection of complementary ideas. In Chapter 3, we advanced our theoretical understanding of innovation under constraints, again from the perspective of social entrepreneurs, by creating bridges between the literatures of innovation and institutional and resource theory. Innovation Model 2 revealed a mix of social, technological and institutional innovation. This too revealed nuances in the ways social entrepreneurs view innovation under constraints differently in relation to motivation and approaches that can be thought of as a collection of complementary ideas.

The coherence and cohesiveness of our empirical findings can be linked to the emerging concept of frugal innovation, as discussed by our sample of social entrepreneurs. In other words, we are not merely labelling our findings 'frugal innovation', but developing a more nuanced understanding of innovation under constraints as both 'social' and 'frugal'.

4.1 INTRODUCTION

Frugal innovation is a potentially challenging paradigm for innovation, with a wide range of entrepreneurs, firms and other institutional actors (for example, foundations and policy institutes) embracing the term 'frugal innovation' perhaps without necessarily understanding its precise, conceptual, theoretical or operational meaning. Based on the insights in this chapter, we offer in the next chapters and specifically in Figure 6.3 definitions of frugal innovation at these three different levels of abstraction. In this integrative chapter, we propose to develop a theory based on our two models of innovation under constraints. We call this a theory of frugal innovation and draw conceptual inspiration from both of the previously developed models, but with an emphasis on Model 2 as it specifically addresses contextual challenges or constraints. In the next chapter, we bring back the relevance of Model 1 in using both models to understand secondary case examples. In developing a theoretical model of frugal innovation based on the empirical data from this study, we also draw support from published descriptions of innovation. By developing an insight into the drivers, determinants and dimensions of innovation, this work paves the way towards identifying and evaluating frugal innovations more objectively. The theory also offers a grounded framework that can serve as a cornerstone for further studies focusing on the sources, diffusion, process and outcome of frugal innovation.

4.2 APPROACH TO THEORY DEVELOPMENT

Marshall Scott Poole and Andrew H. Van de Ven (1988; 1989) suggest that a paradox involving different assumptions can be exploited in theory development. For instance, Eric Abrahamson (1991) used the paradox resolution approach to develop a theory of management. In a similar fashion, we take advantage of the contrasting assumptions about innovation made by social entrepreneurs to generate new theoretical perspectives for understanding innovation under constraints among social entrepreneurs.

Poole and Van de Ven define paradoxes as 'interesting tensions, oppositions and contradictions between theories which create conceptual difficulties' (1989, p. 564). They suggest clarifying the level of analysis, taking time into account and introducing new terms as tools to stimulate theoretical development through paradox exploitation. Abrahamson (1991, p. 601) believes that this technique can 'generate tailor-made theories for varied innovations or contexts'. In contrast to the contingency approach of paradox resolution, this approach works because it does not assume that different perspectives apply to some but not other innovations or contexts. The Van de Ven and Poole approach to theorising is powerful because it allows for the 'flexibility necessary to generate theories that incorporate assumptions that match the innovation or context they study and, thereby, provide for stronger empirical findings' (Abrahamson, 1991, p. 601).

We adopt the term frugal innovation to stimulate theoretical development through paradox exploitation. As part of this approach, we have tried to be consistent and clear about each of the different levels of analysis. Observations were made at the level of individual entrepreneurs, rather than firms, but many entrepreneurs were speaking for their firms. The focus of analysis has been at the conceptual level of innovation. We inferred from the findings captured in Model 1 that social innovation was best understood to occur at the community level of analysis, efficiency-based innovation at the firm level, user-based innovation at the individual level and challenge-based innovation at the sectoral level. As this was not a process study, we did not introduce time (not possible, in any case, as there were missing data for the years 2008–2010, due to computer theft). We can nevertheless attempt to use paradox resolution for theory development because two of the three suggestions Poole and Van de Ven recommend have been adopted. In particular, the theoretical approach we attempt here has strong potential for explanatory power, particularly because the assumptions of innovation under resource constraints, institutional voids and affordability concerns that underlie this approach match the context (Abrahamson, 1991) in which we hope researchers will test this theory.

Table 4.1 *Contradictory assumptions among social entrepreneurs*

How to balance?		
Profit maximisation	×	Social impact
More is better	×	More with less
Cost	×	Quality
Constraints	×	Slack
Localisation	×	Globalisation
Inst. Voids	×	Inst. Complexity
Adaptable	×	Efficiency
Sustainability	×	Scale

Much like social entrepreneurs, many for-profit and non-profit organisations are looking to meet the needs of people who are under-served by existing businesses and non-profit organisations (see for instance Collier, 2007; Easterly, 2006; Novogratz, 2010; Polak, 2008; Prahalad, 2005). While some organisations follow a for-profit model, others use a non-profit or even a hybrid organisational approach. These organisational models stem from fundamentally contradictory assumptions about profit maximisation on the one hand and social impact on the other. Social entrepreneurship offers a middle ground, where the two are not necessarily contradictory (Elkington and Hartigan, 2008), and yet there is a continued struggle to balance the degree of focus on profit maximisation and social impact (see example of iMerit Inc. in Chu and Barley, 2013). Social entrepreneurs also commonly face challenges of dichotomous philosophies around delivering 'more with less' or achieving 'more is better', lowering cost and maintaining high quality, functioning creatively within constraints or benefitting from access to slack resources, focusing on localisation or eyeing globalisation strategies, filling institutional voids or resolving institutional complexities, pursuing adaptability or optimisation and efficiency and achieving scale or maintaining sustainability (see Table 4.1). Indeed, mainstream entrepreneurs may also be concerned with these challenges, but because of the hybridisation strategy of profit maximisation and social impact, social entrepreneurs may be even more concerned about balancing these tensions.

Our findings suggest that these contradictory assumptions partly stem from differences across the logics of justification that social entrepreneurs rely on when viewing innovation models. We identify these contrasting logics as an opportunity to propose that we may need a new theory that can better explain innovation as conceptualised by the respondents in this study. We draw upon common themes across these contrasting logics and use the new concept of frugal innovation to develop a cohesive view that provides some common ground for varied perspectives.

Our methodology includes one caution: these views of innovation reveal models that are 'socially constructed' among social entrepreneurs. Consequently, these views may not be seen in the same way by those who are not social entrepreneurs or even by social entrepreneurs who do not share the same contextual characteristics as the informants in this study. Nevertheless, although the models themselves are not necessarily universally and materially 'objective', as is often the case with qualitative studies based on critical realism, we argue that these models and ideas can lead to material outcomes that will help to develop a theory, which can be further tested to ascertain its degree of robustness and generalisability.

The first model of innovation arose from an empirical investigation of the first sub-question: *How do social entrepreneurs conceptualise innovation?* This revealed a model that captures the sources, drivers or motivations for adopting four types of innovations, and which find support in the existing literature. The second model arose from the next two sub-questions, which in turn built upon the first sub-question by asking: *How do social entrepreneurs conceptualise innovation under (a) resource scarcity and (b) institutional voids?* In other words, while the first sub-question focused on innovation in general, the latter two focused on innovation under constraints.

As previously mentioned, the concept of frugal innovation can serve as a boundary object, linking innovation by social entrepreneurs to more mainstream concerns about innovation, including those affecting large, for-profit corporations. The contesting and negotiation (cf. Hess, Breyman, Campbell and Martin, 2007; Smith, 2007) of boundary spaces (Lamont and Molnar, 2002; Star, 2010), where different motivations, agendas and definitions of innovation spaces occur, promises to support the growth of the subfield of frugal innovation in innovation studies (Bhatti, 2012; Bhatti and Ventresca, 2012).

We expand on that possibility by showing how conceptions of innovation among social entrepreneurs relate to mainstream examples of innovation found in the existing literature. We hypothesise that our proposed theory of innovation may apply to a broader set of globally networked and recognised social entrepreneurs involved in innovation under constraints often described as frugal innovation (Knorringa et al., 2016; Prabhu, 2017; Prahalad and Mashelkar, 2010).

4.3 DEVELOPING A THEORY OF FRUGAL INNOVATION

Social entrepreneurs described that they use technological innovation to address resource constraints, social innovation to address affordability constraints and institutional innovation to address institutional voids. However, these three forms of innovation taken separately cannot deal with the challenges of innovating for the underserved, a common theme across all discussions of social entrepreneurship. Those innovators face a mixture of different constraints. It may be possible to use the assumptions that underpin different conceptualisations of innovation under constraints to build a theory of constrained innovation for underserved populations.

To accomplish this, we draw upon a number of existing theories, including the resource-based view (Barney, 1991; Petcraf, 1993), resource-dependence (Pfeffer and Salancik, 1978), competitive advantage (Porter, 1995) and creating shared value (Kramer, 2011; Porter and Kramer, 1999) to understand how social entrepreneurs navigate resource, institutional and social barriers and challenges.

From a process perspective, it can be shown that technological innovation helps to address or resolve the challenge of resource constraints, institutional innovation helps to address the challenge of institutional voids and social innovation helps to address the challenge of affordability constraints. Together, these three constitute necessary parallel approaches when innovating for the underserved in extreme contexts marked by institutional voids and resource constraints.

From an outcome perspective, we find that broadly speaking and not exclusively, technology innovation in combination with a process of designing solutions helps to make an innovation *adaptable* to specific contexts. Likewise, social innovation that considers economic and environmental sustainability and self-sufficiency can become more *affordable*, while institutional innovation that rethinks soft and hard distribution challenges, such as advocacy, legitimacy and infrastructure, can make an innovation more *accessible* (see Figure 4.1).

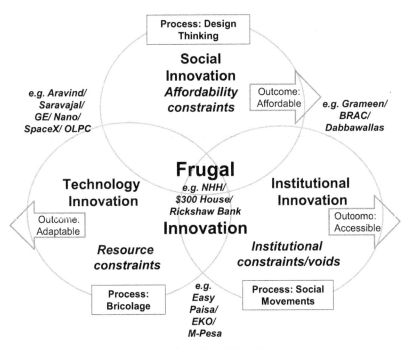

FIGURE 4.1 Theoretical model of frugal innovation

Schumpeterian or technology innovation is primarily concerned with profit, social innovation with creating greater social value and institutional innovation with mitigating discontent by introducing new practices, norms and regulations. If social entrepreneurs focus on generating and retaining growth or dividend profits, they do this while also improving social value creation. If social entrepreneurs focus on changing existing institutions, they do so in a way that preserves or builds on local social values. Innovators who focus on greater social value creation do so in a manner that is economically sustainable and scalable for the growth of the organisation.

We analyse the intersections among these three innovation streams as fertile spaces where a hybrid form of innovation occurs – one which our respondents referred to as frugal innovation. In support of hybridisation, Jerker Denrell, Christina Fang and Sidney G. Winter (2003, p. 11), drawing on the work of Herbert Simon, write about using existing systems to create new ones: 'A complex system is unlikely to emerge if it requires that numerous elements are simultaneously combined. It is much more likely to emerge if it can be assembled via existing subsystems.'

At a very basic level, our theoretical approach, which involves juxtaposing different perspectives on existing notions of technology innovation, institutional innovation and social innovation, helps us not only to understand each approach individually but, perhaps more important, also to develop an understanding of where frugal innovation can occur – namely, in contexts shaped by constraints. The relevance of frugal innovation as a relatively new term reflects the uniqueness of this overlapping space. It offers tools to build new insights from the merger of existing elements. Developing this theory may help us to understand how innovation migrates between different settings – between process and outcome, product and service, profit and not-for-profit, start-up and large MNC and developed and emerging markets.

Several passages from the data support the notion of overlapping approaches to innovation and merger that extend beyond the traditional boundaries of innovation. Based on this supporting data, we hypothesise that frugal innovation lies at the overlap or intersection of technology, social and institutional forms of innovation. In the next three subsections, we explore these intersections and overlapping concerns as spaces for paradox resolution and frugal innovation theory development.

4.3.1 Intersection of Technology and Social Innovation

The empirical data reveal that technology and social innovation have overlapping concerns. The following quotations are drawn from different data sources and support the triangulation of these findings. For additional data quotations from sources that support the overlap between Schumpeterian or technology and social innovation, see Table 4.2a at the end of this chapter.

> Originally energy was not a developed goal. But now we realise that all priority issues of health, education and income are alleviated through access to energy.

> We are not a technology company but a business development house that uses technologies innovatively for socio-economic benefits. I stress the fact that it's not about the technology, but it's about how technologies should facilitate the most basic human needs. We get bogged down on solving the problems of the world through a gadget rather than identifying the problems first then introducing the appropriate technologies to enrich human lives.

In this overlap between technology innovation and social innovation, we exploit the paradox linking two contrasting assumptions behind technology or Schumpeterian innovation and social innovation, arguing that there is a need for theory development in this space. We begin with Schumpeter's (1934b) seminal notion of innovation, which is often associated with technology innovation (see for example, Christensen, 1997; Geroski, 2003; Utterback, 1994). Schumpeter's earliest ideas about innovation emphasised the role of entrepreneurs in creating waves of 'creative destruction'.

However, he later became convinced that lack of access to financial resources would prevent entrepreneurs developing successful innovations as technology became increasingly complex, and hence that large corporations would be the dominant source of technological innovation. Yet today, innovation is considered a playground for entrepreneurs. Regardless of who innovates, there is little debate on the need to access and control resources for innovation to occur. The procurement, control and combining of labour, skills and material are crucial to the creation of new products and services (Schumpeter, 1934a; 1934b; Shane and Venkataraman, 2000).

The unstated assumption behind Schumpeterian innovation is the pursuit of profit and the ability to innovate when resources are available and controlled. Take, for instance, entrepreneurs who need to mobilise resources to innovate and start new ventures (Shane and Venkataraman, 2000). Entrepreneurship researchers have analysed how new ventures mobilise resources (Hsu, 2008; Shane, 2000; 2003). The probability of success in procuring resources depends on conditions such as the nature of the opportunity (Low and Abrahamson, 1997; Shane, 2000), venture legitimacy (Aldrich and Fiol, 1994; Meyer, 1983), founder experience (Amit, Glosten and Muller, 1990; Boeker, 1989) and the technological capability of the new venture (Shane and Stuart, 2002; Westhead and Storey, 1997). The literature has focused on the mechanism of resource-seeking, while assuming that resources are available in the environment.

Yet, the contexts in which social entrepreneurs function may not have the necessary resources or means to access and control potential resources. An environment is resource constrained if it provides new challenges, whether opportunities or problems, without providing additional or new resources (Baker and Nelson, 2005). In such contexts, both entrepreneurs and large corporations face resource constraints. Despite working in resource-constrained environments, the social entrepreneurs in our research sample claimed to be creating affordable and innovative products and services. So how might they be doing this, given the resource constraints?

Geoffrey Desa and Suresh Kotha (2006) carried out a case-study-based analysis of social enterprises to investigate how social ventures use technology in resource-limited contexts. Although the study sheds some light on technological innovation, it does not fundamentally explore the nature of innovation, looking instead at the process of and factors that influence opportunity identification and evaluation. Desa's further work (2009a; 2009b) on technology social ventures suggests that entrepreneurs are able to provide services and products where none existed before because of bricolage processes. Both Desa and Lisa Gundry et al. (2011) show that, even while lacking viable opportunities, legitimacy or intellectual property, many ventures stubbornly survive in penurious environments and are able to provide valuable products and services by relying on bricolage (Baker and Nelson, 2005; Lévi-Strauss, 1967) as a resource-mobilising mechanism. Bricolage involves using friends, family and volunteers for labour, purposely looking for pre-existing materials for reuse and building upon existing skills to enable a venture to originate and build sustainable capabilities. Social entrepreneurs who deploy bricolage are able to mobilise resources for their operations and thereby provide solutions that would otherwise be unavailable to users, for instance because of poverty or lack of access. Desa (2009a) writes, 'by rendering unique services in resource-poor environments and by finding ways to maintain financial sustainability, entrepreneurs can create markets for services where previously none existed' (p. 201).

The notion of entrepreneurs creating markets for underserved populations where none existed before ties Schumpeterian innovation to another approach – social innovation. Social innovation is defined in the *Stanford Social Innovation Review* as a 'novel solution to a social problem that is more effective, efficient, sustainable or just than existing solutions and for which the value created accrues primarily to society as a whole rather than private individuals' (Phills et al., 2008, p. 36). Authors James Phills et al. differentiate social innovations from ordinary innovations because the world is already amply equipped to produce and disseminate ordinary innovations. They argue that when markets fail to produce public goods, for example, social innovation offers a way to meet needs and create value that would otherwise not be possible.

In contrast to the Schumpeterian pursuit of profits, the assumptions in social innovation stem from a growing consensus on the need to address social objectives that can improve living conditions. Coimbatore Prahalad (2005) interprets social entrepreneurship as including entrepreneurship in emerging and developing markets, which improves the economic and social conditions of poor and underserved communities. Definitions of social entrepreneurship have ranged from the non-profit definition to a broader mission to achieve positive social change. These social aspects can extend from societal needs, such as justice and fairness, to health, education and environmental and cultural preservation. Phills et al. (2008) define social value as the creation of benefits or a reduction in societal costs that go beyond the private gains and general benefits of market activity. These social objectives extend to society as a whole, including the underserved. They highlight the need to deal with resource constraints within the innovation process and affordability constraints as an outcome of innovation.

Underserved and neglected populations are unable to pay for basic goods and services such as healthcare, food and housing. Consequently, unfettered markets will not produce such goods and services for these populations. However, with greater cooperation among non-profits, governments and businesses, new models of funding are triggering even profitable social innovations (Phills et al., 2008). Social innovation embodies creative and innovative solutions to social problems, which are often operationalised through entrepreneurial activity. Concomitantly, social innovation encompasses new means and processes, including ideas, strategies and organisations that enhance the social aspects of human functioning and civil society.

One example of social innovation is Ibrahim Abouleish's Sekem Initiative in Egypt. This community scheme reduces poverty, generates employability for rural farmers and conserves natural resources. By applying organic agricultural techniques, Sekem contributes towards maintaining the regional natural environment (Seelos and Mair, 2005). A financial return for profit, although important, is often equally balanced or outpaced by the desire to achieve social impact. Although we do not discount private gains through market activity, the awareness of opportunities to serve the underserved has attracted several efforts to address the problems of the poor through a combination of market and non-market means (Mair and Martí, 2006).

Citing the example of community-based co-housing models, Gill Seyfang and Adrian Smith (2007) explain that these are primarily social innovations, although they also foster sustainable technologies. They write, 'social innovations and the diffusion of technological innovations are intimately linked' (p. 588). Combine social innovation concerns with technology innovation and a space develops for products and services such as those offered by the Aravind Eye Hospital and the Jaipur Knee. The Aravind Eye Hospital has merged market and non-market approaches into a hybrid business model that serves upscale patients profitably and uses the surplus revenue to subsidise free eye surgery for the bottom of the pyramid (Mehta and Shenoy, 2011; Rubin, 2007). When social innovation serves the underserved, it has to lower costs to accommodate the purchasing power of the target market. Aravind Eye Hospital reinvented the intraocular implant to avoid an import cost of $200, building local capacity to manufacture it at just $5 a unit. According to two of our research respondents, Aravind was able to become a successful social enterprise by frugally innovating. This activity took place at the intersection of social and technological innovation, where technology was reinvented to overcome the resource constraints incurred in procuring expensive intraocular lenses. At the same time, social innovation built a hybrid model to meet the needs of all strata of patients. This embodies Aravind's mission, 'To see all as one; to give sight to all'.

Joel Sadler, co-designer of the initial Jaipur Knee, previously worked at Apple. When interviewed, he argued that working under formidable business constraints is what enables the development of 'extreme' products such as the Apple MacBook Air, iPad and iPhone. Although Apple is more focused on performance metrics than on price, working for the company taught Sadler to innovate under the constraint of price-points demanded by low-income customers. As a result, he and classmates Eric Thorsell and Vinesh Narayan in the Biomedical Device Design and Evaluation course at Stanford University were able to redesign a prosthetic knee joint, reducing the price from as much as $10,000 to as low as $20 (version 1) and transforming it into a simple, easily manufactured, high-performance device. In 2009, it was cited as one of the top fifty inventions of the year by *Time* magazine. Since then, there have been several iterations of the frugal innovation after D-Rev, a non-profit product development company focused on the needs of the poor, acquired ReMotion, the company that the graduate students had founded (Figure 4.2a). More recent conversations with Rob Weiss, Product Manager of the ReMotion Knee, have revealed that, based upon years of iteration on the original Jaipur Knee design, the product was launched commercially in 2017 by D-Rev, is International Organization for Standardization (ISO) and Conformité Européene (CE) certified, and is sold worldwide for $80 (source: http://remotion.d-rev.org/).

History of the ReMotion Knee

JaipurKnee (v1)

Students at Stanford University developed the v1 ReMotion JaipurKnee for production and fitting by the JaipurFoot Organization, the largest provider of prosthetics in India and the world.

ReMotion Knee (v2)

The v2 ReMotion Knee was manufactured in Menlo Park and distributed through Fundación Protesis Para la Vida in Ibarra, Ecuador.

ReMotion Knee (v3)

The v3 ReMotion Knee is our first version that is designed to be mass produced for world-wide scale.

FIGURE 4.2A Development from Jaipur Knee to ©ReMotion Knee (used with permission)

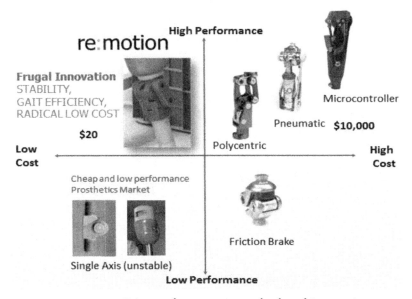

FIGURE 4.2B Price-performance space for frugal innovation ©ReMotion Knee (used with permission)

Figure 4.2b shows the frugal innovation space along performance and cost dimensions that the ReMotion knee is positioned in – a space that was revealed in responding to the contextual constraints faced by its social enterprise partner, Bhagwan Mahaveer Viklang Sahayata Samiti (BMVSS)/Jaipur Foot in India. Figure 4.2c depicts a commonly held assumption that low performance and low cost are associated with cheapness while high performance bears high cost, often representing very expensive or luxury items. But Figure 4.2c overlays nicely on Figure 4.2b, as shown in Figure 4.2d. This supports the contention by many of our respondents that 'frugal' does not mean 'cheap'. In contrast to the common expectation that high performance incurs high cost (top right quadrant), our frugal innovators contend that they deliberately try to position themselves in the top left quadrant where high performance can be delivered at what might be considered cheap rates but without compromising performance or quality. The lower left quadrant resembles typical cheap solutions

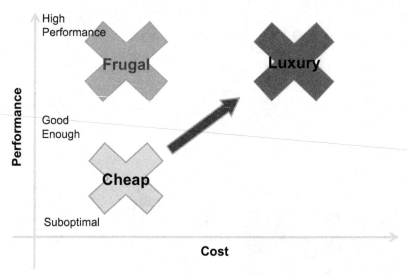

FIGURE 4.2C Frugal innovation is not cheap

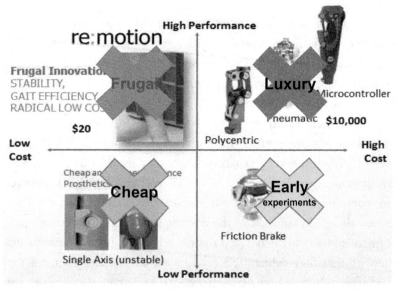

FIGURE 4.2D Overlay of two figures in support of the finding that frugal innovation is not cheap

with low quality and lower right quadrant resembles what we might call early experiments. These are initially expensive and may not have a clear value proposition to be market worthy but nevertheless through further design and innovation could lead to more or better solutions. We therefore believe that limiting frugal innovations as low cost or simply affordable and worse, labelling them as cheap innovations (e.g. Darzi, 2017) may not do justice to their true value proposition, risks discrediting the offerings, and raises cognitive barriers in the early and critical stages of adoption (Harris et al., 2017; Keown et al., 2014; Rogers, 2003).

In support of the feasibility of combining high quality with a low price, Carlos Haertel, the managing director of GE's European Global Research Centre, says that cheap does not mean low quality. In fact, 'a doctor's option for a stethoscope is either to have a cheap one or nothing. An unreliable one is just not an option at all' (Woodward, 2011, online). Since that claim, Tarek Loubani, a Palestinian-Canadian doctor working in Gaza during an Israeli blockade, developed under emergency conditions and constraints a 3D-printed stethoscope for around $5, which is purported to match or exceed in performance compared to popular retail ones costing around $150–200 (Porup, 2015). There are countless other examples of high-performance and high-quality frugal innovations increasingly being developed, particularly in the healthcare sector (Barlow 2016, Bhatti et al., 2017a; 2017b; Prime et al., 2017).

Entrepreneurs and firms seeking to resolve both the economic and social problems facing extreme customers, such as those at the base of the pyramid, do so in extreme environments marked by resource and affordability constraints. Working under these business and social constraints forces innovators to rethink both the process and outcome of innovation, i.e. both means and ends. As suggested by Poole and Van de Ven's (2004) paradox resolution approach to development, this rethinking needs to be reflected in new concepts and terminology. Our respondents used the new term, frugal innovation, to capture this hybrid form of innovation. Social entrepreneurs make Schumpeterian or technology innovation part of the process of overcoming resource constraints, doing the most with the little their firms control and using social innovation to ensure that the outcome is affordable and accessible and can improve the lives of underserved people. We therefore contend that a mix of economic and social concerns can bring about a change of attitude in those who innovate at the intersections of technology and social innovation spaces; this leads us to formulate the following propositions:

Proposition 1: A mix of technology and social innovation creates a hybrid form of innovation marked by distinctly different processes and outcomes, as exemplified by frugal innovation.

Proposition 1a: Social entrepreneurs combine technology innovation and social innovation as part of the process of dealing with resource constraints and affordability constraints.

Proposition 1b: Social entrepreneurs combine technology innovation and social innovation to ensure that the outcome of innovation is adaptable and affordable.

4.3.2 Intersection of Institutional and Social Innovation

The notion that institutional innovation and social innovation share overlapping concerns was revealed by the empirical data. The following two quotations are drawn from different data sources and thus support the triangulation of findings. Additional quotations from data sources that confirm the overlap of institutional and social innovation are included in Table 4.2b at the end of this chapter.

> Kenya currently does have local alternatives to insurance, but these are often mobilised after a catastrophe. So we show our prospective farmer clients the benefit of formal insurance.

> Our innovative approach has led to the development of pioneering methodologies that promote community leadership, locally driven natural resource management and a communicative culture that encourages our partners to share best practices and skills with each other, fostering true regional collaboration and sustainable development.

In the overlap between institutional innovation and social innovation illustrated by Model 4.3, we exploit the paradox between two contrasting assumptions underpinning institutional and social innovation to develop a theory of frugal innovation, as proposed in the preceding section. Chapter 3 shows that social entrepreneurs are not just innovators of products, services and technologies, but also innovators of institutions. Although institutions are the hardest entities to change, they are also where the greatest opportunities lie, since those few who are able to change them possess capacities that are very rare (Haque, 2011). In researching over 250 companies, Umair Haque found fewer than twenty (about 8 per cent) that were institutional innovators. These companies did not just marginally outperform their rivals, they structurally disrupted the competition. In markets where institutional voids exist, market failures offer fertile ground and new spaces for business activity as well as for institutional innovation.

One stream of entrepreneurship literature looks at whether social entrepreneurship happens through or in opposition to existing institutions. Institutions that achieve consistency, impartiality and reliability in their enforcement allow entrepreneurs to form expectations about the future, such as whether to invest in innovation, by removing some of the uncertainty as to whether they will be able to capture the value they create (Baumol, 2002). While most ventures operate on the assumption that their activities will be supported by formal institutions, other ventures emerge despite a lack of institutional support (Sarasvathy, 2006). Research on institutional effects has shown that institutions can both support and preclude actors, entrepreneurs and ventures.

Saras D. Sarasvathy (2006) points out that social enterprises are sometimes forced to oppose existing institutions and come up with creative mechanisms that incorporate the best of both market and non-market solutions. Thomas J. Dean and Jeffery S. McMullen (2007) show how, according to the entrepreneurship literature, entrepreneurs can seize opportunities inherent in environmentally relevant market failures. Social enterprises may serve as bridges between underserved communities and existing institutions (Bayliss, 2004; Wallace, 1999). Bricolage, as outlined above, often goes against the norm and occurs in the absence of institutional support (Baker, Miner and Eesley, 2003; Baker and Nelson, 2005). Yet as social entrepreneurs act to mobilise resources, they brush up against existing political (lobbying), legal (business regulation) and technological (human development) institutional environments, or the lacks thereof. In the process, they may build upon existing fragments to create new structures. Furthermore, several needs or problems that social entrepreneurs take on are not addressed or even recognised by existing public or private institutions. For this reason, social entrepreneurs often have to cope with or operate within an institutional void.

In such cases, institutional entrepreneurs often emerge because they are needed. Institutional entrepreneurship happens when entrepreneurial actors change institutional structures or create new ones (DiMaggio, 1988; Fligstein, 1997). Institutional entrepreneurs 'lead efforts to identify political opportunities, frame issues and problems and mobilise constituencies' (Rao, Morrill and Zald, 2000, p. 240). An institutional entrepreneur develops new institutions or facilitates changes in existing institutions, securing the resources to achieve these changes. Institutional entrepreneurs are actors with an interest in modifying institutional structures and norms, or in creating new institutions, structure and norms (DiMaggio, 1988; Fligstein, 1997). While we do not argue that our social entrepreneurs are necessarily institutional entrepreneurs, those who adopt institutional innovation practices may be. A novel difference in form, quality or state over time in an institution, or an unprecedented departure from the past, constitutes institutional innovation (Hargrave and Van de Ven, 2006).

When social entrepreneurship happens in opposition to existing institutional arrangements, the creation of a venture may in itself cause those arrangements to change (Mair and Martí, 2006). An example taken from our own data and described in Chapter 3 involves a social entrepreneur who faced failure when working to provide sanitary pads in a community where they were taboo; she consequently failed to sell or even give them away. The social entrepreneur then moved to institutional innovation by focusing on advocacy and raising awareness of the benefits of sanitary pads, not only for girls, but for society as a whole. She slowly and gradually initiated a localised social movement to change institutions of culture and meaning that were an obstacle to the sale and use of sanitary pads.

This early clash with existing institutional arrangements occurred in the early days of the Grameen Bank (Yunus, 2007). Microfinance (the form of social entrepreneurship pioneered by Muhammad Yunus and the Grameen Bank, who shared the 2006 Nobel Peace Prize) was widely touted; however, we believe that social entrepreneurship is better explained as operating at the intersection of social and institutional innovations (see Figure 4.2). The formation of a new microfinance institution that changed the capital flows, lending and savings patterns of the poor involved parallel efforts in institutional and social innovation. In addition, social entrepreneurship often takes place at the intersection of multiple institutions, dealing simultaneously with the government, market and community (Shaw and Carter, 2007). Johanna Mair, Ignasi Martí and Marc Ventresca (2012), remembering their work on BRAC in Bangladesh, call this having to deal with institutionally complex environments. In creating microcredit organisations such as Grameen Bank and BRAC, these social entrepreneurs engaged in institutional entrepreneurship by altering existing cultural, economic and regulatory institutions (Dacin, Dacin and Matear, 2010; Mair and Martí, 2009; McMullen, 2011).

The overlap between institutional and social innovation can also be seen in historical accounts of the emergence of the US recycling industry. Environmental degradation can result from a market failure caused by existing institutional arrangements (Desa, 2009a; 2009b; Desa and Koch, 2014). In analysing the development of the US recycling industry, Michael Lounsbury, Marc Ventresca and Paul Hirsch (2003) show how social movements helped to transform socio-economic practices, paving the way for the recycling industry and its market development. Social movements and entrepreneurs jointly develop proofs of concepts for the creation of sustainable businesses. As such proofs develop, public perception is changed and the institutions controlling those perceptions are reconfigured to accommodate the new market.

Institutional analysis, when linked to social movement theory in sociology (e.g. Armstrong, 2002; Clemens, 1997; Rao, 1998; Strang and Soule, 1998), helps to explain how political struggles shape cultural meaning systems, socio-economic processes and industry emergence (Espeland and Stevens, 1998; Heimer, 2001; Lamont and Molnar, 2002). The radical social movement for recycling promoted marginal practices by inspiring non-profit recyclers; recycling then became a central practice for technology and for-profit actors (Weinberg, Pellow and Schnaiberg, 2000). During the emergence of the recycling industry, labour-intensive and often ad hoc, non-profit, voluntary recycling efforts were supplanted by more organised curbside collection efforts promoted by for-profit models. However, these continued to rely on free household labour to clean and sort waste, thereby lowering the overall cost of the recycling process (Weinberg et al., 2000). The ability to leverage mainstream policy negotiations along with grassroots activism was the key to the eventual success of the recycling movement (Lounsbury et al., 2003).

In this section, we have argued that social entrepreneurs seek to resolve both institutional and social concerns for customers at the base of the pyramid and in extreme environments shaped by institutional voids and resource constraints. Working under these institutional and social constraints forces them to rethink the process and outcome of innovation, which needs to be reflected in new concepts and terminology, as Poole and Van de Ven (2004) have argued. We adopt our respondents' terminology to discuss the hybrid form of innovation they call frugal innovation. Social entrepreneurs talk about using a hybrid mix of institutional forms of innovation as part of the process of overcoming institutional voids by reconfiguring old or creating new institutions and structures. They propose to use social innovation to ensure that the outcome of innovation is relevant, affordable and accessible, genuinely improving the lives of the underserved.

Proposition 2: A mix of institutional and social innovation creates a hybrid form of innovation marked by distinctly different processes and outcomes and exemplified by frugal innovation.

Proposition 2a: Social entrepreneurs combine institutional and social innovation as part of the process of dealing with institutional voids and affordability constraints.

Proposition 2b: Social entrepreneurs combine institutional and social innovation to ensure that the outcome of innovation is accessible and affordable.

4.3.3 Intersection of Technology and Institutional Innovation

In Figure 4.2, we look at the overlapping intersection between Schumpeterian or technology innovation and institutional innovation as another fertile space to exploit, using the paradox resolution approach. We use two contrasting assumptions behind technology and institutional innovation to argue once more for a theory of frugal innovation. Our empirical data supports the theory that technology and social innovation have shared concerns. The following sample quotations are drawn from different data sources and support the triangulation of our findings. Additional quotations from various data sources that support the overlap of technology and social innovation are shown in Table 4.2c at the end of the chapter.

> We are not setting up a micro-insurance industry. We are using technology to link the insurance providers to those who need it.

> The biggest obstacle to future growth is overcoming the 'Aid' mentality – this mentality exists on two levels: In the communities where the Solar Sister Entrepreneurs are trying to sell their products, they have to convince customers that improved technology is something they can purchase for themselves rather than expect some NGO to come and provide for them.

Both social movements and technology innovation management researchers have studied the institutional arrangements that enable change to take place, as well as the efforts of social activists and technological entrepreneurs to enact those arrangements. Timothy J. Hargrave and Andrew H, Van de Ven (2006) juxtapose technology innovation literature with social movement literature to propose a collective action model of institutional innovation. Entrepreneurs and social activists both engage in political processes that often resemble social movements (DiMaggio and Powell, 1991; Fligstein, 1996; 2001; Rao, 1998; Snow and Benford, 1992). At this macro-level field of inter-organisational studies, the processes of technological innovation and entrepreneurship have many similarities to social movements (Aldrich and Fiol, 1994; Lounsbury and Ventresca, 2002; Schoonhoven and Romanelli, 2001).

The co-evolution of institutional policies and rules through such as professional associations, governments and markets, alongside technological development, has been documented in the works of Thomas P. Hughes (1983) and William Walker (2000). Kenneth Green (1992) has examined how a market may not exist for a new technology and may have to be shaped. For a market to exist, institutions must be in place to establish prices, inform customers and suppliers and provide distribution arrangements. Entrepreneurs developing radically new technologies must cooperate with others in collective action to create such institutions. Joseph L. Bower and Clayton M. Christensen (1995) have examined the case of disruptive technologies, where information about potential customers, dimensions of product performance important to customers and acceptable pricing levels can be acquired only by experimenting with ways to develop both the product and the market.

Tim Brown, the founder of IDEO, and Jocelyn Wyatt, the head of IDEO's Social innovation group, 'Design Thinking for Social Innovation,' have pointed out that those designing for developing nations must consider not only form and function, but also distribution channels (Brown and Wyatt, 2010). They cite the example of northern Ghana, where a programme that provided free nets to pregnant women and mothers with children under age five was so successful that the nets became difficult for everyone else to obtain as the market collapsed. In this example, the neglect of the whole system had a detrimental effect on those within the scope of the current distribution scheme, making the eradication of malaria impossible.

In the previous section, we discussed how Grameen specifically (and microfinance in general) exemplified a hybrid form of innovation that incorporated both institutional and social innovation. Over the past decades, microfinance has used mobile technologies to achieve even greater penetration and broader scope of service. Mobile phone banking companies in emerging markets, such as M-Pesa in Kenya, Telenor EasyPaisa in Pakistan and EKO in India (all technology companies) innovate at the frontiers of technology and institutions. They help to connect the poor 'unbanked' and underserved segment of the market to existing financial institutions (or alternatives) by leveraging the ubiquity of mobile technology. Telenor EasyPaisa worked with the government to devise the world's first regulatory mobile banking model. In 2011 Pakistan had fewer than 10,000 traditional bank branches (State Bank of Pakistan, 2011) to serve a population of 180 million. The EasyPaisa model quickly surpassed that figure in 2011 by offering 12,000 mainly rural franchisees serving as financial agents and bank kiosks. By 2017, the population had grown to 208 million and while the number of bank branches increased to just over 13,000, EasyPaisa outlets had increased to more than 70,000 (State Bank of Pakistan, 2017). EasyPaisa have used their mobile technology infrastructure to bring more people into the formal economy through this unique 'lowcal' (both local and low-cost) strategy (Bhatti, Khilji and Basu, 2013), than could ever have been achieved through traditional institutionalised bank models. All major telecom companies have followed suit by offering competing services such as Mobilink's JazzCash, Zong's PayMax, and UFone's UPaisa. Major banks as well as startups are now entering the space. This market building activity (Geroski, 2003) should complement efforts towards greater financial inclusion.

In another example, respondent EKO bypassed the mobile companies to create a technology-based mobile phone app that works on any network (and any phone), linking major banks such as ICICI with thousands of mom-and-pop shop owners who serve as bank tellers. EKO's CEO, Abhishek Sinha, informed us that their most socially valuable customers are household domestic maids, who can now save money in their own bank accounts and access their own funds virtually throughout India. These frugal innovations have created different business models in each of their respective environments, from Kenya, where the banks are not involved, to mobile-led Pakistan and entrepreneurial, broker-led India. All help to lower entry barriers for the financially underserved, enabling them to benefit from savings, investments and insurance markets to achieve inclusive growth.

Even in the United States, the emergence of new Internet business models introduced by Ebay for everyday selling and by E-Trade for investment options for those excluded from the markets involved innovating at the intersection between technological and institutional arrangements. Ebay and E-Trade used Internet technology to restructure the market institutions for buying and selling goods and services. Ebay and some similar companies began as grassroots solutions to personal problems faced by their founders. In addition, Eric Topol (2011; 2016), the Chief Academic Officer of Scripps Health and Professor of Genomics at the Scripps Research Institute, cites as an example of frugal innovation $8,000 pocket ultrasound devices (Mobisante and Vscan) which create visual scans of the heart as good as the $200,000–300,000 professional and technical scans carried out by standard machines in a US laboratory. Topol estimates that this innovation could save the US$50 billion per year in ultrasound procedures. But he believes that, although such frugal innovations abound in the healthcare sector (e.g. Barlow 2016, Prime, Bhatti and Harris, 2017; Prime et al., 2016a), their wide-scale use or adoption is hindered by the reimbursement rules and economic models that physicians, insurers and hospitals rely upon. Matthew Harris, Yasser Bhatti and Ara Darzi (2016) argue that the country of origin of an innovation poses a significant challenge in the diffusion of healthcare innovations. Eventual adoption therefore depends, not only on the technological strengths of frugal innovations, but also on the ability of entrepreneurs to restructure and work around existing institutional structures and cognitive perceptions.

This section demonstrates that social entrepreneurs coping with resource constraints and institutional voids can make us rethink both the processes and outcomes of innovation. As part of this rethinking, we argue that frugal innovation reflects the new hybrid approach to innovation. It emerges when social entrepreneurs use a hybrid mix of technology innovation to overcome resource constraints and institutional innovation to overcome institutional issues or voids:

Proposition 3: A mix of technology innovation and institutional innovation creates a hybrid form of innovation marked by distinctly different processes and outcomes and exemplified by frugal innovation.

Proposition 3a: Social entrepreneurs combine technology innovation and institutional innovation to create a process that can deal with resource constraints and institutional voids.

Proposition 3b: Social entrepreneurs combine technology and institutional innovation to ensure that the outcome of innovation is adaptable and accessible.

4.3.4 The Technology–Social–Institutional Nexus

Finally, the overlapping concerns of all three forms of innovation – technology, social and institutional – were also revealed by the empirical data. The following quotations are drawn from different data sources and support the triangulation of the findings. See Table 4.2d for additional quotations that reflect the overlap between institutional and social innovation.

The development of GSMA standards helped to lower the cost of technology for all to be able to afford. And mobile is probably the only sector through which MNCs have innovated widely for the BoP.

Unlike other online marketplaces, e-Mobilizer is organised into local communities, bringing buyers and sellers together for face-to-face transactions. This solution is especially tailored to a market where 1) cash is still the main method of payment with no credit cards or other payment systems in place; 2) a poor logistics system makes long distance shipment difficult; 3) fear of fraud prevents people from doing business with someone they don't trust; 4) culturally, bargaining prices and negotiating deals are part of business practice.

We contend that innovations lie along a spectrum of values. At the social innovation end, social value is the main concern. At the other end are ordinary innovations, producing profits and value for individuals who are often privileged and taking advantage of known markets. The two extremes recall the paradigm of paradox resolution helping to resolve conflicting assumptions. In the middle of the spectrum is frugal innovation, which draws social value from a mix of social, technological and institutional innovation. Innovation blossoms at the intersections where the sectors converge, strengthened by the exchange of ideas and values, shifts in roles and relationships and the integration of private capital and public and philanthropic support (Phills et al., 2008). Social enterprises are routinely positioned at the nexus of the public and private sectors (Dees, 1998).

Gill Seyfang and Adrian Smith (2007) support this pattern of multidimensional integration by citing Staffan Jacobsson and Anna Johnson (2000), who argue that 'specific social and technical practices are embedded within wider, facilitating infrastructures, which subsequently restrict opportunities for alternatives' (p. 587). Johanna Mair, Jeffrey Robinson and Kai Hockerts (2006) and Scott Shane and Sankaran Venkataraman (2003) challenge researchers to apply theories of management to situations that are relevant to social and technology entrepreneurs. What they have missed is the potential relevance to institutional entrepreneurs. Although isolation frees an emerging system from the institutional constraints of existing technologies and industries (Astley, 1985) and permits the system to develop its own distinctive institutional forms (Rappa, 1987), it is best considered in combination with social and technology concerns.

In technological innovation research, knowledge that crosses a boundary-spanning mechanism can produce radical innovations and creative products (Hargadon and Sutton, 1997; Hsu and Lim, 2006). Given that ventures operate at the boundaries of resource availability, facing affordability and institutional constraints, we propose that knowledge-bridging mechanisms across the three types of innovation – social, technical and institutional – can help to explain the development of frugal and other kinds of innovations, particularly among social entrepreneurs, although without being limited to this type of entrepreneurial activity.

One interview example involves the Rickshaw Bank project in India, which holds a prominent position at this nexus of social, technical and institutional innovations. Pradip Kumar Sarmah (2010) set out to enable rickshaw drivers, most of whom are immigrant workers from rural regions, to own rather than rent rickshaws. In the process, he used technology to redesign the rickshaw, social innovation to restructure the prevalent practise of renting (rather than owning) the asset and institutional innovation to license and recognise rickshaw owners as formal contributors to the local economy. The rickshaw community was drawn from a bleakly structured informal economy into the folds of the formal economy. This led to rickshaw owners renting clean energy LPG cylinders at subsidised government prices instead of using firewood or expensive kerosene. Sarmah's rickshaw bank enterprise did more than simply convert rented rickshaws into purchased ones; it also provided damage and healthcare insurance. In isolation, none of these three innovations would have been carried out. Yet by combining all three, Sarmah helped more than 30,000 rickshaw drivers benefit from the scheme. Plans are now underway to use the micro-franchise model and scale to other parts of India to reach the remaining 8 million or so rickshaw drivers. Although the model seems scalable, we need to know the extent to which Sarmah's business model will diffuse to the majority of market clients. The Rickshaw Bank project has redefined business models, reconfigured value chains and redesigned products to create more inclusive markets.

Another example comes from the United States in the mid-1990s when Self-Help, a community development finance organisation, pioneered the secondary market for mortgage-backed securities, based on loans to low-income households, to enable greater access to homeownership. With cross-sector partnerships between the non-profit Self-Help, commercial banks, the federally chartered Fannie Mae organisation and private investors, the scheme grew from $50 million in 1998 to $2.5 billion in 2008 (Phills et al., 2008). Such a sophisticated scheme that relies on robust and varied institutions is unlikely to work in emerging and developing markets. By contrast, through a combination of technical, social and community-based social innovations, low-income housing schemes (for example) are being tested in emerging markets. Bahria Town of Pakistan, purported to be the largest private real estate developer in Asia, has packaged technical innovations to lower the cost of housing construction, institutional innovation to enable financing for low-income household ownership and social innovations that make low-cost housing schemes acceptable, within larger housing schemes designed for the ultra-rich (Bhatti, Khilji and Basu, 2013).

These research findings suggest an initial set of forces that drive and help to explain the rise in frugal innovation activities; these are the social, efficiency, user and challenge-based drivers. Furthermore, an analysis of innovation under constraints suggests that a mix of innovation approaches can be used to overcome constraints involving resource, affordability and institutional voids. The spaces where innovations merge to cope with simultaneous constraints point to fertile spaces where a new form of innovation occurs – one occasionally labelled by informants as frugal innovation. Whatever it is called, this form of innovation stems from a hybrid mix of approaches: technology innovation to overcome resource constraints, institutional innovation to overcome institutional concerns and voids and social innovation to address challenges of scale and affordability. We therefore propose the following:

Proposition 4: A mix of technology, institutional and social innovation creates a hybrid form of innovation marked by distinctly different processes and outcomes, exemplified by frugal innovation.

Proposition 4a: Social entrepreneurs combine technology, institutional and social innovation as part of the process of coping with resource constraints, institutional voids and affordability constraints.

Proposition 4b: Social entrepreneurs combine technology, institutional and social innovation to ensure that the outcome of innovation is adaptable, accessible and affordable.

4.4 SUMMARY

In a nutshell, an understanding of frugal innovation can stem from an innovation process perspective or from an innovation outcome perspective. The process approach alludes to frugal innovation as drawing on myriad existing approaches to overcome institutional voids (either lack of institutions deemed important for efficient markets to function or the presence of localised and complex institutions deemed not to be conducive to efficient markets), resource scarcity (such as constraints to business resources or scarce environmental resources) and affordability constraints (the lack of purchasing power) to create more inclusive markets. The outcome understanding of frugal innovation can relate to the development of affordable, adaptable and accessible solutions to serve and fulfil the needs of underserved market segments. With both process and outcome perspectives encapsulated in the proposed models and theory, we can study a range of issues around the frugal innovation phenomenon, including its sources, development, diffusion and impact.

In the next section, we provide support for this theoretical model of frugal innovation, based on published accounts of innovation. A review of published examples can help to test the applicability and relevance of the theoretical model to cases beyond the ones from which it was drawn.

Table 4.2a *Data supporting the intersection of Schumpeterian and social innovation*

Interviews

Initially, we imported pads but found that the pads were clogging toilets and were not biodegrading, creating greater health risks. So we came up with a patent pending chemical-less process to manufacture biodegradable pads.

In an ideal situation you would need different size interfaces. But in a resource constrained environment you can't do 100% efficiency. Ninety-five per cent efficiency is good enough. So the willingness to compromise doesn't really exist in the United States, which isn't suitable if you want to take the technology to the developing world. And plus, looking at the device's low cost, it isn't really a super-viable business. To provide it at a dollar or two at small scale to Bangladesh and India means it is hard to make ends meet.

There is one group I would really like to partner with. There are two orphans who learned from this Swiss guy who supported an orphanage and they have plenty of capacity to do good engineering. They use the workshop also as a vocational school for people to teach manufacturing skills.

I agree we cannot design in isolation of the USA for developing country applications. Our cook stove was first developed by Engineers w/o Borders at Berkeley. But our engineers went back and forth to Sudan and worked with a local engineer. Through this back and forth, our cook stove went through fourteen iterations and we reached the current price of $16. So I don't think we designed and developed it just in Berkeley and just dumped the cook stove – rather we tweaked it over and over again as necessary.

Aurolab was initiated because we wanted the poor to have the same high-end lenses, so it was a major contribution but not alone. For scalability, we needed to match global technologies with local applications. Among such global technologies was the Aurolab and TIER IT service from Berkeley, which integrated Aravind's fifty remote villages.

And for the 'techie' students, the frugal contexts present interesting challenges of different performance dimensions, as well as an understanding of the whole ecosystem embodying engineering for humanity as opposed to just the role of technology. Take, for instance,

Table 4.2a (*cont.*)

the case of a bridge that was designed and constructed by our engineers. When the team left, the bridge was rendered useless because the landowner took possession and started to charge, at which the community was furious!

Western engineering schools have not addressed these because designers here don't understand the problems and contexts in developing economies. However, equally, engineers in developing markets are not the best designers, so they need partnerships to match problems in developing markets with designers in developed ones.

Documents

The need for locally relevant, language-specific content on the World Wide Web exists in every developing country (not to mention developed countries). XayanIT is currently developing a Bangla-language 'portal to the World Wide Web', designed to increase the participation of Bangladeshis in the Information Age and expose Bangladesh to the world community.

These technologies – like the hand-driven oil-expellers, biogas plants and smokeless stoves – have been evolving for decades, but have not received much attention from larger political movements.

While many organisations promote technology transfer, EnterpriseWorks almost alone, complements such technical activities with the development of a complete market for these locally manufactured technologies.

Table 4.2b *Data supporting the intersection of Schumpeterian and institutional innovation*

Interviews

Good innovators can find markets for their inventions. The truth is, people will buy these if they are designed properly and efficiently distributed. So distribution will be the real key source of frugality. I've learned in this programme that I need to help my distributors have the capacity to distribute, such as with access to financing.

Table 4.2b (*cont.*)

Our business model would not have existed five years ago because (i) people were not talking about this opportunity, (ii) rural broadband was not available and (iii) water and health technologies were not ready.

Here in the Indian centre we have to be more deliberate about it. So part of my research deals with improvisation and what I see is that people here improvise quite easily. It is that element of rigor and process that needs to be brought in ... versus when I deal with engineers in the United States, they already have a structured approach and we have to loosen them up a bit more. There is that contrast to some extent.

It was part of our goal to have it locally manufactured. Just for two reasons: one, I personally think it is better for a product that is made for Ethiopians is to be made by Ethiopians in Ethiopia, so that if it breaks people know it is manufactured locally; and two, Ethiopia has very high import tariffs. So to try and make it somewhere else where manufacturing might be easier, like I can easily send drawings to India or China, but then I incur 100–300% import tariff. The economics work out better if we manufacture locally.

Documents

In most cases, however, it is less that the technology or even the basic idea itself is new than that the technology is applied creatively to a wide variety of environmental conditions.

Even in the developed world, SMS is an effective communications medium for reaching vulnerable groups such as low-income families and frequent movers, for whom their mobile phone is their most reliable 'address'.

ONergy creates and manages the distribution and service of appropriate renewable technology – effectively and creatively – by eliminating the middlemen. RECs are set up in partnership with MFI and NGOs. RECs operate in a sustainable (also financially viable), decentralised and scalable manner. The distribution and servicing network is managed by ONergy leveraging the network, infrastructure and local knowledge/goodwill of the partner.

Table 4.2c *Data supporting the intersection of institutional and social innovation*

Interviews

Over the years, Engineers w/o Borders and other initiatives have made people aware of projects around the world. For instance, in El Salvador and Nicaragua, we do projects where SCU has Jesuit partnerships. These relationships and partnerships are crucial for our projects' implementation and success.

In the USA, if I ask people how much they pay for their water bill, they have no clue. But if I ask them how about their cable bill, they know exactly – $102.67! This means we take for granted some of our very basic human rights, such as water and we consequently waste it. The water here costs only 1/2 cent per gallon and the quality of tap water is even better than bottled, because it is so much more heavily regulated. Yet we pay $1 for a small water bottle.

I got involved in 'frugal' in the early 1990s, when I was the first female professor at the engineering school here, with very few female students. I took them to Housesafe near Santa Clara, a community programme for battered women and tried have my students solve some of their needs. Inequities lie everywhere and, relatively speaking, the differentials are worse in Silicon Valley where the rich-poor divide is huge.

A challenge to VCs here (in the West) is that most social enterprises in developing countries are family-run small businesses which will grow, but will probably never grab huge market shares to become the next high growth MNCs. In fact, many of the developing markets do not have a culture of large firms.

The obvious answers that I am not giving you are capital for instance or funding. I think it may come from the fact that I sit in a very privileged context here where if there are great ideas, I feel confident that those ideas will gain access to capital. I don't even think that the typical entrepreneur sitting elsewhere in the United States feels that way. So funding is a big hurdle, but for me I believe there is enough capital to help solve these problems, but it is just speculation from my privileged position.

The government does not like slums and generally has a policy of relocating or removing them. So while they say they will do slum upgradation, at the same time they don't want to invest in permanent

Table 4.2c (*cont.*)

sewage infrastructure, which makes these slums permanent.
They don't want to sanction or legitimize a lot of these neighborhoods, but they understand they are a threat to healthcare. So you don't want sewage systems but they are a source of cholera that spreads to the whole city.

Documents

It is possible that we could patent our system for online p2p microfinance. For instance, in the early days of the Internet, a man patented online auctions and won a huge settlement from Ebay.
Kiva will pursue a patent only for defensive reasons. It is against Kiva's ideals to offensively litigate against another organisation seeking to do good in the world. If awarded a patent, we would be very free in terms of licensing it to others in the space.

At least two aspects of our innovation are replicable. First, we have found that a franchise-based growth strategy with clear toolkits and mini-grants for students is an excellent way to build a movement on campuses quickly and consistently. Second, we have found that new models of engagement for students that emphasise localised, concrete returns and professional development tap the contemporary student zeitgeist. Both of these innovations could be used to mobilise and engage youth effectively on issues other than foreign policy, such as healthcare, tax policy or campaign finance.

Table 4.2d *Data supporting the social–Schumpeterian–institutional nexus*

Interviews

Based on lessons from 139 business models, we found that cost reduction strategies include: 1) Local labour and materials (meaning close to beneficiaries); 2) De-skilling to use local and low-cost labour; 3) Partnering with local experts, especially for manufacturing and distribution; 4) Disintermediation by eliminating the middle man; and 5) M-commerce to leverage mobile phone ubiquity.

The BoP wasn't taken seriously by mainstream VCs. Either the entrepreneurs there will have to find local investors or the VCs in Silicon Valley will change their strategies. The latter could happen if the VCs realise the benefit of developing products for large developing market populations. But overall, it is hard to convince traditional non-impact VCs to invest in developing markets based on technology and financial impact.

Jugaad or FI cannot work in the USA because those kinds of cars and tractors would not be allowed to run on the roads here. Plus, used cars are so affordable here that the need for a Tata Nano seems to not exist.

Documents

Instead of advocating a new technology or material, Build Change makes low or no-cost modifications to existing, common, culturally appropriate and preferred ways of building to create long term change and reduce deaths, injuries and economic losses during earthquakes.

Lastly, to address the problem of affordability, the Scojo Foundation has commoditised reading glasses by making them a consumer product that is easily sold by women entrepreneurs, thereby taking them out of the exclusive hands of eyecare professionals. This mimics the successful shift that occurred in the West that made reading glasses a commodity item rather than one wholly controlled by eyecare professionals. Through relationships with large-scale optical manufacturers, the Scojo Foundation is able to source reading glasses at very low cost. These low costs, coupled with efficient distribution systems, allow the Scojo Foundation to sell reading glasses to the entrepreneurs at 50 per cent margins. The profits from these margins will support investment in program replication and reduce dependence on traditional sources of grant funding.

Table 4.2d (*cont.*)

Fund raising and scaling-up, EnterpriseWorks is committed to establishing sustainable supply chains for technology transfer by training local manufacturers and assisting them to promote technologies at a price that ensures a profit for them and a benefit for the end user.

Build Change empowers homeowners to design and build homes themselves with technical assistance. Build Change works with local builders to incorporate disaster-resistant building techniques that are easy to adopt with limited training and education.

The approach begins with an active stakeholder dialogue to refine technology development and dissemination strategies; it ends with technical assistance and capacity building to enable local businesses and organisations to implement Envirofit solutions long after we have left.

The contribution of our work can be assessed from three perspectives:

1) Poverty reduction – We have been able to help more than seventy-five families establish oil collection businesses. These businesses supply us with used oil. The families earn money, which they are able to use to meet their needs.

2) Environmental conservation – We have so far been able to collect 45,000 litres of used oil, which would have been disposed of in water systems in Kenya. Despite the fact that this may appear to be a small effort, it is contributing to the fight against water pollution in Kenya.

3) Economic – The recycled oil is sold off to buyers. Our organisation is able to generate revenue from the sale of used oil.

Information technologies increase business efficiency, organisational impact and beneficiary scope while improving the economic, social and political participation of individuals.

Competition from knock-off and imitation products – Quality must be kept high to establish a strong brand and price must be competitive to handle any potential knock-offs. Our initial lighting product, the Angaza SoLite, is the brightest in its price range, the most accessible for our customers due to our rural distribution networks and the most affordable through our unique leasing model, allowing even the poorest families to prosper from clean, bright light.

5   Test of Models Using Secondary Cases

Thus far, we have developed the models and suggested steps towards theory development based on our empirical data. In this chapter, we attempt to investigate whether or not the proposed models and theory applies to popular published accounts of social entrepreneurship. We show how the perceptions and conceptions of innovation revealed in this study relate to popular examples found in the existing literature. We hypothesise that our proposed models of innovation apply to a broader set of globally networked and recognised innovators, entrepreneurs and organisations involved in frugal innovation. We have selected ten cases that represent diverse types of organisations (large and small social enterprises, MNCs, local corporations and networks), sectors (healthcare, finance, ICT, transportation and housing) and countries (in Asia, Africa and North America) but all with the common theme of serving underserved markets. The published accounts help to test the applicability and relevance of the theoretical model to cases beyond the ones from which it was drawn.

5.1 INTRODUCTION

Insofar as was possible for us as researchers, our knowledge of the following cases did not influence the development of our theory. To carry out a first test of the applicability of the findings, models and theory proposed in this study, we reviewed ten frequently cited cases of innovation for underserved markets. Recall that underserved markets were a main cross-cutting theme mentioned by the social entrepreneurs who participated in this study. We selected ten diverse cases, representing large social enterprises (Aravind, Narayana, Dabbawalas and Grameen Bank), small social enterprises (One Laptop per Child), large multinational corporations (GE and Tata), local corporations (M-Pesa and EasyPaisa) and networks involved in challenge competitions or prizes (Ansari X Prize and $300 House). They also represent diverse sectors such as healthcare (Aravind, Narayana and GE), finance (Grameen Bank, M-Pesa and EasyPaisa), information technology and communications (One Laptop per Child), transportation (Dabbawalas, Tata and Ansari X Prize) and housing ($300 House). And they represent global contexts from Asia (Bangladesh, India and Pakistan) and Africa (Kenya and Tanzania) to North America (Canada and the USA) and the world. Though diverse, the common theme linking these cases was their aim to serve underserved markets.

We categorised the ten cases in accordance with the two models of innovation presented in Chapters 2 and 3. Model 1 was for innovation in general while Model 2 was for innovation under constraints. Model 1 speaks to the different sources and drivers of innovation while Model 2 speaks to the different types of innovation used in resolving constraints. Table 5.1 shows the positioning of the cases as per their relevance to the social, efficiency, challenge or user-based innovations in Innovation Model 1 and to the overlapping space(s) of technology, social and institutional innovations in Innovation Model 2. We find that these popular cases do support the relevant dimensions in the two models. The table below shows the complementary nature of the two models, which allow cases to

Table 5.1 *Categorising case examples in accordance with Innovation Models 1 and 2*

Model 2 / Model 1	Technology–Social intersection	Institutional–Social intersection	Technology–Institutional intersection	Technology–Institutional–Social
Social	Aravind	Grameen		Narayana
Efficiency-based	GE		EasyPaisa/ M-Pesa	
Challenge-based	Tata Nano Ansari X Prize One Laptop per Child (OLPC)			$300 House
User-based		Dabbawalas		

be categorised using the two models together. We next describe how these published cases exemplify support for the models of innovation.

5.2 INTERSECTION OF TECHNOLOGY AND SOCIAL INNOVATION

In discussing the next five cases, we describe how each fits into one of the four quadrants of Innovation Model 1, using examples that reflect social, efficiency- and challenge-based innovations. We then describe how the cases fit into the overlapping area between technology and social innovation in Innovation Model 2. We also suggest how, with reference to Proposition 1 in Chapter 4, these cases show how a mix of technology and social innovation creates a hybrid form of innovation marked by distinctly different processes and outcomes, as exemplified by frugal innovation. The processes involve using technology innovation to deal with resource constraints and social innovation to deal with affordability constraints. The outcomes of these processes should lead to frugal innovation that is adaptable and affordable.

5.2.1 Aravind Eyecare System (Social)

Since 1976, the Aravind Eye Hospital has been on a mission to end blindness in India, seeing 2.5 million patients a year (Mehta and Shenoy, 2011). Today, Aravind is the largest eye-surgery provider in the world. Amongst its highly touted technical and social achievements are replacing imported intraocular lenses costing $200 apiece with locally produced lenses costing $5, charging $10 to conduct a cataract operation that lasts just twenty minutes, carrying out 300,000 eye surgeries a year and maintaining a gross margin of 40 per cent, despite the fact that 70 per cent of patients receive free or heavily subsidised rates. With less than 1 per cent of the country's ophthalmic manpower, Aravind accounts for 5 per cent of the ophthalmic surgeries performed nationwide (Aravind, 2011). The hospital network uses broadband for rural screenings. 'We are going from village to village to provide eye care to the unreached', says Aravind's chairman, Dr P. Namperumalsamy (Rubin, 2007).

By comparison, the average cost for this eye procedure in the United States is about $1,650. The key to these achievements has involved constantly cutting costs, increasing efficiency and building a market base. The high scale and high efficiency are made possible through a Fordist assembly process: 'Doctors have created equipment that allows a surgeon to perform one 10–20-minute operation, then swivel around to work on the next patient, who is already in the room, prepped, ready and waiting. Post-op patients are wheeled out and new patients are wheeled in' (Rubin, 2007). The hospital's Aurolab pioneered the production of high-quality, $5 intraocular lenses – producing 700,000 lenses a year, of which three-quarters are exported all over the world. However, these lenses are not exported to the United States, since Aravind cannot afford the costly US FDA clinical approval process (Rubin, 2007).

Aravind's *social* mission is 'sight for all and to see everyone as one', which embodies the creation of value for inclusive markets. The organisation's guiding principle is to achieve wide-scale social improvement of common sight problems through affordable eye surgery, never turning away any patient – poor or rich – who knocks at Aravind's door. The technology outcome is to provide adaptable solutions in the Indian context, where resources and skills are lacking. This is accomplished through redesigning products and services and reconfiguring the surgery value chain. The outcome of these social and technical processes is a frugally innovative eye care service that is widely accessible and highly affordable to everyone.

5.2.2 *General Electric's Electrocardiogram and Ultrasound Machines (Efficiency-Based)*

It may not be conventional to identify or label a multinational corporation as a social entrepreneur, but we refer to GE and later to Tata Corporation as such because some of their projects focus on resolving the problems of underserved consumers. When explaining their conceptions of innovation and frugal innovation in particular, some of the social entrepreneurs we interviewed referred to both GE and Tata. There is evidence that this usage is accepted among social entrepreneurs themselves.

In a case study entitled, 'How GE is disrupting itself', by GE chairman Jeff Immelt, Vijay Govindarajan and Chris Trimble (2009), the authors say, 'If GE doesn't master reverse innovation, the emerging giants could destroy the company'. The authors argue that the long-pursued glocalisation strategy of innovating in developed markets and distributing to the rest of the world with adaptations to local conditions must pave the way for a reverse innovation strategy. Glocalisation limited GE to skimming off the top emerging market opportunities by focusing only on the high-paying wealthy segment. In the reverse innovation strategy, solutions are designed and developed for the broader markets in emerging economies. Products such as the $1,000 handheld electrocardiogram machine (ECG) and the portable ultrasound device (which costs 15 per cent as much as GE's contemporary ultrasound devices) are finding their way to new applications in the United States. Another example is a low-cost baby warmer developed for Nepal by Embrace, a start-up from Stanford University, which is being considered by GE for use in cold regions of the United States. Organisationally, this means that the centralised and product-focused structure has to change to a more decentralised and local market-focused structure.

Given the threat from low-cost competitors in emerging markets, GE is driven both by the pursuit of *efficiency* in cost leadership and by the prospect of new mass markets in developing countries. Immelt et al. (2009) use the case of GE to show how reverse-innovation products are creating new markets in both the emerging and developed worlds by offering two main differentiators: dramatically lower price-performance points and a search for new applications.

For GE, the guiding principle is to achieve large market capture by improving the efficiency of solutions for problems in developing markets. However, problems in these markets often include affordability constraints that have to be resolved before social conditions can be improved through more affordable solutions. In the cases of the ECG, ultrasound and baby warmer technologies, the technology outcomes involved designing solutions that could be adapted to the Indian context, where resources may be scarce. This was accomplished by redesigning products and services and reconfiguring manufacturing and distribution value chains. The outcome is frugal innovation making healthcare technologies affordable and well adapted to the Indian context.

5.2.3 Tata Nano (Challenge-Based)

The reality in India and neighboring South Asian countries is that it is not uncommon to see a family of five riding on a single motorcycle or scooter. While MNCs such as Mercedes and BMW tap the luxury market, Ratan Tata, entrepreneur and the CEO of the Tata conglomerate looked at this unsafe yet very common transportation practice and commented:

> I observed families riding on two-wheelers – the father driving the scooter, his young kid standing in front of him, his wife seated behind him holding a little baby ... It led me to wonder whether one could conceive of a safe, affordable, all-weather form of transport for such a family. Tata Motors' engineers and designers gave their all for about four years to realise this goal. Today, we indeed have a People's Car, which is affordable and yet built to meet safety requirements and emission norms, to be fuel efficient and low on emissions.
>
> (Foster and Malhotra, 2008)

The result of this challenge that Ratan Tata gave to his motoring division was the $2,000 Tata Nano car targeted at people using scooters, who can now make what was once considered an impossible leap to car ownership. The Tata Nano is the least expensive car in the world, sold in India as well as in neighbouring countries, such as Sri Lanka. A book was dedicated to this product with the promise that such a little car could teach the world to think big and act bold (Freiburg, Freiburg and Dunston, 2012). A European version called the Pixel, built on the Nano platform, was showcased in Coventry, UK with innovations that included being able to turn all four wheels ninety degrees to facilitate parking.

For Tata Motors, the guiding principle was to meet the technical *challenge* of producing a car for the masses at a price that was inconceivable in the industry. The price of the car was paramount, given the inability of masses of people in India to afford a car, an example of an affordability constraint. What made the car socially affordable was technology innovation that used processes, tools and resources to redesign the car, as well as to reconfigure the value chain away from the traditional assembly and distribution network. Coimbatore Prahalad and Raghunath Mashelkar (2010) point out that strict parameters – about price, safety and environmental standards, space and design – formed the Nano's 'innovation sandbox' (Prahalad, 2006). In terms of business model, the company rethought the traditional manufacturer-assembly-to-dealer-distribution value chain to consider an IKEA type model of flat packing the car in a modular fashion and shifting the final assembly to local auto-mechanics who could put together, sell and service the vehicle in their local and often rural contexts. The outcome has been a frugally innovative car that is affordable and significantly adapted to the needs and constraints of the local context and market.

5.2.4 Ansari X Prize (Challenge-Based)

The Ansari X Prize announced in 1996 offered $10 million in prize money for the first non-governmental organisation to launch into space a reusable manned spacecraft – twice in two weeks. A typical space shuttle mission costs on average $450 million (John F. Kennedy Space Center, 2000) and a space-tourism ticket on the Russian Soyuz costs about $20 million, both of which are far beyond the reach of mainstream civilians. The prize hoped that competition would breed innovation and the discovery of new low-cost methods of space exploration. The *challenge* was to demonstrate that spaceflight can be affordable and accessible, not just to the government but also to corporations and (more importantly) to civilians.

The technical design criteria were reusability, reliability, simplicity and low cost. In 2004, Mojave Aerospace Ventures and Scaled Composites won the prize. Today, a civilian space launch such as Virgin Galactic could cost as little as $200,000 per ticket for a space flight. When compared with the $20 million charged by the Russian Space Agency, this equates to a radical 99 per cent cost reduction. Virgin Galactic's Spaceship 2 holds six passengers and the average cost of a single mission amounts to around $1.2 million (Virgin Galactic, 2012). Compare this to NASA's $450 million and we experience a 99.7 per cent cost reduction. Success continues to mount in this contest and challenge for affordable and more convenient space flight. In early 2018, Elon Musk's private firm SpaceX demonstrated the viability of lifting to orbit more than twice the payload of the next closest operational vehicle at one-third the cost (SpaceX, 2018).These technical improvements combined with significant cost reduction reflect the constructs of 'radically improved performance' and 'design breakthroughs' that constitute challenge-based innovation in Model 1.

Luciano Kay (2011) studied inducement prizes and found that teams attempting to find simple, low-cost solutions to problems focused on using existing technologies or the 'make-do' construct. In fact, since prizes have strict deadlines and do not provide up-front funding for research and development, low-cost solutions and short timescales end up being the most important design and development criteria (Kay, 2011). The downside, however, is that prizes cannot guarantee that entrants with the best ideas will be motivated to participate or that the best idea will be selected at the minimum cost (Scotchmer, 2005). However, by using technology innovation to do more with fewer resources and social innovation to bring space travel within the affordable reach of mainstream society, the outcome here is frugally innovative space travel that is affordable and adapted to a resource-limited environment.

5.2.5 One Laptop per Child (Challenge-Based)

The One Laptop per Child (OLPC) project was initiated by Nicholas Negroponte of the MIT Media Lab. We have not covered this case in detail because it is quite similar to the previous two. The project *challenge* was to design a laptop for the world's schoolchildren and to offer it to them at the affordable price of $100. This case can be positioned in the space where technology and social innovation overlap; the aim was to design a frugally innovative laptop that was adaptable and affordable. Although OLPC has struggled to achieve that goal, it did initiate the challenge and demonstrate proof of concept by instituting technical breakthroughs and a radical improvement in price-performance. Recently, however, Google began to offer a laptop for $100, something that OLPC has been unable to achieve.

5.3 INTERSECTION OF INSTITUTIONAL AND SOCIAL INNOVATION

We suggest how the next two cases fit into the four quadrants of Innovation Model 1, with the first example reflecting social innovation and the second, user-based innovation. We also describe how they fit into the area of overlap between institutional and social innovation in Innovation Model 2. With reference to Proposition 2 in Chapter 4, these cases show that a mix of institutional and social innovation creates a hybrid form of innovation marked by distinctly different processes and outcomes, as exemplified by frugal innovation. The processes use institutional innovation to deal with institutional voids and social innovation to deal with affordability constraints. The outcomes of these processes are designed to lead to frugal innovation that is accessible and affordable.

5.3.1 Grameen Bank (Social)

Microfinance has been revolutionary, not only in how it has affected people and communities on the ground, but also in raising awareness of the needs of the poor. This awareness was brought into the mainstream when the 2006 Nobel Peace Prize was awarded to the Grameen Bank and its founder, Muhummad Yunus, 'for their efforts to create economic and social development from below' (Nobel Prize, 2006). The microfinance phenomenon has provided access to financial resource-lending to people who have traditionally been excluded from the mainstream banking sector. This reflects an institutional void, as well as the unavailability of collateral, which constitutes affordability constraints.

The primary social objective of Muhummad Yunus was to provide this access to capital, which he deemed was necessary to improve the *social* wellbeing of underserved, rural or deprived communities. Microfinance extends inclusiveness to all groups, particularly poor women in developing countries, for whom access to finance was considered inconceivable two or three decades ago. The popularity of microfinance has gained traction as a social movement to help eradicate poverty. The enabling institutional innovation that deals with the institutional voids of collateral, risk assessment and recovery mechanisms lies in lending not to individuals, but to community and women's groups. Every person in the group essentially insures each of the others, and the collective dynamics help to ensure that the whole group is under pressure to perform and repay loans. The outcome of these social and institutional processes is a new market for microfinance, which can be considered a frugal innovation that makes capital accessible and affordable to virtually everyone.

5.3.2 Mumbai Dabbawalas (User-Based)

Professor Karl Moore (2011) of McGill University, also a Fellow of Green Templeton College, Oxford, explains how the dabbawalas of Mumbai exemplify frugal innovation by maximising the efficiency of the supply chain to meet personal *user* requirements. A network of independent lunchbox-delivery people, known as dabbawalas, have formulated a method and a system that allow workers to deliver meals on time with unmatched efficiency. The system is efficient at a rate of only one error per 16 million transactions. In 2001, *Forbes* magazine awarded a Six Sigma certification to the dabbawalas.

Although the business model is simple – delivering freshly home-cooked meals in lunch boxes to family members at work and at school – the delivery process is anything but simple. Five thousand dabbawalas deliver more than 200,000 lunch boxes every day using a complex supply chain that comprises collection, sorting and delivery zones, trains, bicycles and communication through manual codes. Since most of the dabbawalas are illiterate, only numbers and colours are used for the coding system, which was designed by the users themselves. Over time, the dabbawalas have innovated further by adopting website and mobile text messaging to receive delivery requests.

Moore holds that sometimes less is indeed more. The dabbawalas use few literacy skills, almost no fuel, no capital investment and almost no modern logistical technology and yet offer a high quality of service which Moore terms, 'frugality at its best'. Furthermore, the operating context matters immensely to frugal innovation. The dabbawalas have been extremely successful for decades in Mumbai but have not expanded to other cities – a finding of limited scalability we referred to in Chapter 2 when discussing user-based innovation. Moore believes that one reason for this is the fact that their system is built on a combination of characteristics, including codes, proximity, density, train networks, bicycles and other factors that are unique to the city of Mumbai. The dabbawalas have innovated to fulfil the needs of their own users by transporting tins to the right place on time. Often, user-based innovations are so idiosyncratically specific to a particular user and context that it is difficult to replicate or scale them up to accommodate other users or contexts.

Socially, the long-term sustainability of Mumbai dabbawalas' livelihood is ensured by the efficient and cost-effective delivery of home-made lunches to 200,000 people in Mumbai. Institutionally, the dabbawalas are able to do this through a system that both overcomes and taps into the complexity of Mumbai's crude and dilapidated infrastructure, as well as into their own inability to read and write. The outcome of these social and institutional processes is a frugally innovative system for transporting lunch boxes that is highly efficient, making the delivery of tins possible, accessible and affordable to virtually everyone in Mumbai.

5.4   INTERSECTION OF TECHNOLOGY AND INSTITUTIONAL INNOVATION

The next case, relating to mobile phone banking, is primarily efficiency-based, reflecting Innovation Model 1. It also fits into the overlapping area between technology and institutional innovation described in Innovation Model 2. With reference to Proposition 3 in Chapter 4, this case shows that a mix of technology and institutional innovation creates a hybrid form of innovation marked by distinctly different processes and outcomes, as exemplified by frugal innovation. The processes involve using technology innovation to deal with resource constraints and institutional innovation to deal with institutional voids. The outcomes of these processes lead to frugal innovation that is adaptable and accessible.

5.4.1 Mobile Phone Banking (Efficiency-Based)

Colin Mayer (2011) says 'a revolution is taking place in finance and it is a revolution that is not happening in the streets of New York or London, but in the slums of Nairobi in Kenya [through] what is termed mobile banking'. Mobile phone technologies, with their impressive affordability and wide-scale availability in even the most remote parts of Africa and Asia, provide a technical means to formulate and deliver banking services. Using this mobile platform, several multinational mobile firms are entering the banking sphere, to provide banking services more *efficiently*, effectively and affordably than the traditional bricks-and-mortar banking sector.

In just the four years since M-Pesa's launch in 2007, about 14 million Kenyans (70 per cent of the adult population) were brought into the banking sector (Daily Nation, 2011). According to the International Monetary Fund, in October 2011, M-Pesa conducted more transactions domestically within Kenya than Western Union does globally. The project began in 2003 as an initiative of the UK development agency, DFID, in cooperation with Vodaphone. In Pakistan, only 12 per cent of the 170 million population in 2008 was served by the formal banking system (Sambandaraska, 2010). Two local organisations, including Telenor (a leading mobile phone operator) and Tameer (a local microfinance bank) created a joint venture to offer banking to virtually every adult, making it accessible throughout the country. This is known as the 'EasyPaisa' (or EasyCent) service. Telenor and the State Bank of Pakistan sought to help billions of people in developing countries break out of the cycle of poverty by providing low-cost, convenient financial services.[1]

The role of legal systems (or lack of any, which creates an institutional void) is also crucial in understanding the socio-political process of operationalising such novel financial platforms. Mayer believes that M-Pesa has taken off so dramatically in Kenya in part because of how the regulatory authorities have responded. Conventional banks do not like mobile phone transactions since they bypass the banking system. Although there have been calls for mobile banking to be regulated like ordinary banks, the Kenyan authorities have resisted. 'If it is regulated like a bank and goes through the banking system it's very expensive. If it's kept outside of the banking system and just involves mobile phone transactions, it's incredibly cheap' (Mayer, 2011).

---

[1] Telenor has extended its partnership model to offer services in other sectors such as healthcare with DoctHERs. The award-winning start-up improves access to healthcare through telemedicine in Pakistan by connecting marginalised and remote communities with female doctors often residing in urban areas but whose expertise, for various social and cultural reasons, is left untapped. While women account for almost 70% of medical students, only 23% are registered or practicing doctors. The model helps to re-integrate this vast untapped resource into the medical workforce by allowing the docters to work from anywhere (Ajadi and Bayen, 2017).

Pakistan's introduction of some of the world's first regulations for branchless banking in March 2008 has produced more than eleven competitors in the pipeline; it is described as a 'laboratory for innovation' for this emerging sector (Bold, 2011), not only in terms of technology innovation but perhaps more importantly in terms of institutional innovation and alongside, new market formation (Geroski, 2003). State Bank of Pakistan regulations have helped to implement a bank-led sustainable and profitable 'branchless banking' model that prioritises services for low-income consumers in rural areas (Bold, 2011), something Bhatti, Khilji and Basu (2013) describe as a 'lowcal' (low-cost and local) strategy.

This form of banking, which bypasses the banking system, may worry regulatory authorities in Western countries concerned about the potential for money laundering. However, mobile phone banking, as well as allowing instantaneous transactions, also provides transparency on all transactions, which creates trust and therefore stymies money laundering:

> What could happen in the developing countries is that this form of technology could leapfrog ahead of existing monetary payment systems that we have. So instead of spending three or four days clearing a check, as typically happens in this country (the UK), one has a mechanism for instantaneous transmission of money. One of the reasons why it's been so successful in Kenya is that people can observe straight away what's happening to their money ... you instantaneously can see on your phone that you've been credited for the money you handed over. So it creates trust, and trust in financial markets is absolutely critical.
>
> *(Mayer, 2011)*

As discussed earlier, Mayer believes that mobile banking will be even more exciting than microfinance for social improvement. Instead of placing an emphasis on people borrowing and getting into debt, mobile banking can help people accumulate savings: 'And that (savings culture) I think in the long term is actually going to be more transformational than the emphasis on lending through microfinance which has been featured so prominently to date' (Mayer, 2011). Even Adam Smith (1904) argued long ago that frugality is important for accumulating savings and generating capital for investment.

This case shows that a combination of technology innovation and institutional innovation can be used to deal with resource constraints, such as a lack of savings and the need to lend to poor communities, as well as addressing soft institutional voids, such as the mobile banking regulatory mechanisms, and hard institutional voids, such as the lack of brick-and-mortar bank branches in developing countries. The outcomes of these processes prove that mobile phone banking as a frugal innovation is adaptable to specific contexts and yet accessible to mainstream society.

5.5 THE TECHNOLOGY–SOCIAL–INSTITUTIONAL NEXUS

In examining the next two cases, we show how they fit into the four quadrants of Innovation Model 1 and the area of overlap between technology, institutional and social innovation of Innovation Model 2. The first case is an example of social innovation and the second of challenge-based innovation. With reference to Proposition 4 in Chapter 4, these cases show that a mix of technological, institutional and social innovation creates a hybrid form of innovation marked by distinctly different processes and outcomes, as exemplified by frugal innovation. The processes involve using technology innovation to deal with resource constraints, institutional innovation to deal with institutional voids and social innovation to deal with affordability constraints. The outcomes of these processes can lead to innovations that are adaptable, accessible and affordable.

5.5.1 Narayana Health Cardiac Hospital (Social)

Dr Devi Shetty, dubbed the 'Henry Ford of Heart Surgery' by the *Wall Street Journal* (Anand, 2009), was Mother Teresa's cardiac surgeon. Shetty uses process innovation and economies of scale to increase efficiency and drive down the costs of cutting-edge medical care in India, in ways that benefit society as a whole: all social classes. His flagship heart hospital, the Narayana Hrudayalaya Hospital (NHH) in Bangalore, has 1,000 beds, charges $2,000 for open-heart surgery, performs 600 operations a week and carried out 3,174 complicated cardiac bypass surgeries in 2008. Compare these to the statistics for an average hospital in the United States, with 160 beds, a $20,000–100,000 charge for heart surgery and (in the case of US leader, the Cleveland Clinic) 1,367 cardiac bypass surgeries carried out in 2008. In the same year, Shetty's hospital operated on 2,777 paediatric patients, more than double the 1,026 surgeries performed at Boston's Children Hospital. Not only are the procedures numerous, the success rates are better than those in developed countries; for example, in 2008 the thirty-day mortality rate after coronary artery bypass graft surgery at NHH was 1.4 per cent, compared to the US average of 1.9 per cent. This supports our finding described in Chapter 4, that frugal innovators strive to deliver high performance and quality. Shetty says, 'Japanese companies reinvented the process of making cars. That's what we're doing in healthcare' (Anand, 2009, para 6). To scale this model, Shetty's group has expanded to a 1,400-bed cancer hospital and a 300-bed eye hospital in his homeland. He has also expanded internationally, by setting up in the Cayman Islands to serve patients in North America.

Although most published references to the NHH tout healthcare efficiency, Dr Shetty's primary motive and objective resemble those of Dr Venkataswamy and his Aravind Hospital: to reduce inequity in healthcare services for the poor in order to achieve social improvement. About one-third of NH hospital patients receive almost free healthcare. With an insurance premium costing just $3 a year per person, through an insurance plan that Shetty developed with the state authorities, the NHH adapts health insurance to the context and needs of its people. Through this insurance plan, the NHH provides services, not as a handout, but as an empowered and affordable right through affordable health insurance. Dr Shetty not only provides technology innovation in the surgical procedures and processes he helps to improve, but also employs institutional innovation, for example by co-opting insurance providers to cover non-traditional customers, who are mainly poor patients. Where necessary, poor patients are subsidised through the higher margins paid by wealthier patients. As in the Aravind Hospital, few people (if any) are denied world-class healthcare. What sets the NHH apart from Aravind is the way it has co-opted the insurance industry into its business model. The outcome of this complicated mix of techno-logical, social and institutional innovation is the ability to provide a frugal innovation healthcare system that is affordable, adaptable and accessible to all, both rich and poor.

5.5.2 $300 House (Challenge-Based)

The $300 House was proposed in 2011 as a design challenge by Vijay Govindarajan, a professor of Management at Dartmouth College and Christian Sarkar, an innovation and strategy consultant. Initially, they introduced the idea on the Harvard Business Review (HBR) blog; the challenge quickly gained traction among individuals and com-panies representing different sectors globally, as a way of coming up with a viable solution to the world's housing problem. Because so many different actors have come together to take on the challenge of designing a $300 house for the world's homeless, it is difficult to isolate the main motivation of participants. Some individuals may have joined the project to resolve what they see as personal needs; designers and engineers may be motivated by the prospect of challen-ging design criteria; companies may be hoping to create and test efficient designs, while others may be attracted to the project as a social cause that resolves a major human need. Overall, we are calling this an example of challenge-based innovation, as the creators do – a prize-driven design challenge meant to reveal a proof of concept, as in Innovation Model 1.

In terms of Innovation Model 2, the project is perhaps more interdisciplinary and complicated than any of the other examples cited thus far. The initiators of the challenge describe the involvement of various actors as follows:

> By helping create this ecosystem, we believe companies can make money while providing services needed by the poor at an affordable cost. The poor deserve a chance, a real chance, to make it out of poverty. To do this, we'll bring together people, institutions and businesses in a 'creation space' to:
>
> 1) turn this idea into a reality and
> 2) test it out in the field. (www.300house.com/concept.html)

The $300 House considers not only the technical challenge of design, construction and manufacture under resource constraints, but also the associated challenges of housing, including the need to achieve social improvement for residents and the institutional challenges of leasing or buying land and distributing the homes to far-flung corners of the world. Different actors have come up with varying proposals on how a mix of technological, social and institutional innovation can deal with the resource and affordability constraints and institutional voids associated with housing. The outcomes of these processes should lead to a frugally innovated house that is adaptable, accessible and affordable.

Executives are increasingly designing for innovation (Van de Ven, Ganco and Hinings, 2013). Leaving behind the engineering and analytical approaches of the past, they are pursuing more artistic and generative approaches to design (Boland and Collopy, 2004) through design thinking (Brown, 2008). In the last decade, such design thinking has spread beyond the field of product design to become widely adopted in the social field (Brown and Wyatt, 2010).

5.6 SUMMARY

Having shown that the models of innovation and theory proposed in this section can be used to understand ten secondary cases, we assume that our models and theory can also be used to gain greater insights into other innovations taking shape under institutional conditions and constraints akin to those revealed in this work. In the next chapter, we outline the ways in which the conception and definitions of frugal innovation based on our empirical data compare with the version of frugal innovation found in the existing literature, as well as with related terms such as reverse innovation, grassroots innovation, inclusive innovation and *jugaad* innovation.

6   Emerging Concepts in Innovation

In the domain of knowledge generation and the contest for ideas, several emerging concepts of innovation continue to arise. We are particularly interested in those innovation ideas and concepts that help to explain innovative activity under complex institutional conditions and resource constraints. A bibliometric search of Google Scholar explored the use of related concepts since 1990; these findings are presented in Figure 6.1. We find there are several popular terms which have complementary meanings and yet also have subtle variations both across and within the terms. In this chapter, we discuss and highlight these similarities and differences in light of the models we have presented and in light of the conception of frugal innovation based on our empirical data.

6.1 INTRODUCTION

We used Google Scholar to identify patterns in the popularity of emerging concepts of innovation through bibliometric search because of its focus on scholarly literature, including peer-reviewed papers, theses, books, preprints and abstracts, as well as technical reports from practitioners and policymakers representing broad areas of research. In addition, Google Scholar has the ability to extract references in several languages. Concepts linked to fewer than twenty publications since 1990 were not included. We have carried out this search every two years since 2012. In terms of cumulative numbers, grassroots innovation is ahead with publications mounting since early 2000s. Reverse innovation has rapidly gained second place with inclusive innovation in third place. Frugal innovation is quickly catching up as is evident from 2017 publications outnumbering those

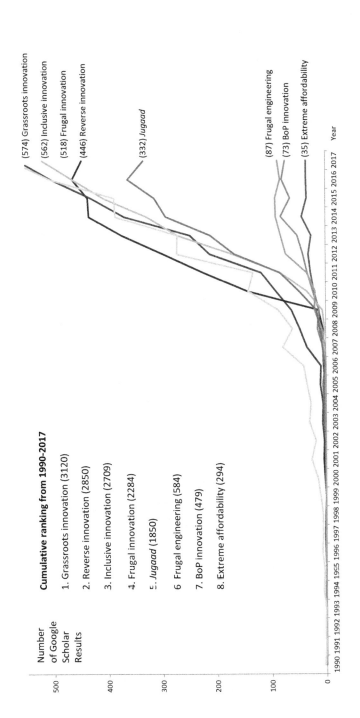

FIGURE 6.1 Growing trend in articles related to frugal innovation 1990–2017 data retrieved in January 2012; 2012, 2012 and 2013 data retrieved in February 2014; 2014–2015 data retrieved in August 2016; 2016–2017 data retrieved in January 2018.

Note: Google Scholar search results may vary over time.

related to reverse innovation, Both reverse and frugal innovation have grown steeply since 2010 in comparison to grassroots and inclusive innovation which have had a headstart since 2000s. Our last search was conducted in early January 2018, so some of the dips in the number of publications in 2017 may be explained by the fact that Google Scholar may not have found all publications in the closing months of 2017. The five top terms therefore are grassroots innovation, reverse innovation, inclusive innovation, frugal innovation, and *jugaad*. Although there are others, we focus on describing and critically discussing these variants, which are often discussed in relation to each other.

Before moving on, we acknowledge there are other terms that could also relate to frugal innovation. Coimbatore Prahalad (2005) refers to 'BoP innovation'; Lisa Gundry et al. (2011) and Clayton M. Christensen, Heiner Baumann, Rudy Ruggles and Thomas M. Sadtler (2006) refer to 'catalytic innovation'; Pradeep Kanta Ray and Sangeeta Ray (2010) cite 'resource-constrained innovations'; Ming Zeng and Peter J. Williamson (2010) mention 'cost innovations'; and Coimbatore Prahalad and Raghunath Mashelkar (2010) discuss 'Ghandian innovation'. What these generally have in common is the idea that innovations should be low-cost, simple yet useful services for people ignored by traditional social sector organisations. However, the evidence in bibliometric analysis suggests that these terms have not been picked up by practitioners or the academic literature to the same extent as those we discuss in this chapter.

6.2 REVERSE INNOVATION

Reverse innovation is defined as 'any innovation that is adopted first in the developing world' (Govindarajan and Trimble, 2012, p. 4). Reverse innovation follows from an understanding of how innovation differs in developing versus developed markets (cf. Van Agtmael, 2007). In developing an evolutionary model of reverse innovation, Vijay Govindarajan and Ravi Ramamurti (2011) propose that 'competitive advantage is likely to shift from emerging MNEs (multi-national enterprises) to developed world MNEs as the onus shifts from developing products to marketing them globally' (Sarkar, 2011, p. 239). Woolridge, who introduced frugal innovation to mainstream discourse, supported the idea of reverse innovation: 'Frugal innovation radically redesigns products and services to make them much cheaper for the emerging middle class – and then re-exports them to the West' (2011, p. 6). Govindarajan and Ramamurti discuss the implications of reverse innovation for global strategy, as well as for the organisational design of multinational enterprises.

In the discussion of Model 1, we described that the drive for efficiency improvement was supported by the literature on reverse innovation. In reverse innovation, commercial firms based out of developed countries may seek to become more efficient and productive by using frugal related research, development, practices and opportunities in developing and emerging markets. They then could benefit from bringing back these lessons, products, and services back to their home markets in order to become more competitive globally (Govindarajan and Trimble, 2012; Zeschky, Widenmayer and Gassmann, 2014). In support of this idea, a respondent described reverse innovation as follows:

> We have already been laggards in mobile banking because we have an alternative well-developed infrastructure here. But we will need to catch up and start designing and developing and investing in developing economies to bring back solutions that could be useful for ourselves.

In the shift from developed to emerging markets, Govindarajan and Trimble (2012) cite five needs gaps as the starting points for revising innovation strategies through reverse innovation: the performance, infrastructure, sustainability, regulatory and preferences gaps. As an analysis of the constraints of resource scarcity and institutional voids faced by social entrepreneurs in both developing and developed markets, our research both corroborates and expands

Govindarajan and Trimble's five gaps. The first-order codes from this study that relate to the five gaps are shown in Table 6.1. These make up about half (seventeen of the total thirty-three) first-order codes. While some of the constructs support Govindarajan and Trimble's five gaps, additional constructs identified in our study suggest two new findings about needs gaps.

First, our data suggests that these gaps also exist in pockets of developed markets. Among the social entrepreneurs we studied were several who functioned (either simultaneously or at different times) in both developing and developed markets. Second, while developing vs. developed market comparisons are useful, they cannot provide an understanding of innovation under constraints. Constraints can be faced to varying degrees in either context. The question of innovation under the dual constraints of resource scarcity and institutional voids therefore must not presume that the developing market context exclusively accounts for innovation constraints.

Rather than analysing innovation through the lenses of strategy and international business by studying globalisation, glocalisation and other areas shared by developing and developed markets, we may better understand innovation by focusing on the organisation of innovation under constraints and the innovators who cope with such constraints. This study therefore sets out to describe frugal innovation by exploring what innovation means to social entrepreneurs. This approach moves away from an exclusive focus on developing or emerging markets as the drivers of frugal or reverse innovation.

Indeed, many developing markets experience more constraints to innovation than do developed markets. And so Govindarajan and Trimble drew their inspiration in part from constraints in developing markets, such as performance and infrastructure gaps. However, even in Govindarajan and Trimble's book on reverse innovation, the discussion of constraints as drivers of reverse innovation is somewhat secondary. The book does not cover constraints, apart from acknowledging that, 'In a situation free of constraints ... evolution toward

Table 6.1 *First-order codes that support reverse innovation needs gaps*

	High performance	Improve efficiency	Good enough	Making do	(De)sophistication
Performance gap:					
Infrastructure gap:	Distribution	Supply chain			
Sustainability gap:	Economic sustainability	Environmental sustainability			
Regulatory gap:	(Un)structured	Partnership	Legitimacy		
Preferences gap:	Context	Culture	Aspirational	Needs	Affordable

complexity is almost inevitable' (p. 127). While some of the cases the book cites, including the Deere, Harman and GE corporations and Aravind, the social enterprise organisation, embody several constraining features, the cases of Pepsico, Partners in Health, P & G, EMC and Logitech may not primarily be driven by constraints (Bhatti, 2013a). For this reason, we argue that frugal innovation better addresses the study of innovation under constraints, while reverse innovation better addresses the study of innovation diffusion between developing and developed markets. This was supported by Govindarajan , whereby the former concisely explained the difference between frugal innovation and reverse innovation: 'Frugal thinking creates the innovation in poor countries. Reverse innovation takes such ideas into rich countries' (17 August 2011, personal communication).

The literature on reverse innovation includes a great deal of work on innovation sources and diffusion; few studies address the 'how to' or the 'what is' of innovation under constraints. Frugal innovation helps address this gap as can be seen in the link sometimes outlined between frugal and reverse (e.g. Zeschky, Widenmayer and Gassmann, 2014; Zeschky, Winterhalter and Gassmann, 2014). But we caution against assuming that frugal innovation is a necessary precursor or part of reverse innovation or that it comes only from developing or poor countries. As we have shown, constraints in developed markets also set the conditions for frugal innovation and indeed many have been sourced, developed or first implemented in developed market contexts before diffusing elsewhere (Prime, 2018). For instance, the OLPC described above was conceptualised and primarily developed in the USA but was destined for developing countries, but some of the insights from this venture led to the development and introduction of netbooks globally – smaller, more affordable laptops. Similarly, work by Max Zedwitz and colleagues (2015) shows how reverse innovation can have several typologies and varying patterns of innovation flows or diffusion for different parts of the new product development cycle across a range of low-, middle-, and high-income countries.

6.3 GRASSROOTS INNOVATION

Over the past two decades, most of the literature on grassroots innovation has been rooted in sociology, anthropology and international development, with a focus on poverty alleviation and sustainable socio-economic development (cf. Gupta, 1998; Letty, Shezi and Mudhara, 2012; Monaghan, 2009; Smith, Fressoli and Thomas, 2014; Warren, 1990). More recent work in grassroots innovation has contributed to the literature on information technology development (Bailey and Horvitz, 2010; Hanna, 2011), governance (Gault et al., 2012), transportation (Ross, Mitchell and May, 2012) and other concerns such as frugality and inclusiveness (Pansera, 2013; Pansera and Sarkar, 2016).

Grassroots innovation draws its name from its origins in marginalised, often rural communities (Agarwal 1983) and the informal sector (Cozzens and Sutz, 2012). It aims to make beneficiaries into 'agents, not patients' (p. 2). Tracy Ross, Valerie A. Mitchell and Andrew J. May (2012) explain grassroots innovation as initiatives triggered by individual users or communities trying to solve a personal or societal problem. More generally, Adrian Monaghan cites the grassroots as an 'alternative site for the development of innovations that may contribute to shifts towards more sustainable systems of consumption and production' (p. 1026). Gill Seyfang and Adrian Smith (2007) use the term to describe 'networks of activists and organisations generating novel bottom–up solutions for sustainable development; solutions that respond to the local situation and the interests and values of the communities involved. In contrast to mainstream business greening, grassroots initiatives operate in civil society arenas and involve committed activists experimenting with social innovations, as well as using greener technologies' (p. 585).

Grassroots innovation incorporates both user-led (Von Hippel, 1988) and need-based components (Jain and Verloop, 2012). It is frequently cross-referenced with social innovation (Butkevičiene, 2008; Jain and Verloop, 2012) and with inclusive innovation (Letty et al.,

2012). For wider social change that is adopted by communities, efforts towards local development must involve local people, creating innovation that includes the community process as well as its outcome. Given some of the same contextual constraints faced by social entrepreneurs, grassroots innovators use traditional knowledge, skills and materials to adapt to scarcity (Gupta, 1998; Gupta et al., 2003).

Seyfang and Smith's (2007) broad claim is that bottom-up, community-based innovations are social as well as technology-related and that grassroots innovations are driven by two motives: social need and an ideology more focussed on sustainable innovation than on profit or commercial success. However, although grassroots innovations are useful in showing that alternative processes and outcomes are possible for sustainable development, they have been unable to go mainstream due to a disconnect or inability to diffuse within mainstream socio-technical regimes (Monaghan, 2009). By contrast, this study shifts the focus to a middle ground that bridges the gap between prototyping and scaling up. Our interpretation of Model 1 is that prototyping is the purview of user-based grassroots innovation, while scaling up is the purview of efficiency-based commercial innovation.

6.4 INCLUSIVE INNOVATION

Inclusive innovation is defined as 'the development and implementation of new ideas which aspire to create opportunities that enhance social and economic wellbeing for disenfranchised members of society' (George, McGahan and Prabhu, 2012, p. 663). Inclusive innovation, according to Andre Nijhof, Olaf Fisscher and Jan Kees Looise (2002), refers to the 'inclusion of fundamental social responsibilities in both strategy and operations management in organisations' (p. 84). Nijhof et al.'s (2002) project on 'inclusive innovation' seeks to develop a label for the integration of social responsibility and universal human rights within organisations. More recently, the term has been used to denote inclusive innovation systems that take into account context-specific issues, obstacles and needs in developing countries, such as underserved low-income markets and informal institutions (Altenburg, 2009). Such innovation addresses the needs of the poor by lowering the costs of goods and services, creating income-earning opportunities for poor people and improving the knowledge-creation and absorption effects most relevant for them (Dutz, 2007).

Gerard George, Anita M. McGahan and Jaideep Prabhu (2012, p. 662) warn that 'the field is in a state of infancy – particularly with regard to theory that deals satisfactorily with inequality and the implications of inequality for innovation'. Overall, inclusive innovation is about fostering growth and equality for underserved and disenfranchised people, even if the means by which this is achieved are unclear (George et al., 2012). Like reverse innovation, inclusive innovation tells us what should be done but not necessarily how or in what form to do it. Some scholars draw from other approaches to fill this gap by referring to frugal innovation as one way forward to take concrete steps towards greater inclusiveness (e.g. Baud, 2016). Kirsten Bound and Ian Thornton (2012) posit that, while inclusive innovation is more focused on equity, frugal innovation 'ultimately offers a way to resolve the tension between excellence and equity' (p. 23).

6.5 *JUGAAD* INNOVATION

Of the variants discussed this far, the concepts most commonly associated with frugal innovation are reverse innovation and *jugaad*. While reverse innovation is more concerned about the strategy of learning from developing markets and using those applications to identify new market segments or to become more efficient in home markets, *jugaad* innovation explains more about how to create innovation and what it should look like.

Jugaad innovation is defined as 'an innovative fix; an improvised solution born from ingenuity and cleverness' (Radjou, Prabhu and Ahuja, 2012, p. 4). According to proponents Navi Radjou, Jaideep Prabhu and Simone Ahuja (2012), the six principles of *jugaad* are: frugality, flexibility, simplicity, intuition, opportunity in adversity and inclusion of the margin. *Jugaad*'s fundamental principles are synonymous with the third construct of bricolage 'improvisation', which uses work and creative thinking to counteract environmental limitations (Miner, Bassoff and Moorman, 2001; Weick, 1993). *Jugaad* is about the culture and mindset of creative improvisation that is required for frugal innovation (Bound and Thornton, 2012). The ability to do more with less is addressed, but considered a high-level art, culture or mindset, rather than a definitive process and outcome, or means and ends.

Jugaad has its share of critics: 'However, the term *jugaad* has the connotation of compromising on quality' (Prahalad and Mashelkar, 2010, p. 2). Anand Mahindra, CEO of Mahindra and Mahindra, says 'We have to move beyond *jugaad*. Frugal engineering and frugal innovation is fine, but not *jugaad*. The age of *jugaad* is over; we have to do more for less and that is what Mahindra Research Valley will embody. It is not about bridging the gap, it is a new paradigm, which is Indian' (John and Thakkar, 2012). The danger with *jugaad* is that it can be viewed as a quick and temporary fix. And *jugaad* could benefit from greater empirical research to back its claims (Bhatti, 2013b). It provides an entry point in conceptualising frugal innovation but suggests mostly 'making do'. The challenge with this idea or concept is that it can be easily construed as an unstructured process or mindset that 'makes do' to come up with an innovative fix.

Frugal innovation, by contrast, includes *jugaad* as only one of many elements or dimensions that help explain its approach or outcome. Certainly *jugaad* can play a crucial role at the very early phase of ideating or conceptualising a solution. But over the course of the innovation development process, innovators have to move away from the shortcutting, improvising or even compromising approach of *jugaad* to come up with a solution that upholds quality standards to meet customer and regulatory expectations. An example is the Arbutus Medical DrillCover (Prime et al., 2016a; Prime, Bhatti and Harris, 2017, Prime et al., 2018), a medical-grade solution for use in

FIGURE 6.2 Arbutus Medical DrillCover (Image source: http://arbutusmedical.ca/; used with permission)

orthopaedic surgeries (Figure 6.2). The original idea came about as a *jugaad* solution by surgeons in low-resource settings, mainly in Malawi and Uganda, making do by covering a commercial hardware drill with a locally developed cover to make it cleaner, but not entirely sterile for medical purposes. This solution only transitioned from a *jugaad* practice by local surgeons to became a frugal innovation after biomedical engineers in the 'Engineers in Scrubs' programme at the University of British Columbia introduced structured design and engineering processes to develop a fully sterile cover which was rigorously tested and approved by Health Canada, CE marked for Europe and listed and registered with the US FDA. The frugal innovation, costing less than £1,500 while mainstream clinical drills cost as much as £25,000, is backed by venture capital and has been used to treat 30,000 patients, in seventy-five hospitals across twenty-seven countries.

6.6 FRUGAL INNOVATION

The first global scholarly debut of frugal innovation came out in a relatively small section of a book about strategy in China by Anil K. Gupta and Haiyan Wang (2009). This was followed by, substantive coverage in a special report by *The Economist* in 2010. It described frugal innovation as 'not just a matter of exploiting cheap labour (though cheap labour helps), it is a matter of redesigning products and processes to cut out unnecessary costs' (Woolridge, 2010).[1] Subsequently, one of the first journal articles dedicated to helping us understand this idea and concept was published by Marco Zeschky, Bastian Widenmayer and Oliver Gassmann (2011).[2] They characterised frugal innovations as affordable, good-enough products that stem from needs in emerging markets. The first practical test of frugal innovation that we are aware of was the establishment in 2009 of the Frugal Innovation Lab at Santa Clara University by co-author and serial entrepreneur Radha Basu. Sometimes frugal innovation is referred to as reverse, *jugaad* or *shanzhai* innovation (Woolridge, 2010). In fact, the first comprehensive and much recognised account of related phenomenon and set of ideas was published in a book on *jugaad* (Radjou, Prabhu and Ahuja, 2012) followed by one dedicated to frugal innovation (Radjou and Prabhu, 2015). Alongside, the idea of frugality was referred to in terms of reverse innovation flows from the developing or emerging markets to developed markets (Govindarajan and Trimble, 2012).

Almost a decade on, there are still attempts to collate the various definitions, understandings and approaches (Pisoni, Michelini and Martignoni, 2018). And although we are getting there, there is not yet widespread agreement on how frugal innovation should be defined or distinguished from other forms of innovation. But this should not come as a surprise or even as a concern. Concepts that have been popular in the literature for significantly longer, such as social entrepreneurship (Zahra et al., 2008; 2009) and business models (George and Bock, 2011), have yet to settle on a single definition. Understandably, through the

---

[1] Before *The Economist* special report, a brief article in the *Business Standard* magazine (31 July 2009) by Bhupesh Bhandari on 'Frugal Innovation' described General Electric's technology centre in Bangalore as a 'low-cost but cutting-edge facility'. According to another news article, frugal innovation takes the specific needs of base-of-the-pyramid markets as a starting point and then works backwards to develop appropriate solutions that may be significantly different from existing solutions designed to address the needs of upmarket segments (Silicon India 2010).

[2] At the time of first online publication, this paper's title did not contain the label 'frugal innovation', and was later revised to its current form.

course of our intellectual and practical journeys, we learn, revise, and redevelop our understanding For instance, Radha Basu's perception and use of frugal innovation in practice has evolved from identifying five core competencies needed to innovate in the developing world to eight and now ten core competencies (cf. Basu, Banerjee and Sweeny, 2013; these are outlined in Appendix B). What is important is that as we and others had earlier on evisaged, this continues to gain popularity in both practitioner and academic circles (cf. Bhatti, 2012; Bhatti, Khilji and Basu, 2013; Bhatti and Ventresca, 2012; 2013; Crabtree, 2012; Tiwari and Herstatt, 2012; Woolridge, 2010).

From the perspective of social entrepreneurs, innovation think tanks NESTA and the SERCO Institute in the UK praised frugal innovation for helping to improve the effectiveness and efficiency of the public sector and in providing solutions where traditional markets fail (Bound and Thornton, 2012; Singh et al., 2012). Ten years on, this research and the findings among social entrepreneurs of variant approaches to innovation suggests that some of the terminological confusion comes from a shifting focus in the way people think about innovation – from artefact to value chain, mindset and impact – while some of the confusion comes from shifts in the process of innovation, which incorporates technological, institutional and social aspects. Strategies include redesigning products (e.g. Zeschky, Widenmayer and Gassmann, 2011), reconfiguring value chains (e.g. Sharma and Iyer, 2012) and rebuilding entire ecosystems (e.g. Bound and Thornton, 2012). The study of frugal innovation can be placed within international business (e.g. Radjou and Prabhu, 2015), competitive strategy (e.g. Prahalad and Mashelkar, 2010), social entrepreneurship (e.g. Bhatti, 2014), design (e.g. DePasse et al., 2016), engineering (e.g. European Commission, 2017), or sustainability (e.g. Rosca, Arnold and Bendul, 2016). In essence, frugal innovation is a label that captures a range of heterogeneous activities which cut across different sectors. For this reason, perhaps, four other concepts are sometimes also labelled frugal innovation: reverse innovation, grassroots innovation, inclusive innovation and *jugaad*.

6.6.1 Conceptualising Frugal Innovation

How is this study's conceptualisation of frugal innovation similar to or different from the abstractions previously discussed and those found in the existing literature? Before we try to answer this question, please note that we use the term frugal innovation to connote the phenomenon, process or activity while frugal innovations connote outputs of the process.

In the bibliography at the end of the book we list works on frugal innovation chronologically based on our updated search in January 2018. The field is evolving rapidly, with ten articles published in a special issue of The European Journal of Development Research investigating the role of frugal innovation in development (Leliveld and Knorringa, 2018) just around the time we were finalising this book. While we have cited in the text more than half of all those listed in the bibliography, we detail links to many others in order to acknowledge the growing community dedicated to a decade of scholarship in frugal innovation (2008–2018). This bibliography should also serve as a resource for those setting out to review and conduct research and on this topic and keep up the momentum for knowledge generation and application.

The definitions of frugal innovation prevalent in the existing literature involve low cost and sourcing from developing or emerging market countries. Ernst and Young (2011) define frugal innovation as the economical use of resources to provide products affordable to those on a lower income. In the academic literature, scholars consider frugal innovation a category of 'toned down' and 'good enough products' (cf. Hang et al., 2010), or low-cost products (Govindarajan and Ramamurti, 2013; Hesseldahl, 2013). Definitions provided by Anil K. Gupta and Haiyan Wang (2009), Marco Zeschky, BastianWidenmayer and Oliver Gassmann (2011), Rajnish Tiwari and Cornelius Herstatt (2012) and George et al. (2012) reinforce those also mentioned in Govindarajan and Trimble's work on reverse innovation.[3]

---

[3] Carlos Ghosn, CEO of Nissan and Renault, uses the term 'frugal engineering' to denote low-cost input innovation. He says 'Frugal engineering is achieving more

In a 2009 book entitled, *Getting China and India Right: Strategies for Leveraging the World's Fastest-Growing Economies for Global Advantage*, Gupta and Wang write, 'by frugal innovation, we mean innovation that strives to create products, services, processes and business models that are frugal on three counts: frugal use of raw materials, frugal impact on the environment and extremely low cost' (p. 214). They stress that this type of innovation is a profound contrast to the ordinary products, services and processes produced in advanced developed economies, which are energy inefficient, raw-material inefficient and environmentally inefficient. Consequently, a significant portion of literature has associated frugal innovation with sustainability and environmental impact (e.g. Levänen et al., 2015). Zeschky, Widenmayer and Gassmann (2011) focuses on how Western companies are organising their frugal innovation activities in emerging markets and define frugal innovations as products with extreme cost advantages in comparison to existing solutions, developed in response to severe resource constraints. They compare such products with Christensen's concept of low-end disruptive innovation (1997), which assumes that frugally innovated products, made with limited functionality and simpler, cheaper materials, are initially inferior to existing solutions.. Consequently, they do not identify a conceptual distinction between frugal and disruptive innovation. Likewise, Balkrishna C. Rao (2013) attempts to describe the disruptive potential of frugal innovations. George et al. (2012, p. 1) define frugal innovation as 'innovative, low-cost and high-quality products and business models originating in developing countries and exportable to other developing countries or even the developed world'. Tiwari and Herstatt (2012, p. 97) define frugal innovations

with fewer resources. The cost of developing a product in the West is high since engineers there use more expensive tools. In India, they achieve a lot more with fewer resources' (Nair, 2008). Suma Athreye and Sandeep Kapur (2009, p. 214) contend, 'some firms from India and China have acquired a niche in "frugal engineering" – the ability to manufacture low-cost versions of goods for mass markets'.

'as new or significantly improved products (both goods and services), processes, or marketing and organisational methods that seek to minimise the use of material and financial resources in the complete value chain (development, manufacturing, distribution, consumption and disposal) with the objective of reducing the cost of ownership while fulfilling or exceeding certain pre-defined criteria of acceptable quality standards'. Tiwari and Herstatt's (2012) work has focused on India as a lead market for frugal innovations, raising concerns similar to those of reverse innovation. Like Zeschky, Widenmayer and Gassmann (2011), they focus on frugal innovations from emerging markets as low-cost and disruptive innovations.

In *The Frugal Innovator*, Charles Leadbeater (2014) narrates stories of individuals from developing countries around the world, highlighting four characteristics of their innovations: leanness, simplicity, social relevance and cleanliness. Many of these innovators, we believe, could be classed as social entrepreneurs; however, he also cites examples from mainstream businesses and even the public sector, including major urban centres. More recently, Radjou and Prabhu (2015), as in their first book, *Jugaad Innovation* (Radjou et al. 2012), seek to draw lessons from and for developed-world businesses and industries that are pursuing frugal innovation strategies (mainly Accor, Aetna, Giffgaff, General Electric, GlaxoSmithKline, Pearson, PepsiCo, Renault-Nissam, Saatchi and Saatchi, Siemens, SNCF and Unilever). They use these examples to elucidate six principles of frugal innovation, focusing on what international corporations can learn from these principles to become more competitive. They argue that, although consumer needs are changing rapidly, corporate structures are lagging behind in fulfilling those needs. For the latest systematic literature review of frugal innovation please see Alessia Pisoni, Laura Michelini and Gloria Martignoni's (2018) study.

Fundamentally, there are variations in conceptions and understanding of frugal innovation and indeed between terms popularly linked with frugal innovation (reverse, grassroots and inclusive innovation and *jugaad*). Reverse innovation is international and strategy-driven (aiming to innovate in developing markets and diffuse learning to developed markets). Grassroots innovation is bottom-up and source-driven (community rather than commercial or corporate initiatives). Inclusive innovation is outcome-driven (benefits accrue to all levels of society) and *jugaad* is process-driven (the belief that obstacles can be circumvented through the creative use of whatever is on hand).

In support of these variations, in Chapter 2, we found a diverse range of economic orientations, ranging from non-profit to for-profit and many different solutions, from simply making do, to making things good enough, to surpassing expectations and even striving for radical or breakthrough improvements. Some innovators thrive in the market economy and others in the social economy. Some are motivated by profit (Schumpeterian rent) and others by social need or ideological pursuits. Some use the traditional organisational form of competitive firms, while others rely on informal associations or formal but hybrid organisations, such as social enterprises, coops and networks. Some attract commercial investment and generate profit, while others receive grant funding and voluntary contributions, in addition to generating profits.

Table 6.2 captures some of these differences between the dimensions outlined in Innovation Model 2, specifically in relation to the three constraints – institutional voids, affordability constraints and resource scarcity. This table illustrates our analytical assessment of how well each innovation alternative fares in either seeking to address or successfully addressing these three constraints. Reverse innovation's primary focus is on adapting solutions to resource scarcity in developing or emerging markets; it may or may not address institutional voids and affordability constraints in the process (depending on which market segment is being targeted). Grassroots innovation's primary focus is on addressing affordability and resource scarcity; it may or may not deal with institutional voids (depending on the nature and degree of community or grassroots involvement).

Inclusive innovation is similar to grassroots innovation in this ana-lytical assessment; the two are frequently cross-referenced in the literature. *Jugaad* innovation's primary focus is on affordability and overcoming resource scarcity. It rarely (if at all) addresses institu-tional voids to make solutions more widely accessible. Perhaps the *jugaad* process is not well placed to scale up solutions emanating from this approach to innovation.

Indeed, Table 6.2 highlights that few of the alternatives to frugal innovation focus on widespread *accessibility* or incorporate institutional innovation. As some of the examples cited in this study demonstrate, frugal innovation addresses all three contextual con-straints through a mix of social, institutional and technological innovations in order to provide solutions that promise affordability, accessibility and adaptability.

All five emerging models of innovation are fundamentally simi-lar, in that they aim to demonstrate that an alternative way is pos-sible, beyond mainstream innovation practices. Frugal innovation also seeks to exemplify alternative visions and practices. However, it captures a range of differences highlighted by other constructs in their desire for independent identity. Our models provide a holistic, diverse and encompassing theoretical framework that captures both the similarities and differences in earlier conceptions of frugal innov-ation. We state in Chapter 1 that there is still scope to contribute to clear and crisp conceptual, theoretical and operational definitions and frameworks at various micro-meso-macro levels of analysis.

In Chapter 2, we used three lenses – functional, process and institutional – to better understand the myriad perceptions reported by social entrepreneurs of mixed/hybrid innovation, something we refer to as frugal innovation, based on our respondents' use of the term and in light of the myriad perceptions they provided. The func-tional, process and institutional levels suggest that slightly different issues and concerns pertain to individual innovators, organisations and sectors. Although the functional lens reveals differences in the motivations and goals of frugal innovators, the process and

Table 6.2 Comparing frugal innovation with related concepts

Constraints	Affordability constraints	Institutional voids	Resource constraints	Differentiator
Components	Social innovation	Institutional innovation	Technology innovation	
Outcomes	Affordable	Accessible	Adaptable	
Reverse innovation	SOMEWHAT	SOMEWHAT	YES	International strategy-driven
Grassroots innovation	YES	SOMEWHAT	YES	Bottom-up source-driven
Inclusive innovation	YES	SOMEWHAT	YES	Outcome-driven
Jugaad	YES	SOMEWHAT	YES	Process-driven
Frugal innovation	YES	YES	YES	Bridges above domains

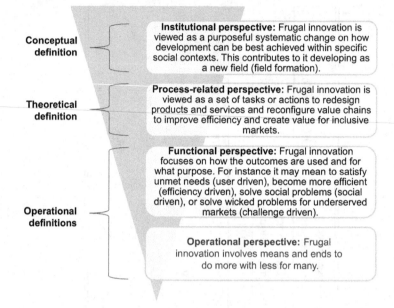

FIGURE 6.3 Definitions of frugal innovation at different levels of abstraction

institutional lenses reveal commonalities that bind all of these notions of innovation around a set of related ideas. Here we add another layer that should help operationalise frugal innovation. Figure 6.3 shows how we can propose definitions of frugal innovation at different levels of abstraction: from a high-level conceptual perspective to a mid-level theoretical perspective and further down to an operational perspective

From an institutional perspective, frugal innovation is viewed as a purposeful systematic change in the way development can be best achieved in specific sectors or social contexts. Policy leaders and development activists leverage such approaches to espouse need for change in how growth can benefit more people, more equitably. From the process perspective, frugal innovation is a set of activities for organisations to redesign products and services and reconfigure value chains to create value for inclusive markets. Organisations seek to achieve cost leadership as a competitive advantage by generating high profits through low costs and high scalability as a form of efficiency-based innovation. From the functional perspective, frugal innovation inspires innovators to solve their own problems and aspire to share those solutions for social improvement. Individual or grassroots innovators meet their own or local user needs without necessarily aiming to achieve high profits or scaling For-profit organisations may formalise these solutions to improve their own efficiency or improve value for users. Not-for-profit community organisations may seek to scale these solutions to solve societal level problems. Innovators may come together as part of a network to take on the challenge to prove that notorious problems can be solved by exhibiting proof of concept for a challenging concern.

The strength of this empirically embedded and analytical approach is that Model 1 captures the differences within frugal innovation, with aims to satisfy unmet needs (user-based), become more efficient (efficiency-based), resolve social problems (social) and produce solutions for the underserved (challenge-based). Salient similarities in this study help to consolidate the construct despite these differences, by showing how the four approaches recombine to create a common, higher-level approach and objective, as reflected in process and institutional definitions.

A simple operational definition of frugal innovation supported by the findings in this study is: means and ends to do more with less for many or more people. We adopt this definition because it resounds with and complements some of our previous or parallel work by colleagues (cf. Bhatti and Ventresca, 2013; Bhatti, Khilji and Basu, 2013; Bound and Thornton, 2012; Prabhu, 2017; Prahalad and Mashelkar, 2010; Radjou and Prabhu, 2015). We outline how our core characteristics of affordability, adaptability and accessibility revealed in the empirical-based models relate to the individual components within this definition (see Table 6.3). This is a powerful definition because it encompasses a wide range of perspectives on motivation, process and outcome. The phrase 'means and ends' describes the component of innovation that can be a process as well as an outcome

Table 6.3 *The definition of frugal innovation has many facets*

Definitional components	Encompasses	Outcome
Means and ends	Process and outcome	Affordable
To do more with less	Efficiency and/or bricolage	Adaptable
For many	Social and economic value	Accessible and scalable

to achieve affordability. Frugal innovations can incorporate manufacturing and service delivery processes as well as products and services (Bhatti, Khilji and Basu, 2013; Bound and Thornton, 2012). 'To do more with less' suggests efficiency in process and outcome through for instance *jugaad* (Radjou, Prabhu and Ahuja, 2012) and as we find through the use of bricolage (Lévi-Strauss, 1967) to get more out of few resources in the contextually constraining environment in order to achieve adaptability. 'For many' describes the generation of economic and social value that achieves accessibility and high scale (Prabhu, 2017; Prahalad and Mashelkar, 2010). In fact, some emerging scholars are beginning to explore 'how to do more with less for many *with* many', by looking at issues of co-creation and co-design.

The outcome of these motivations, processes and ends are frugal innovations that are affordable for consumers, adaptable to contextual circumstances and accessible to vast populations. This book's empirical findings that the core characteristics of frugal innovation are affordability, adaptability and accessibility are supported by practice-based claims made by our co-author Radha Basu, who was founding Director of the Frugal Innovation Lab (Basu, Banerjee and Sweeny, 2013), which are summarised in Appendix B.[4]

---

[4] Basu et al. (2013) in an earlier work cite 'appropriate' as another characteristic dimension of frugal innovation. Our respondents mentioned appropriate technologies, often embedded in the work of Ernest Friedrich Schumacher (1974). We assume this to be relevant and similar to 'adaptable' technologies.

As these findings show, frugal innovation can perhaps be deemed to be a boundary object, helping to create a bridge between traditional and alternative practices and bringing together actors motivated by different precepts but sharing a common drive to overcome the shortcomings of the past. These shortcomings include failures of markets, government, management and technology. Social movements, civil society, academic researchers, commercial enterprise and government departments all have their own motivations that drive separate agendas. However, the core objective is always the same in frugal innovation: to innovate in a way that uses means and achieves outcomes to do more with less for many or for more people.

In any case, this book is not competing to win construct identity or ownership. The value of our work is not to arbitrate what frugal innovation is or is not. This book strives to provide a deeper understanding of the various perspectives of social entrepreneurs, as depicted in the models of innovation developed here. And we argue for a more systematically plural conception of how these innovations under constraint come to be assembled. As a source, the models provide fresh insights on critical research issues of innovation under constraints, for the underserved, for equitable growth and indeed innovation for humanity. We next move to explore and understand the mechanisms that create different perceptions of innovation.

6.6.2 Mechanisms Enacted in Frugal Innovation

One may ask how frugal innovation, which according to this study embodies social, technological and institutional concerns, occurs within extreme environments marked by resource and affordability constraints and institutional voids. The answer could emphasise the role of social needs recognition, design thinking, resource mobilisation and the use of bricolage, collective action processes and social movements. The three processes or mechanisms (design thinking, bricolage and social movements) by which frugal innovation addresses constraints are depicted in Figure 4.2.

Using design thinking to better understand local needs may help to capture appropriate ways to improve the social status of communities. Design thinking (Brown and Wyatt, 2010; Rowe, 1991) refers to methods and processes used to investigate problems in a structured manner, by acquiring information on need, gaining empathy, analysing knowledge and iterating solutions for quick experimentation. Particularly in the context of extreme environments, design thinking offers the ability to combine empathy for the context in which the problem exists with creativity in generating insights and solutions to suit that particular context and rationality to analyse and fit solutions to the specific context.

Our interviews with the designers of the Jaipur/ReMotion knee joint revealed that patterns of empathy led them towards success, even before the particular technology was considered. By comparison, Scott Summitt of Bespoke Innovations also set out to design prosthetics at low cost for developing market applications (see www.summitid.com). Based on our conversation, Summitt was by and large focused on the technology. By using materials and tools he was used to working with in the United States, he was able to bring down the cost of a prosthetic from $50,000 to $5,000, only later realising that the price-performance point he was offering was not acceptable to his target market, which demanded levels closer to $500.

Technologically, there may be few resources available for the innovation process; feature-laden innovations may be unaffordable. Existing solutions may have to be stripped of all unneeded, superfluous and expensive features and redesigned to suit local contexts. Resource mobilisation processes such as bricolage try to make do with what one controls and has access to by combining pre-existing resources to accomplish an immediate task (Baker and Nelson, 2005; Lévi-Strauss 1967). Another approach – resource-seeking – involves procuring standard resources meant for a specific task. Desa (2011) demonstrates that social ventures originate, develop and grow through bricolage in the absence of external financing or even when faced with low levels of institutional support. One way in which bricolage has helped to create a paradigm shift in price-performance is by moving markets away from customised hardware-centric design towards off-the-shelf components and sophisticated software. GE's $8,000–15,000 portable ultrasound machine versus its high-end $100,000 machine shifted from a hardware- to a software-centric design by using a standard laptop. Software has virtually no marginal cost and costs have been lowered through development by open source communities and by leveraging the availability of software talent in emerging markets.

This leads us to Panagiotis Louridas' (1999) claim that design thinking is a form of bricolage, which exploits the combinatory nature of frugal innovation by drawing on both social and techno-logical concerns. Design thinking plays a role here, not only because of its human-centric approach but also because it is able to quickly and iteratively prototype. Given the uncertainty involved in innov-ation endeavours, it is more important to learn quickly by testing and readjusting assumptions than to meet solid performance metrics (Immelt, Govindarajan and Trimble, 2009). GE's ultrasound team in China discovered through rapid prototyping and field tests in rural clinics that ease of use was much more important than they had at first assumed. This led to simpler keyboards, built-in presets for routine tasks and additional training. Rapid prototyping and field testing means shorter product-development cycles, made possible in emerging markets by less stringent regulatory regimes and govern-ment approval processes. GE's development of ultrasound in China reflected this shorter development cycle, which benefitted from the country's less intricate approval process (Immelt et al., 2009).

Although the reversibility potential of frugal innovations has been much acclaimed, Mokter Hossain, Henri Simula and Minna Halme (2016) find that only in rare cases have frugal innovations diffused or scaled globally – and even more rarely into developed markets. (Our current research seeks to help accelerate this diffusion, particularly in the healthcare sector, see for instance Bhatti et al.,

2017a, 2017b). Desa (2009a) empirically found that technology social ventures had a limited ability to scale, particularly when they employed bricolage. However, collective action processes that leverage existing institutions or offer new ones can have a moderating effect and achieve high scalability despite the use of bricolage. This finding reinforces the point that frugal innovation draws from both technological and institutional concerns.

Institutionally, innovation may have to deal with local norms, rules and institutional arrangements to ensure the spread and adoption of new products, services and solutions. Collective action processes stem from social movements. Scholars of social movements have focused on the collective political processes of institutional change that remedy perceived social and ecological problems, barriers or injustices. Brayden G. King and Nicholas A. Pearce (2010) demonstrate how social movement theory explains the emergence of market heterogeneity (Schneiberg and Lounsbury, 2008). Dieter Rucht (1999) defines a social movement as 'an action system comprised of mobilised networks of individuals, groups and organisations which, based on a shared collective identity, attempt to achieve or prevent social change, predominantly by means of collective protest' (p. 207).

Social movement research shows empirically that contentiousness can be a source of market dynamism, for instance by encouraging innovation and by changing what is deemed acceptable practice (Rao, 2009). The rise of the market for organic and grass-fed beef and dairy (Weber, Heinze and DeSoucey, 2008) is attributed to social movements helping to create consumer audiences for these once-ignored products (King and Pearce, 2010). Social movement literature has expanded from movements triggered by the poor and frustrated masses to resource and capability-empowered mobilisation by the middle classes and beyond – to the new social movements fostered by elites who shape discourse and agendas.

We find support for the argument that social movements form markets – that in the case of frugal innovation, a coalition of academics, idealistic students, global policy people, business elites, funders,

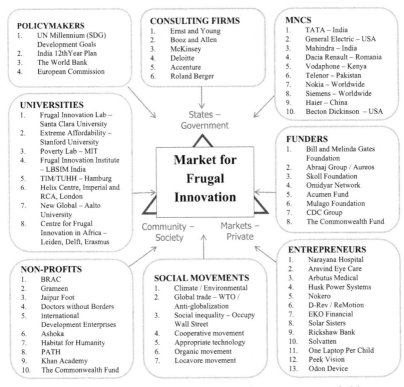

FIGURE 6.4 Mapping the ecosystem for an emerging field

foundations and ventures are collaborating, contending and negotiating to serve the unmet needs of the world's underserved and to create a market for frugal innovations. The major players identified in the course of our research are shown in Figure 6.4. We see a myriad of state, market and community actors and institutions involved in shaping this emerging market and field.

6.7 SUMMARY

Jeffery S. McMullen (2011) offers a theory in which development entrepreneurship lies at the intersection of social, institutional and business entrepreneurship. Similarly, we have argued that frugal innovation is perhaps best understood as existing at the intersection of social, technology and institutional innovation. All three innovation subfields are emerging fields in themselves; together, they offer challenging opportunities for scholarly research: to test and refine theories of entrepreneurship, innovation and strategy in unique contexts, such as developing and emerging markets or pockets of context in developed markets that are marked by resource and institutional constraints.

The concept of frugal innovation is a useful way to conceptualise the integration of existing innovation types in extreme contexts. We refer to 'extreme contexts' because of the contextual constraints; frugal innovations in these contexts have to tolerate harsher conditions than regular innovations do. Unlike those at NASA or SpaceX, the mission here is mundane: to create offerings for people who live and work at the least privileged interfaces of the modern world. This is the 'why' of frugal innovation: a broadly shared desire to provide consumer value and amenities with the feature of 'extreme affordability'. As the data and models show, these may be created for philanthropic, social, challenge-related, market or efficiency-seeking reasons.

The plurality of elements and means made visible in this study from giving social entrepreneurs voice suggests that concepts like social, grassroots, inclusive, reverse, *jugaad* or frugal innovation in fact represent heterogeneous assemblies of innovation for humanity. This challenges the too frequent view that frugal innovation is simply about cost reduction or affordability. Our work is an invitation for scholarly and practical attention to more plural sources and elements in the study of models of innovation.

7 Implications for Research, Practice and Policy

In the preceding chapters, we provided a detailed account of models of innovation based on the views of social entrepreneurs who function under constraints. We described the findings in terms of frugal innovation and compared our understanding of this concept to other constructs in the literature. We suggested steps towards theory development for frugal innovation based on our empirical data and attempted to apply it to published cases often cited in support of emerging concepts in innovation. In this chapter, we consider the implications of our models of innovation and attempts in developing theory to research, practice and policy.

The overarching research question of this study has been: *How do social entrepreneurs conceptualise innovation broadly and specifically under constraints or extreme conditions marked by institutional voids and resource scarcity?* This has been broken down into three research sub-questions, each with specific objectives and significance for existing theory and practice. We have investigated the research questions using qualitative methods by studying two communities of globally networked and formally recognised social entrepreneurs (although most of the data we ended up using in this work came from one community). Overall, this study contributes to developing models of innovation based on the conceptions of social entrepreneurs who function under constraints in contexts marked by institutional voids, complexities and resource scarcity.

7.1 INTRODUCTION

On social entrepreneurs, this work has helped to reveal social entrepreneurs' perceptions of the conceptual drivers, determinants and features of innovation. We found that they were involved in more than simply social innovation; they used a combination of existing innovations, were more likely to be concerned about institutional and social innovation than technology innovation and packed combinations of innovations into a new emerging concept – frugal innovation.

On constraints to innovation, we found that extreme contexts marked by constraints are not unique to developing or emerging markets. They also exist in pockets of developed markets. Social entrepreneurs and their customers face a combination of constraints to innovation, including institutional voids and resource and affordability constraints. Social entrepreneurs are more focused on resource challenges, while investors are preoccupied with institutional challenges.

On methods, this work is one of few qualitative studies that acknowledges the use of retroduction, as opposed to a purely inductive grounded theory approach. This approach benefits from an iterative deductive-inductive process that helps to make the research transparent and rigorous. There is no shortage of works that purport to use a purely grounded theory approach but remain of questionable value because the researchers have not been able to completely let go of various preconceived notions of what they are looking for or might find.

One of the main goals of this study has been to reveal insights into how organisational theorists and strategic management scholars can frame models of innovation for contexts marked by resource scarcity or constraints and institutional voids. To do so, we have captured the perspectives of social entrepreneurs who often work in such conditions. In Chapter 2, we found that social entrepreneurs vary in how they view and justify innovation. This suggests that a sole focus in the existing literature on one type of (mainly social) innovation needs to be viewed with greater suspicion. In Chapter 3, we found that social entrepreneurs have varied concerns and approaches to innovation under constraints. We found that social entrepreneurs use a combination of existing innovations and repack them to address problems and challenges in their markets. Innovation Model 1 is introduced in Chapter 2; Innovation Model 2 is discussed in Chapter 3. The two models of innovation we developed are neither contradictory nor necessarily complementary. Although they examine and portray different aspects of innovation as perceived by social entrepreneurs, together they support the emergence of a new innovation phenomenon, that of frugal innovation. This emergent concept brings some cohesion to the seemingly disparate notions of innovation among social entrepreneurs described in Models 1 and 2. Chapter 4 integrates lessons from these two models of innovation to propose first steps towards a theory of frugal innovation under constraints.

This study suggests that innovation among social entrepreneurs can be conceptualised as a multidimensional construct with three innovation components – social, institutional and technological – that help to achieve three outcomes: affordability, accessibility and adaptability, all in an effort to address three main constraints or challenges, namely institutional voids, resource scarcity and affordability constraints. A multidimensional construct consists of a number of interrelated attributes that exist in multidimensional domains (Weerawardena and Mort, 2006). Kenneth S. Law, Chi-Sum Wong and William H. Mobley (1998, p. 741) argue, 'In contrast to a set of interrelated uni-dimensional constructs, the dimensions of a multi-dimensional construct can be conceptualised under an overall abstraction and it is theoretically meaningful and parsimonious to use this overall abstraction, as a representation of the dimensions'. Along the same lines, we use the term frugal innovation to refer to the overall abstraction of social, institutional and technological innovation that helps achieve outcomes that are affordable, adaptable and accessible. The proposed empirical models capture the conceptual characteristics of innovation among social entrepreneurs within broad environmental and operational constraints marked by resource scarcity and institutional voids.

Operationally, we define frugal innovation as *'means and ends to do more with less for many'* (Table 5.4).[1] We adopted this definition based on our previous work and from parallel work by colleagues (cf. Bhatti and Ventresca, 2013; Bhatti, Khilji and Basu, 2013; Bound and Thornton, 2012; Prabhu, 2017; Prahalad and Mashelkar, 2010; Radjou and Prabhu, 2015). The 'means and ends' (Bound and Thornton, 2012) describe the components of innovation that can be a process and/or an outcome. 'To do more with less' (Radjou and Prabhu, 2015) describes the notion of efficiency in process and outcome as well as using bricolage to get more out of few resources. 'For many' (Prabhu, 2017; Prahalad and Mashelkar, 2010) describes the generation of highly scalable economic and social value. We expect the findings and theory development proposed in this work to have important implications for theory, practice and policy. A brief overview of these implications and lessons is outlined in Table 7.1 and described in detail in the next three subsections.

7.2 IMPLICATIONS FOR RESEARCHERS

This research and the findings outlined here may contribute to theory-building in innovation among social entrepreneurs (Mulgan, 2006) and understanding innovation management concerns (Leonard-Barton, 1988; Van de Ven, 1986) in extreme environments marked by constraints. We have applied Poole and Van de Ven's (1989) logic of paradox resolution to develop a theory of frugal innovation, which better captures the complexity of the different assumptions involved in understanding the phenomenon of innovation in extreme environments, as perceived by social entrepreneurs. We offer the findings embodied in these models to help future researchers develop a more theoretically grounded and programmed body of research in the emerging field of frugal innovation. To recognise the space for frugal innovations and understand how it can be organised, we

---

[1] Mainly for scholars, we offer other definitions that are conceptual and theoretical in nature (see Figure 6.3).

Table 7.1 *Implications of two models in relation to theory, practice and policy*

	Model of Innovation 1	Model of Innovation 2
Researchers	Theoretical framework for understanding 'innovation for the underserved' or social innovation; a finding of drivers and sources	Theoretical framework for understanding 'innovation under constraints for the underserved'; a finding of frugal innovation
Practitioners	The three constraints exist not only in developing but also in developed markets; the innovation life cycle may go through different phases	Overlapping spaces and hybridisation of innovation are necessary to tackle different contextual constraints
Policymakers	Policy should help the field evolve, rather than focusing on best practices	Involvement of different stakeholders: public, private and civil

propose two models to help us theoretically conceptualise frugal innovation – the first based on drivers of innovation and the second on constraints to innovation. We explored resource constraints, affordability constraints and institutional voids to develop a conceptual framework for analysing innovation under constraints.

In Model 1, we conceptualised the sources and determinants of innovation along two key characteristics or dimensions: need or vision and proof of concept or scalability. The literature has, for the most part, relegated social entrepreneurship and social innovation to the ideational and globally scalable – the top right-hand quadrant of Model 1. This study empirically reveals that social entrepreneurs perceive their innovation activities as fitting into the other three quadrants, all of which find corroboration in the existing literature – grassroots and user-based innovation, efficiency and corporation-based innovation and challenge and network-based innovation.

Yet these are not generally associated with social entrepreneurship or social innovation. This suggests that a broader view of social innovation could better align different theoretical assumptions with actual conceptualisations in practice.

In Model 2, we conceptualised the nexus of social, institutional and technology innovation as fertile overlaps that help to identify, understand and position frugal innovations. These spaces reflect our theoretical assumption that social entrepreneurs and their customers face a combination of constraints to innovation, including institutional voids and resource and affordability constraints. The examples that fit the various intersections of typology in Model 2 are based on empirical data and published accounts. Although ours is an exploratory research project with findings that need further testing, this exercise demonstrates how the overlapping spaces within which frugal innovation activities are carried out can help us understand existing case studies. Further research can assess the successes and failures of frugal innovation strategies and the capabilities firms need to adopt them. The theoretical propositions outlined here can be tested in future to analyse innovation trends among social entrepreneurs in unique contexts marked by resource constraints and institutional voids.

In terms of theory, there is potential to demonstrate that social entrepreneurs are articulating a more plural and encompassing view of innovation (as a concept, idea, framework or process) – i.e. frugal innovation – the impact of which may diffuse to mainstream entrepreneurs and large corporations. Frugal innovation could present an opportunity to disrupt prevalent innovation assumptions. For instance, instead of innovating only when the right components of a National Innovation System (Freeman, 1995; Lundvall, 1992) are present, the idea of frugal innovation enables recognition of an approach to innovation that is catching on in extreme environments despite or because of resource constraints and institutional voids. In contrast to the view that innovation occurs only when slack resources and supporting institutions exist, with high-income users the first target segment of choice, frugal innovation suggests that all three of these components may not be necessary to produce globally useful solutions. Empirical studies that test this theory and its ability to generalise beyond social entrepreneurs could be a next step.

On methods, this is one of few qualitative studies to acknowledge the use of retroduction in a significant research project of this scale and scope, as opposed to taking a purely inductive or deductive approach. Most research has clearly differentiated between purely inductive and deductive approaches. However, Ragin (1994) argues that in many research settings, it is neither possible nor beneficial to argue for one approach over another. Instead, an iterative combination of induction and deduction makes it possible to acknowledge the evolving understanding of phenomena and theory that researchers develop simultaneously. In retroduction, we used an inductive–deductive, iterative approach that helped achieve both reliability and validity. On the one hand, the criterion of reliability induces analysts to derive standard categories from theory that can be used repeatedly. On the other hand, the criterion of validity calls for analysts to inductively develop original categories that stem from the phenomenon (Druckman and Hopmann, 2002; Srnka and Koeszegi, 2007). Through retroduction, we acknowledge how prior knowledge of innovation studies shapes our initial codes and constructs, helping to determine what we initially look for in our data, as a part of template analysis (King, 1998; 2004a; 2004b). However, as the process has progressed, we have iteratively changed and adapted the template of codes and constructs to better address the research problem and match the themes gathered from the data. This back-and-forth process of using theory for deductive and then inductive analysis generates new theoretical models of innovation. Essentially, it helps researchers be more honest with themselves: acknowledging and making use of a limited theoretical understanding, while also searching for a new or at least an extended theory.

We found retroduction to be a powerful methodological means to acknowledge the limitations of purely deductive and inductive approaches in long-term and emergent studies such as this one. Although initially we tried to pursue a grounded theory approach, we found it difficult to enact in practice. Instead, we found the retroductive approach more honest and reflective of the iterative sense-making process of research design, defence and implementation through which our research progressed. Furthermore, this methodological approach helped to avoid some of the complications of perceptions being considered purely 'socially constructed'.

Among the world's most influential social scientists is Daniel Kahneman, who won the 2002 Nobel Prize for 'having integrated insights from psychological research into economic science' (Goldstein, 2011). According to Google Scholar, Kahneman and Tversky's paper on prospect theory has been cited in scholarly journals more than 45,000 times since 1979. Jevin West of the University of Washington helped to develop an algorithm for tracing the spread of ideas among disciplines and comments: 'Kahneman's career shows that intellectual influence is the ability to dissolve disciplinary boundaries' (Goldstein, 2011). We believe that this attempt among social entrepreneurs to understand innovation through the proposed theoretical models similarly dissolves long-standing disciplinary boundaries in the technological, social and institutional innovation literatures.

7.3 IMPLICATIONS FOR PRACTITIONERS

Scott Keller and Colin Price (2011) argue in their McKinsey study of business performance that innovation and change have replaced scale and stability as determinants of organisational survival and success. Today, executives are searching for distinctive and competitive ways to increase innovative capacity both within and outside their organisations (Van de Ven, Ganco and Hinings, 2013). In terms of practice for enhanced business performance, our theoretical models for understanding frugal innovation can help firms and entrepreneurs innovate in extreme contexts characterised by resource scarcity and institutional voids. The models enable innovators to analyse and categorise different approaches to innovation, based on the nexus of constraints they need to address and leverage. In Chapter 5, we showed how the two models can be used to map existing popular cases. Should contextual factors and demands change or firms wish to enter different or home markets, an awareness of the need to reposition to other complementary innovation subsets can be valuable for strategy reformulation.[2]

To exemplify this, we can briefly think about how the two models can be used to explain Ebay's evolution. Some scholars (cf. Martin and Osberg, 2007) suggest that Ebay can be considered a social innovation that has globally changed the way society buys and sells, allowing people to extract value by reusing goods otherwise destined for garbage dumps. It may also be thought of as a frugal innovation that allows buyers and sellers to find each other in the most convenient way possible and to exchange otherwise hard to find items, often used, at the most reasonable price agreeable to both parties. Model 1 suggests that organisations may face different innovations at different times and in different contexts throughout their life-cycles. Model 2 suggests that functioning within overlapping innovation spaces can be necessary for growth, but also may be very challenging. Like many entrepreneurial projects, Ebay started in the lower left-hand quadrant of Model 1, where it began as a project by Omidyar to test a proof of concept that fulfilled his girlfriend's need to collect, buy and sell 'Pez' dispensers. The proof of concept caught the attention of the start-up system in Silicon Valley, which moved the project up to the top left-hand quadrant of Model 1. Over time, as the business model evolved with the acquisition of Paypal, itself an institutional innovation through which money was transferred and

---

[2] Although the models can be useful strategically for practice, we caution here that this research mainly addresses models of perceptions of innovation and the emergent definitional concerns about frugal innovation, based on a qualitative analysis of cases, without any consideration of success or failure, as opposed to an evaluation of business performance.

deposited, Ebay was able to reach out globally to locations where the banking sector was not conducive to online transactions, enabling cross-border transactions of goods and services. By combining Internet technologies with institutional change in monetary transactions, Ebay and Paypal together were able to change social behaviour to make goods and services more affordable, accessible and adaptable to local contexts but with global integration. The core lesson – to be positioned in the centre of Model 2, where all three innovations meet – can be epitomised, but is also the most challenging goal, which may require progression over time through the various quadrants of Model 1.

Another lesson for practitioners is the increasing effort needed to create a bridge between social entrepreneurs and mainstream businesses. On the one hand, we found social entrepreneurs more likely to be concerned about institutional and social innovation than about technological innovation when pursuing social value. On the other hand, social entrepreneurs mentioned examples of mainstream large businesses using technology innovation to build social value. Despite these differences of approach, the use of frugal innovation as a concept by social entrepreneurs and mainstream businesses suggests that both have common concerns. As a conceptual term, the idea of frugal innovation helps to bring business into the activities of social entrepreneurs and social needs into the activities of corporations (Figure 2.4). This also shows, by way of background, that frugal innovation is not an entirely new or different concept or approach to innovation. This makes it easier to bridge two business communities (i.e. social entrepreneurs and large corporations), which ostensibly have little in common.

This work also showed that extreme contexts marked by institutional voids and resource constraints are not unique to developing or emerging markets but also exist in pockets of developed markets. Although the level of both is higher in the latter, the former markets can be fertile spaces for frugal innovation activity. As the West looks to the East for innovation, ideas and entrepreneurship (Cappelli et al.,

2010; Chen and Miller, 2010), frugal innovation can offer fresh ideas and new perspectives on cost minimisation and innovation maximisation to a world slowed down by recessions, i.e. by doing more with less (Bhatti and Ventresca, 2012; 2013; Prabhi, 2017; Radjou and Prabhu, 2015). Adrian Woolridge (2011) argues that frugal innovation will change the world in the same way Japanese lean manufacturing once did.

In many ways, the activity of frugal innovation is already catching on in the West in its own way, possibly due to changes in the preferences and needs that stem from demographic changes. Firms may recognise and adapt to these changes. For instance, aging populations and changing immigration patterns are putting increasing pressure on public finances through the UK National Health Service and the US Medicare programme. Govindarajan and Ramamurti (2013) argue that the United States can learn from innovative low-cost and affordable healthcare models in India. There is an increasing preference among young adults for collaborative consumption; cars (Zipcar and Uber), houses (Airbnb) and shared baby clothes (Plumgear) are brokered by web start-ups in San Francisco, using existing publicly owned assets. These are some of the many forms and practices reflective of frugal innovation (Bhatti, 2012; Hesseldahl, 2013; Radjou and Prabhu, 2015).

There is also evolving work in international management by Govindarajan and Trimble (2012) on reverse innovation strategies for firms seeking to internationalise. Many, although not all, features of reverse innovation resonate with frugal innovation. Jeffrey Immelt, the CEO of GE, and his colleagues (2009) argue that reverse and frugal innovation strategies help GE to not only to flourish in India and China, but also to bring back to the United States lessons learnt for new applications, new market segments and future recessionary periods that require cost minimisation and impact maximisation.

Overall, the strength of social value-enhancing strategies and frugal innovations that revolve around the three main outcome factors – adaptable, accessible and affordable – suggests that firms can discover new applications and market segments previously over-looked. For instance, firms equipped to implement strategies for adaptability, accessibility and affordability can better capitalise on periods of recession and not just have to ride them out and struggle to stay afloat. As cyclical waves of growth and recession are an almost inevitable law of economics, firms may benefit from learning new ways to capitalise not only on growth, but also on recessions.

Some firms, for instance, budget retailers such as Tesco, Primark and Walmart, do well not only when the economy is growing but also (and sometimes even more) during times of deceleration. The predominant lesson these firms bring to times of recession and depression is to cut costs and do more with less. Combine this with ever-rising energy and raw material prices and firms are seeking ways to become more efficient and do more with less. Institutionally, developed markets are regulating harder and heavier, forcing firms to meet tight environmental standards. Functioning under resource constraints may help firms meet these tighter environmental regula-tions. As ambidextrous organisations (Tushman, Anderson and O'Reilly, 1997) seek to balance the exploration of new product devel-opment and the exploitation of breadwinners, we propose that firms can embrace frugal innovation strategies alongside their conventional innovation pursuits.

Firms that adopt frugal innovation strategies are better equipped to compete in the emerging and growth markets of the world. Tiwari and Herstatt (2012) use the theory of 'lead markets' to explain the rise in sourcing frugal innovations from India. Edward Tse, John Jullens and Bill Russo (2012) cite examples of an emerging category of high-growth, low-price, medium-quality Chinese com-panies that are shaking up the global competitive landscape. Tse et al. and Eric Thun (2006) cite reasons for this emergence: China's enormous size and the complexity of its customer base, among other political, economic and infrastructure characteristics. The goal for these companies is 'Mercedes-level quality and attractiveness, Toyota-level durability and margins and Skoda-level prices' (p. 36).

Carlos Haertel of GE says that the rising popularity of frugality can be attributed to a demographic tipping point. He cites changes in the size of the market opportunity: 'These products were always technically feasible. The fundamental change is that in India and China you now have mass markets that are price-sensitive but have a massive purchasing power' (Woodward, 2011). Such frugal innovations pose opportunities, not only for emerging markets, but also for developing and developed markets.

We have hinted at the ways in which global firms such as GE and Tata seek to learn from opportunities that force them to do more with less, by developing strategies that are socially equitable, ecologically sustainable and economically profitable, i.e. that meet the triple bottom-line for benefitting people, the planet and profits (e.g. Altamirano and van Beers, 2018; Annala, Sarin and Green, 2016; Brem and Ivens, 2013). However, frugal innovation is not a panacea for all problems or needs. Indeed, there are situations where it may not always be a good idea (e.g. Hyvarinen, Keskinen and Varis, 2016; Nielsen and Wilhite, 2015). As Joan Woodward (1965) and Paul R. Lawrence and Jay William Lorsch (1967) discovered while studying why different organisations had different organisational designs, there may not be 'one best way'. Take, for instance, the desire for low-cost medicines or food supplements (Topol, 2011) – overly processed, low-cost, mass-produced food has been criticised for its long-term detrimental effects, which include obesity and cancer. Generic low-cost medicines that have escaped rigorous testing standards have been involved in criminal neglect and dangerous consequences. The negative aspects of frugal innovation deserve further investigation (Knorringa et al., 2016).

Another interesting finding that has practical implications, particularly for entrepreneurial firms, is that social entrepreneurs are more focused on resource challenges, while investors are more focused on institutional challenges. This may explain why investors and social entrepreneurs have a difficult time speaking to each other in the same language and facilitating greater investment in social ventures. These differences in the way social entrepreneurs and investors perceive their sources of challenge may be explained through differences in their own situationally 'perceived contingencies'. Investors are wary about the institutionally underdeveloped contexts in which they invest. Social entrepreneurs seem more focused on the need for greater resources to, in part, overcome these contextual constraints. This suggests that the problem might be one of chicken and egg – would greater resources help to ameliorate institutional challenges, or would fixing the institutional challenges attract more resources?

7.4 IMPLICATIONS FOR POLICYMAKERS

We have investigated how innovation differs and have sought to understand how institutionally complex and constraint-based innovations in low-resource settings for underserved market segments differ from prevalent models of innovation. Frugal innovation is a potentially challenging paradigm, with a wide range of entrepreneurs, firms and other institutional actors (foundations and policy institutes) embracing the term 'frugal innovation' without adequately theorising or understanding what it actually means or how to adopt related activities and strategies. This study offers an in-depth understanding of the drivers, determinants and dimensions of frugal innovation. As shown in Figure 6.4 (Mapping the ecosystem for an emerging field), different players from the public, private and civil sectors are in the process of negotiating the space and terrain of frugal innovation. The fact that social innovation and frugal innovation in particular have caught the attention of researchers, practitioners and policymakers suggests that this developing field of innovation studies will reach a wider community of impact and offer scope for timely and relevant policymaking.

India's government was bold to include frugal innovation and solutions in its twelfth five-year plan as a means to achieve inclusive growth. The European Commission Directorate-General of Research and Innovation in Brussels commissioned a study to investigate how to achieve greater economic competitiveness and social inclusion through 'Frugal Innovation and the Re-Engineering of Traditional Techniques'. In the UK, innovation think tanks NESTA and the SERCO Institute promote frugal innovation to UK public-sector institutions such as the NHS (Bound and Thornton, 2012; Singh et al., 2012).

Professor of Surgery Lord Ara Darzi of Denham, who served as Parliamentary Under Secretary of State in the Department of Health during Prime Minister Gordon Brown's government, is a proponent of adopting frugal innovation in the UK's National Health Service for efficiency gains and abroad for universal health coverage. He led the establishment of the Helix Centre (Healthcare Innovation Exchange) in 2014 in one of London's busiest hospitals, St Mary's, and has co-located professional designers to address complex healthcare issues through co-design and co-creation. Ministry for Foreign Affairs for Finland and Tekes, the Finnish Government's Funding Agency for Technology and Innovation (now known as Business Finland), have supported The Nordic Frugal Innovation Society which organises InnoFrugal, a forum for sharing best practices, policy analysis, latest thinking and successes in frugal innovations from around the world. The Innovation Centre Denmark, under the auspices of the Ministry of Foreign Affairs of Denmark, seeks to impart lessons in frugal innovation (particularly in emerging markets) to Danish companies.

The Scandinavian approach to frugal innovation, including aspects implemented by the Innovation Centre Denmark and the Universe Foundation, began by looking at market segmentation for lower-cost products but has evolved to enhancing national R&D in order to become more competitive globally. In general, the core focus continues to be on strategies associated with the design and production of technology for mid-tier markets. Should Danish companies wish to learn from and tap into opportunities in extreme settings, this study suggests that other localised social and institutional dimensions are critical factors, in particular for lower-tier market segments. Additionally, many Scandinavian frugal innovation projects involve a top-down mindset of scaling down or de-featuring luxury goods to mid-tier consumers, whereas indigenous firms in developing markets pursue a bottom-up strategy, starting with lower-tier market segments and gradually improving their offerings for mid- and even top-tier market segments. Consequently, the current research and development policies in Scandinavia, which are geared for highly sophisticated and often luxury products and services, may have to be reconsidered for frugal innovation to flourish, whether for exporting to emerging markets or for catering to local concerns that require frugal solutions.

Healthcare is arguably the most important sector that could make use of frugal innovations for global impact. But affordable or low-cost products are only part of a more interesting and unexpected process of value creation and appropriation. Instead of focusing only on low-cost healthcare products or tools, the models of frugal innovation in this study take into account the wider value creation or value chain processes supporting those products. This study's lens on frugal innovation permits fuller attention to the challenges and opportunities present in institutionally complex contexts, such as those that lack efficient markets or public health services. Our most recent work (Bhatti et al., 2017a, 2017b) suggests that alongside the development of new products and tools for diagnostics or treatment, there needs to be a focus on care delivery models at the national and system level. For instance, community health workers build up trust in their communities and serve as a main conduit for the delivery of healthcare straight into homes, even in the most remote places. They are better placed to harness the potential of frugal innovation products and tools for diagnostics, communication and treatment, but their widespread use can only be facilitated by national level policymaking, as in the case of Brazil (Wadge et al., 2016).

There are few, if any, frameworks available to policymakers to benchmark and evaluate frugal innovations. The models of innovation proposed in this study can help practitioners and policymakers discover, synthesise and document designs and implement projects and policies in several public sectors, including healthcare, transportation and housing. For instance, the models can be useful in identifying and evaluating projects around several constructs that coalesce into the key outcome dimensions of affordability, adaptability and accessibility (we share in Appendix A a toolkit developed from the findings in this study and subsequently successfully used to find and shortlist hundreds of healthcare innovations) (Prime et al., 2016b).

In Figure 6.3, we allude to the conceptual abstraction of frugal innovation as a purposeful systematic change, showing how development can be best achieved within specific social contexts. This then leads to more operational abstractions that seek to identify and benchmark the phenomenon. While the detailed constructs explored in this book are a first step towards identifying and measuring frugal innovations, policymakers also need to help the field to experiment and evolve, rather than trying to benchmark 'ideal' frugal innovations. Given the rapidly changing understanding of innovation under constraints or in extreme contexts, policymakers should cautiously epitomise and tout the benefits of this phenomenon, which is still in flux, lacking a fully established professional identity (Abbott, 1988). There remains much to research in the emerging trend or field of frugal innovation. Most accounts of frugal innovation have largely been based on anecdotal accounts. This book has sought to depart from that shortcoming by basing findings, propositions and theoretical arguments on rigorously collected evidence.

Many practitioners and policymakers have tried too early to operationalise lessons from presumed examples of frugal innovation, rather than working to develop a theoretical and empirical understanding to help establish it as a field of innovation worthy of independent research and practice. Some publicly funded studies have moved in this direction. For instance, the pan-European Creating Economic Space for Social Innovation (CRESSI) project seeks to inform future policy by better understanding the economic underpinnings of marginalisation and social innovation in the European Union. As the project embarks on studying 'Social versus Technical Innovation', lessons from our models can inform policy analysis by helping to link social innovation with technology and institutional innovation. The European Commission's (EC) recent study on 'Frugal Innovation and the Re-Engineering of Traditional Techniques', led by Doris Schroecker, Head of Unit, DG Research and Innovation and authored by Henning Kroll at Fraunhofer ISI and Madaleine Gabriel at NESTA and their respective teams has already benefitted from some of the insights presented in this book (European Commission, 2017).[3]

Historically, economic growth has resulted in an increased use of resources. However, frugal innovation decouples growth from the use of resources. Contextual factors, such as environmental impact and limited resources in emerging markets, are changing personal preferences, promoting production and consumption patterns that de-couple this effect. The ambition of a new generation of innovators, both start-up entrepreneurs and large corporations, and the challenge for policymakers is to facilitate inclusive and responsible economic growth without an increased use of resources or being held back by institutional voids.

7.5 LIMITATIONS

Frugal innovation is not just about innovating products and technologies, but also about innovating perhaps the very concept of what innovation is, what it strives to achieve and how it can succeed in the face of constraints. Given the persistent uncertainty about what the concept actually means or refers to, we need to acknowledge some of the limitations of this work, as these may naturally feed into opportunities for further research. As with any bold research study, this work has strengths but also weaknesses and limitations. We outline here the limitations and ways in which we have tried to mitigate those limits, closing with possible avenues for future research.

[3] Between 2015 and 2016, co-author Yasser Bhatti served as an expert on the Steering Group and Scientific Advisory Board for this EC project.

Since this study seeks to uncover the conceptualisation of innovation among social entrepreneurs, it pursues a qualitative research path in which informants give personal accounts of how they perceive and are sometimes involved in innovation. Consequently, this study is exploratory and retroductive. It iteratively and deductively draws on existing theory, as well as inductively analysing empirical data from a group of social entrepreneurs, each serving as a case-study. This is both a strength and possible limitation of the book. The strength lies in first-hand accounts of innovation and in the iterative process of deduction and induction that provides a balanced approach – drawing a conceptual framework from the existing literature and accessing the benefits of grounded theory. The limitation reflects the robustness with which the researcher has been able to triangulate various data sources to make inferences while satisfactorily following the process of retroduction. We have tried to minimise these risks by having multiple researchers review the data and findings.

We researched innovators from two academically hosted programmes in Silicon Valley and the cases are embedded in a distinct socio-political context. This was a critical decision, as we chose to examine the motives and perceptions of a particular population, who are globally networked, formally recognised as social entrepreneurs, geographically and sectorally diverse and generally conversant in the English language. They attend programmes based in the entrepreneurially driven free-market economy of Silicon Valley. The programme organisers draw inspiration and strategies from the free market entrepreneurship model of Silicon Valley, where the logic of property rights, risk and revenue generation through innovative pursuits dominates. This means that their logics may be (and probably are) very different from those of all other possible populations we could have chosen – including local people who aren't globally networked or formally recognised (see Appendix C). Such differences appear in Sylvia Dorado's (2013) work on Latin American entrepreneurs and other literature. It is possible that, if we were to conduct the same study using social entrepreneurs drawn from an academic programme in the East, the findings might differ.

Although we contribute to the literature on innovation, entrepreneurship, strategy, organisational theory, economic sociology and to some extent development studies, we recognise that more work is needed to improve and extend our models of innovation. Our respondents came from different sectors and physical locations, but further research could examine the perception of innovation using more diverse cases and settings. This would allow for greater variation and quantity as well as enabling cross-sector and cross-location analysis. We next outline the limitations of this study, specifically in relation to the three research sub-questions and the three substantive, empirical chapters:

7.5.1 Research Question 1

Both the strength and limitation of this study are that it gathered and analysed data on how social entrepreneurs perceive and talk about innovation, as opposed to what they actually do (as in the works of John Law and Michel Callon, 1988). We don't follow the actor, but observe and interview the actors. Our findings rely on this narration of perceptions and implementation, as opposed to what social entrepreneurs really do on the ground. However, since the objective of this research is to generate models of innovation from the perspective of social entrepreneurs, rather than to benchmark practices or processes, a reliance on perceptions and narration was deemed appropriate for this study's desired goal.

Another word of caution is that our findings reflect the Global Social Benefit Institute's (GSBI®)'s preference for short-listing applicants as social entrepreneurs. The GSBI is more than a decade-old, world-renowned programme that has nurtured many globally prominent social entrepreneurs. The various exercises and steps involved in the application, combined with expert committee reviews, helped to mitigate any individual bias in determining who was a social entrepreneur. Despite this possible limitation, our innovation model provides a stylised view of how globally networked, formally recognised and well-established social entrepreneurs view innovation. Consequently, our typology provides a useful starting point for uncovering the range of innovation types perceived by social entrepreneurs.

We described a variation in responses across entrepreneurs, mentors and investors. A more fine-grained analysis might show how a diverse group of respondents keeps returning to the same themes – is there geographical variation in the responses? Is there an overlap across certain regions or are they distinct?

7.5.2 Research Questions 2 and 3

We used a value chain perspective to analyse how social entrepreneurs perceive innovation activity under (i) institutional voids and (ii) resource scarcity. Although the value chain approach has been useful in outlining these findings, it is most applicable to analysing actual activities. For this reason, our data shows how social entrepreneurs describe the activities they are involved in, rather than activities the researcher has observed first-hand.

Data was gathered for the second two research questions, exploring what social entrepreneurs and their colleagues perceive and claim to do when innovating under constraints. This data does not constitute an objective observation of the activities of social entrepreneurs in action. Instead, it reflects the idiosyncratic views of entrepreneurs who attended the GSBI programme.

Recall that the objective of this research project was to reveal models of innovation under constraints, as perceived by social entrepreneurs; these models have been successfully revealed, based on data, analysis and findings. We believe that our findings and models offer valuable insights into how social entrepreneurs view innovation under constraints and cope with those constraints. This study paves the way for future field research to observe innovation activities under constraints.

7.5.3 Results and Claims

The claims about developing a theory of frugal innovation may suffer from limited generalisability to other similar or extended cases. Although qualitative studies are suitable for theory development, they are less useful for generalising findings. Instead, they provide insights into unique phenomena and/or unique settings. We cannot make explicit claims about the generalisability of our context-specific findings. However, in accordance with Erving Goffman's (1983) 'interaction order', we can assume that patterns and practices in one place will have relevance to other contexts (Streeck and Mehus, 2005). Thus, we can claim that the findings from this study have a wider relevance, beyond those cases and contexts from which they were drawn. The purpose of theory-building in frugal innovation has been to encourage further empirical investigation of this phenomenon in similar and other contexts. We have attempted to do this in Chapter 5 by testing the models on ten popular cases found in the literature. Appendix C alludes to a generalisability test on our second cohort of social entrepreneurs.

In order to enhance the trustworthiness of the data (Lincoln and Guba, 1985) and our claims of robustness, we used multiple data sources that allowed for the triangulation of data (Hartley, 2004; Yin, 1994). However, triangulating data is only beneficial when you can rely on the objective interpretive approach of at least two researchers to cross-reference and validate the constructs and codes generated. If the study were conducted using a purely realist-oriented ontology, one would need to ensure the reliability of the process by using two coders working independently with a significant overlap for the reliability test (Neuendorf, 2002), or at least set the initial template to ensure its validity (King, 2004a; 2004b).

Among the limitations of our research design was the process of coding qualitative themes. We are unable to claim the highest degree of validity, since one researcher was the source of most of the coding analyses. However, our ontological position involves critical realism, which cautions that what we perceive as real might be in part 'socially constructed'. The coding exercise was dependent on our understanding and interpretations of the 'verbatim' responses we gathered through interviews and archival documentation. We took steps to minimise coding bias by following the method of template analysis, leaving an audit trail and soliciting quick and constant feedback on themes already generated through working papers and presentations. To reduce the risk that other researchers might code responses differently, the co-authors reviewed the data and findings to reach consensus on codes and interpretation.

In the post-positivistic tradition, Trochim (2005) suggests that the best way to improve objectivity is to do it within the context of a community of truth-seekers who regularly criticise each other's work. Right from an early stage of developing the initial ideas and performing the analysis, the lead researcher solicited critical feedback from peers and seasoned researchers, including professors and students (Denzin and Lincoln, 2005; Strauss and Corbin, 1998). Findings were reviewed and verified by supervisors and other colleagues and mentors, but these individuals were not asked (and would not have been able) to generate constructs or codes independently, as recommended by inter-rater coder reliability tests.

Nevertheless, this reflexive process of 'using the professional community provides a means to challenge and refine our developing theory and analysis to attain better validity' (King, 2012). We routinely circulated working papers through our own website and presented works-in-progress at several international conferences, such as the Academy of Management annual meetings. We used this repeated process of analysing the data and reworking the findings and theory to help us critically validate the results we have interpreted and revealed in this five-year study.

The results of this study open the way for intriguing possibilities and directions in innovation and entrepreneurship studies. Some of the limitations mentioned earlier may pave the way for future research that can help to overcome them.

7.6 FUTURE RESEARCH

Frugal innovation is not just about innovating products and technologies. It also concerns the very concept of what innovation is – what it strives to achieve and how this can be done when facing constraints. The strength of this work lies in raising an interesting epistemological debate about the differences between scholarly descriptions of innovation among social entrepreneurs – and their actual perceptions of innovation. The future is not just around the innovative aspects, it is also in the scaling of the innovation. This is a subject that is getting lot of attention among entrepreneurs, investors, funders, technologists and social scientists. How does one scale frugal innovation and social entrepreneurship for large scale impact? Scholarly work has attributed social innovation to social entrepreneurs, but has not adequately investigated the perceptions of social entrepreneurs themselves. This work has fundamentally analysed how social entrepreneurs perceive and discuss innovation and scaling under constraints.

In the process, we have learned what social entrepreneurs think of innovation, as carried out by themselves and other actors, including grassroots innovators, commercial entrepreneurs and big business. This study opens up opportunities for future observations of the innovation activities of different types of innovators, seen through a more flexible, encompassing and wider lens that incorporates existing innovation components. The next step may be to use our conceptual frameworks to ascertain what these other actors think about the type of innovation social entrepreneurs engage in. Innovation Model 1 reveals efficiency-based, social, user-based and challenge-based innovations. Innovation Model 2 reveals social, technological and institutional innovation. This study further opens up opportunities for subsequent research on the conceptualisation of innovation, particularly in the context of penurious environments marked by two overarching constraints or limitations, i.e. the resources available and the degree of institutional maturity. Having proposed a set of models and propositions that can be used to generate hypotheses, future research can use quantitative methods to test the models and theory advanced in this book.

Bruno Latour and Steve Woolgar (1986) argue in favour of using ethnography and photography to execute the methodological principle of 'follow the actor' (Latour, 1978). Rosemary Stewart (1972) has introduced a methodological focus on first-hand observations and the analysis of what managers actually do. This has led to micro-studies of scientists and technologists in their laboratories (Knorr Cetina, 1995; Latour and Woolgar, 1986; Michael, 1996). The methodological approach has resulted in the emergence of the field of strategy as practice. Micro-level and first-hand approaches are useful in revealing not only the kinds of work done, but also the kinds of people who do them and the skills involved (Johnson, 1997). Our research has focused on listening to social entrepreneurs who shared their views on innovation orally and in written business plans. We believe that this work is relevant for an understanding of models of innovation – and a good starting point for future research on what social entrepreneurs actually do. The models in this study could be verified or challenged through a comparison with codes and themes generated from what really happens on the ground.

Furthermore, frugal innovation, which we have defined by outlining and defining models, can help to elucidate a possible shift in the innovation paradigm, which is moving from a focus on technology towards social impact, efficiency enhancement and challenge- or need-driven innovation. Most innovation research that looks back through time has identified (in retrospect) fundamental changes in innovation system structures in different periods (Bruland and Mowery, 2005). For instance, the shift from an agricultural to an industrial society and then to a knowledge and service economy brings with it economic and social changes that illustrate the way innovation paradigms evolve. We may question to what extent the shift towards social impact, value creation and shared values in economic activity is a precursor or antecedent of the evolution of new innovation paradigms. The increasing popularity of frugal innovation among both social entrepreneurs and big business creates opportunities to observe shifts in paradigm, logic and practice – not in retrospect, but during the process of evolution.

Traditionally, innovation has relied on incremental improvements in product and process and the achievement of economies of scale to reduce costs through process efficiency for greater widespread affordability. The findings of this study suggest that frugal innovation is also a deliberate effort to reduce prices from the outset rather than rely on eventual but also inefficient or unequally accessible economies of scale. If frugal innovations can be considered disruptive (Hossain, Simula and Halme, 2016), then this poses fundamental questions about the prevalent models of innovation, such as the S-curve, which postulates the eventual 'catch-up' of new disruptive technologies in terms of both performance and price. If, however, frugal innovations are not deemed disruptive, then the strategy of frugal innovators in tackling performance and price together may signal a position on the S-curve that accelerates price reduction beyond that achieved by an economies of scale trajectory. Future research would have to look into the fundamental nature of frugal innovations as simultaneously disruptive and incremental, in order to compare the pursuit of price reduction with mainstream innovation models.

The work of Everett M. Rogers (2003) has long been considered an established theory of innovation diffusion. The idea that frugal innovation might from the outset target late majority or laggard customers challenges the Rogers (2003) diffusion and adoption curve. Recent studies analysing the validity of the Rogers curve in developing contexts (cf. Zanello et al., 2016) could be extended to verify whether or not the curve remains valid for the diffusion patterns of frugal innovations. Figure 7.1 shows how the direction of frugal innovation adoption may be reversed, in comparison with the traditional Rogers sequence of diffusion from A: wealthy and early adopters to lower income and laggard adopters, to B: lower income and laggard or late majority adopters to wealthier and sophisticated early adopters or innovators.

7.7 SUMMARY

This chapter has drawn implications from this work for researchers, practitioners and policymakers. Using social entrepreneurs'

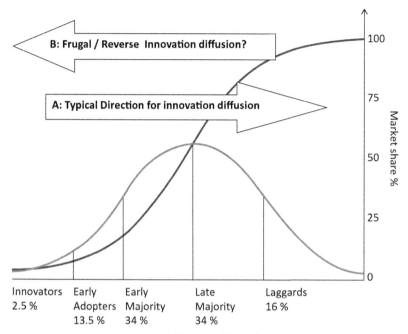

FIGURE 7.1 Reverse diffusion of frugal innovation in the Rogers diffusion curve

wide-ranging responses to innovation under constraints, this book proposes that we move beyond social innovation and recognise other forms of innovation, including user-based, efficiency-based, challenge-based and technological and institutional innovation, all of which we suggest can be captured in the emerging construct of frugal innovation. The field is evolving, but it needs support from researchers who can theorise and ground it in empirical data. It also needs practitioners to operationalise the findings and policymakers who can support system-level research and practice for global impact. This work suggests theory development for frugal innovation by postulating propositions based on empirical analysis, which can be tested in further work. Our hope is that we can collaborate with colleagues to extend this work towards some of the varied and intriguing avenues for future research outlined earlier, for a greater impact on practice and policymaking.

Conclusion

This book starts from distinctive premises and extensive empirical research, to understand innovation under constraints from the perspective of social entrepreneurs. We bring to bear theory and tools from organisation theory and strategic management. Despite recent work in strategy and organisational analysis on entrepeneurship and innovation in complex contexts and some discussion within the development literature about innovation in extreme contexts, few studies have grappled with the simultaneous challenges of institutional voids and resource scarcity for innovation. To extend current work, we connected innovation in extreme contexts with research on social and purposeful innovation. Despite growing interest in social entrepreneurship and social entrepreneurs, the current scholarly understanding of innovation in this space tends to start from the assumption that social innovation is an outcome of the activities of social entrepreneurs. This assumption may have some empirical support but could benefit from a more unified and coherent framework that captures the unique contexts in which social entrepreneurs seek to innovate.

Our work has investigated empirically how social entrepreneurs conceptualise innovation, using empirical insights to generate more fully specified models that start to provide just that kind of integrated framework for the study of sources of and types of innovation among social entrepreneurs in theory and in practice. We argue for two models of innovation, both rich with attention to institutionally complex context and both providing ways to make more precise empirical claims about how innovation takes shape. Model 1 makes explicit plural sources of the innovations described by social entrepreneurs. They in fact speak to four different sources of innovation – social, user, efficiency and challenge concerns. These issues and concerns are linked to different actors such as activists, users, firms, and networked communities of practice at the individual, firm, community, and sectoral levels. Model 2 sets this perspective within contextual constraints and makes explicit the plural types of innovations being pursued as described by social entrepreneurs. Here, they speak to three different types of innovation – technology, social, and institutional innovations to overcome resource scarcity, lack of affordability, and institutional voids. These innovations are linked into a set of overlapping dimensions which relate to different but complementary outcomes such as greater adaptability, affordability, accessibility, as well as appropriateness. This study advances an understanding of innovation among social entrepreneurs in a number of ways. Our contribution begins with the development of empirically derived models of innovation (see Guillén, 1994 and Sarasvathy, 2001 for models of managerial innovation and entrepreneurial action, respectively). We start from the reports and percpetions of social entrepreneurs, and specifically from social entrepreneurs drawn from wide geographic diversity and at the same time linked by participation in crucial training and mentorship programmes sponsored in the United States.

The models capture a hybrid mix of motivations and components of innovation approaches that bring into focus multidimensional constructs in innovation and that may help explain emerging trends in innovation under constraint. Further, we take seriously the sociological view of markets when analysing the market entry story of innovation (Robinson, 2006). We therefore focus on the constraints within which innovation is conceptualised and likely practiced. In doing so, our empirical findings support Perrini and Vurro's (2006) contention that social enterprises originate with a single innovation but assume the innovation as part of their workflow to progressively embrace other innovative services, complementing the initial innovation. Essentially, the nature of social innovation is multidimensional and temporal throughout the social entrepreneurial process.

We focus especially on our contribution in this direction: The models we have developed describe more specific and varied dimensions to consider in both analysing and assessing social innovation in context and making more precise emerging concepts such as frugal, grassroots and reverse innovation. The vantage point from our social entreprenuer informants starts to distinguish among these in fresh ways and potentially to recognise patterns across these different usages in practice In contrast to the singular conception of social innovation sometimes presented in current literatures, we find that social entrepreneurs distinguish the sources and impacts of innovation according to various dimensions. They report a disparate range of understandings that stem from varied motivations, means and outcomes. This variety is critical for theorising and studying innovation in these complex contexts. Moreover, as Kay (2011) argues for mainstream strategy practice, complex goals are often and perhaps best achieved by indirect and diverse means. We find his view of 'obliquity' consistent with the unchartered and unpredictable approaches to innovation described by social entrepreneurs. The variety of motivations and means reflect social concerns but also user, efficiency and challenge concerns (Model 1, Figure 2.3). Furthermore, we find that social entrepreneurs view the adoption of a mix of technological, social and institutional elements for innovations as a way of overcoming resource and affordability constraints and institutional voids (Model 2, Figure 3.2).

In developing and testing Model 1, we found that, beyond social entrepreneurs, large corporations are also involved in social entrepreneurial activities, mainly driven by the need to be more efficient or to achieve cost leadership. This supports the relevance of the reverse and frugal innovation focus on industrial markets and large firms in the strategy and international business literature (Govindarajan and Ramamurti, 2011; Zeschky, Widenmayer and Gassmann, 2011). Alongside, we found support for user-based and grassroots sources of innovation in testing the model, as mentioned in the innovation literature (von Hippel, 2005) and entrepreneurship literature

(Elkington and Hartigan, 2008). We also found support for challenges or prizes as sources of innovation – providing monumental social, economic and technological goals for innovators who either work together or compete against each other to be the first to achieve these goals (Diamandis and Kotler, 2012).

In developing and testing Model 2, we found support for Jeffrey Robinson (2006) who believes that, for social entrepreneurs in particular, 'disequilibria in the economic, social and institutional environment lead to entrepreneurial opportunity' (p. 97). Certainly many innovation and entrepreneurship scholars hold the same view, such as Roger Martin and Sally Osberg (2007; 2015). But we cite Robinson because our findings tie into the economic, social and institutional dimensions as in Model 2, which captures these three aspects of the environment in which social entrepreneurs carry out their Schumpeterian or business innovations, as well as social and institutional innovations. We refined the findings about the forms of innovation in each models by comparing and constasting our findings with existing innovation literatures (mainly Diamandis and Kotler, 2012; Govindarajan and Trimble, 2012; Hargrave and Van de Ven, 2006; Mulgan 2006; Nicholls, 2006a; 2006b; Schumpeter, 1934a; von Hippel, 2005). The variety of sources, concerns and approaches to innovation described by social entrepreneurs pointed us to propose a fresh view of frugal innovation.

Frugal innovation is not a new term (Prabhu, 2017; Weyrauch and Herstatt, 2017). But neither is it an especially well-specified concept, despite several engaged, scholarly accounts (see, for instance, a study by European Commission, 2017; Pisoni, Michclini and Martignoni, 2018; as well as refer to bibliography for many others). In particular, the term is often used interchangeably with a number of other terms (cf. Pansera, 2013; Radjou, Prabhu and Ahuja, 2012; Tiwari and Herstatt, 2012). This ferment and indetermancy suggests that this is both 'live' as a set of ideas and practices, and also captures real issues in the world. Our approach, to more directly take into account two kinds of contextual complexity (institutional voids and resource scarcity), represents a strategy to provide a more robust concept for theory and research. This emerging concept clearly resonates across many communities of policy and practice (cf. Bhutto and Vyas, 2017; Farooq and Farooq, 2017; Howell, van Beers and Doorn, 2017; Khan, 2016; Pansera and Sarkar, 2016; Soni and Krishnan, 2014; Winterhalter et al., 2017 and many more). And our approach reflects a shared account of the seemingly disparate perspectives reported by social entrepreneurs but ones that also provide insights into the activities of other actors, both individual entrepreneurs and large corporations. In proposing these two models, we take a step towards clear models to test and frameworks to use in analysing existing case studies. We hope we have shown how the models can contribute towards the development of a theory of frugal innovation. The models outline factors and dimensions through which frugal innovations can be identified, measured and evaluated along strategic objectives. These models are useful, not only in identifying the motivations and factors that influence the adoption of innovation activities, but also in understanding the life cycle of innovation, as it evolves and progresses temporally over the life cycle of the venture.

We close this book by offering in Appendix A to practitioners and policymakers a toolkit developed from the thematic codes in this study and used very effectively to identify frugal innovations for follow-on projects. In Appendix B, we summarise the ten core competencies espoused by the Frugal Innovation Lab, which has built expertise over the years in training engineers to develop frugal innovations. Finally, in Appendix C, we include an in-depth description of our research and analytical process for the benefit of researchers.

There is much work yet to be done. We trust that this book points to fruitful directions for further research by helping to authenticate the growing, if sometimes confusing, research agenda on frugal innovation for scholars, practitioners and policymakers. While there are increasing efforts to consolidate an understanding of this phenomenon through different approaches including systematic literature reviews (cf. Agarwal et al., 2017; Hossain, 2017; Pisoni, Michelini and Martignoni, 2018; Tiwari et al., 2016; Zeschky et al., 2014), this work drills down to the very basics by studying the core actors working in core contexts that define this activity. The research reported in this book starts from people working to innovation in complex contexts and for diverse purposes. We postulate initial propositions based on empirical data about how social entrepeneurs perceive drivers and determinants, and and key features of innovation. We contend that starting with social entrepeneurs opens up comparative insights applicable to mainstream entrepreneurs, firms, corporations and communities or networks of innovators.

Overall, frugal innovation, together with complementary concepts and approaches by myriad actors, can be identified as part of collective effort towards inclusive innovation, or innovation for humanity. In support of this, we have shown that frugal innovation draws on a multitude of means, methods, and measures that make innovation meaningful not only for the marginalised but also the masses and the mainstream. We hope that the theory, models, propositions and tools provided here will be used to carry out further practical work and scholarly research on frugal innovation in constrained but challenging and promising extreme contexts for the benefit of society, economy and the planet.

PART III

Tools for Practice and Research

Appendices

Although all appendices should be useful for researchers, practioners and policymakers, Appendix A should be most useful for policymakers, Appendix B for practitioners and Appendix C for researchers. Appendix A describes a tool to help identify and evaluate potential frugal innovations and another tool to categorise innovations and trace their stage in the lifecycle from start-up to global scalability. Appendix B outlines the important characteristics and core competencies of frugal innovations. Appendix C is a detailed account of the research methodology and also contains a generalisability test of the findings.

Appendix A Toolkit to Identify and Categorise Frugal Innovations

This appendix provides two tools. The first tool outlined in Table A.1 should be useful for observing and identifying frugal innovationsalong ten subcomponents of the three dimensions of affordability, adaptability and accessibility, as described in this research and based on our definition: 'means and ends to do more with less for many'. The toolkit has been iteratively co-developed, tested and improved by co-author Yasser Bhatti and colleague Matthew Prime to offer a methodical framework for evaluating and documenting whether an innovation can be considered frugal. It has been rigorously tested by Matthew Prime as part of his PhD (2018) and used in other works to shortlist hundreds of innovations (Bhatti et al., 2017a; 2017b). For more information on its effectiveness and limitations, please see the paper by Prime et al. (2016b). We continue to find this tool useful in our ongoing research, as it helps us to shortlist frugal innovations in a relatively rapid manner before carrying out more detailed economic analyses on their potential to be useful in different contexts. The second tool outlined in Figure A.1 is useful to categorise the innovations along the four key dimensions of user-based, efficiency-based, social and challenge-based innovation and to trace the innovations' stage in the lifecycle from start to scalability. By understanding this, strategists can plan on how to get an innovation from where it began to where it should or may end up.

A.1 FRUGAL IDENTIFICATION TOOL

- The innovation has potential to be a frugal innovation if you have at least one 'yes' in each of the dimensions: A, B and C.

Table A.1 *Frugal identification tool*

Name of Innovation: _____
Circle the best option for each of the following factors.

A. **Affordability:** Is the offering more affordable than alternatives in terms of?	
i. Production? (process)	Yes No N/A Unknown
ii. Operation? (process)	Yes No N/A Unknown
iii. Purchasing? (outcome)	Yes No N/A Unknown
iv. Servicing? (outcome)	Yes No N/A Unknown
v. Disposal? (outcome)	Yes No N/A Unknown
B. **Adaptability:** Is it adapted and appropriate to the needs of the context to perform better than, be equivalent to other options or be good enough?	
vi. Outperform? (efficiency)	Yes No N/A Unknown
vii. Be equivalent? (as good)	Yes No N/A Unknown
viii. Be good enough? (bricolage)	Yes No N/A Unknown
C. **Accessibility:** Is it accessible and scalable enough to benefit many in society?	
ix. Currently widely accessible?	Yes No N/A Unknown
x. Has potential for scalability?	Yes No N/A Unknown
Frugal Innovation:	**YES / NO / Unknown**

- Please note that this is not a scale of measurement. Further in-depth analysis is needed to understand the exact reasons why and the degree to which an innovation is frugal. However, we have found this to be a useful way of quickly screening hundreds of innovations for further analysis in subsequent research.

A.2 INNOVATION LIFECYCLE TOOL

Innovation Model 1 in Chapter 2 offers stakeholders a tool that enables them to understand who is backing the innovation and what their motives are. This makes it possible to judge the kinds of resources and stakeholders needed to take the innovation to its next level scale or goal.

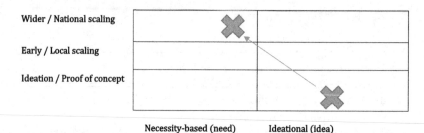

FIGURE A.I Categorising frugal innovations in lifecycle

The two columns are: (i) Ideational, which indicates a visionary idea with the ambition to bring about system-wide benefits, as opposed to (ii) Necessity-based, which suggests that the idea is derived from an effort to meet a personal need, with the initial ambition to provide localised benefits. The three rows indicate the degree of scaling up: (i) Ideation or proof of concept; (ii) In-progress early scaling, perhaps at a local level and (iii) Mass scaling at a national or global level.

Plot the quadrant in which the innovation best fits now and might fit in the future. Then pencil in a possible trajectory, as indicated on the model, to chart a course for how it might reach its intended purpose and scale. Please see Chapter 2 for a detailed account of this model to understand where the innovation starts and is headed.

Appendix B Lessons from the Frugal Innovation Lab

This appendix provides lessons from the world's first frugal innovation design centre and teaching facility, the Frugal Innovation Laboratory at Santa Clara University. It was co-founded in 2012 by co-author Radha Basu and Godfrey Mungal, Dean of the School of Engineering. The laboratory (now rebranded the Frugal Innovation Hub) has designed new products and services by teaching engineers to improve the sustainability and scalability of solutions for greater global impact: 'Basu incubated the idea of the Frugal Innovation Lab as a way to marry instruction, innovation and immersion experiences for SCU students to develop appropriate, adaptable, affordable and accessible technologies, products and solutions to address human needs in emerging markets.' (For more information, visit http://students.engr.scu.edu/~classall/COEN161/FIL_final/)

The space develops products and services using engineering and design principles inspired by the needs of users in emerging markets or the developing world. The principles are captured in the ten core competencies of frugal innovation depicted in Figure B.1 and described in Table B.1. Basu, Banerjee and Sweeny (2013) have illustrated in detail how the ten competencies have been brought to life in examples drawn from around the world. Many of these are based on social enterprise models. Although one example is listed against each main competency, it is characterised by several other competencies. It is advisable to consider all competencies in the design phase. Each competency offers opportunities for differentiating a solution and making it more innovative. We have found that many innovators gradually incorporate more competencies over the life cycle of an offering or in varying degrees. We summarise these examples in Table B.2.

Table B.1 *Ten core competencies of frugal innovation from the Frugal Innovation Lab*

Core competency	Description
1. Ruggedisation	Capable of coping with harsh physical environments (e.g. dust, heat, moisture, pests, electric surges and shocks)
2. Lightweight	Portable and light to be carried over long distances through varying transportation options
3. Mobile-enabled	Connectivity anytime, anywhere and effective instrumentation
4. Human-centric design	Easy-to-use, intuitive designs that require little to no prior knowledge or training to utilise
5. Simplification	Minimalist features and intuitive functionalilty
6. Last-mile distribution	Non-conventional channels for greater access
7. Adaptation	Leveraging existing products, inputs and services
8. Use of local resources	Sourcing using what is available, local labour and reducing imports
9. Green technologies	Powered by renewable energy and resources
10. Affordability	Low input and operation costs

FIGURE B.I Ten core competencies of frugal innovation from the Frugal Innovation Lab

Table B.2 *Examples that support the ten core competencies of frugal innovation*

Core competency	Example	Key features
Ruggedisation	**ToughStuff: Durable Solar Panel Charging System:** Focus on making products that can withstand environmental and physical tribulations	Solar panel charging system for powering LED lamps, mobile phones and radios; uses materials that are nearly indestructible but also are flexible, waterproof and relatively small.
Lightweight	**Cisco and NetHope: Emergency NetReliefKit:** Focus on providing a communications hub in a box for relief and emergency organisations	Uses the joint experiences of 25 partner NGOs to understand design parameters; Light weight allows organisations to transport kit in backpacks to remote areas; condenses lots of equipment into one unit.
Mobile-enabled	**Kopo Kopo Mobile Money Platform:** Offers a mobile money platform that works on various operators	Financial transactions without limiting to specific operators; analysis of transactions for buying and selling trends; offers value-added services on top of mobile phone transactions.
Human-centric design	**Naandi Jerry Can for Safe Water Program:** Integrates water service, product, distribution, payment and awareness campaign	Educates rural communities on the need to store water carefully; local leader to encourage transition to clean drinking water; product use of food-grade 20-litre jerry cans.
Simplification	**TATA Chemical Rice Husk Water Filter:** Aims to be the world's lowest-cost water purifier	Water purifier that is accessible, inexpensive, effective; makes use of local resources with high-tech; ease of use, prevents use once purifying capacity limit is reached.

Table B.2 (cont.)

Core competency	Example	Key features
Last-mile distribution models	**Solar Sister Avon Style Solar Product Distribution:** Revolutionises energy distribution	Provides and empowers rural sellers and customers with solar products; Makes women a key factor in entrepreneurial livelihood development; fosters networking, information spread and lowering energy poverty.
Adaptation	**Awaaz. De Voice Message Board for Education:** Provides rural information delivery systems using existing technology	Gives voice through mobile voice and intermittent Internet; adapts to local technology and customs; overcomes language barriers and literacy constraints; users can create forums around specific topics.
Use of local resources	**Husk Power Systems Rice Husk Gasification:** Generates clean, safe and efficient electricity by sourcing local waste	Increases access to off-grid energy at lower cost; reduces emissions and prevents deforestation; training and operations give rise to small entrepreneurs.
Green technologies	**WE CARE Solar Suitcase Lighting Delivery Rooms:** Uses solar energy to light and power clinics	Provides light primarily in clinics in emergency situations; lowers maternal mortality rate; offers power points for other equipment.
Affordability	**Jaipur Foot $30 Prosthetics:** Provides normalcy to amputees	Offers high value services at a low cost; Ability to pay is waived; durability in design and materials for harsh environments.

Appendix C Detailed Research Methodology and Design

C.1 INTRODUCTION

(Note: Unlike the main text in the book, this appendix is written in the first person from the perspective of the lead author who conducted the fieldwork and data collection.)

A review of the nature of research questions guides the choice of research methodology and methods (Bryman and Bell, 2003; Creswell, 2003; Maylor and Blackmon, 2005; O'Leary, 2004; Punch, 2005 and others). However, the researcher's assumptions about the nature of knowledge discovery, epistemology and the nature of reality or ontology can affect the type of answers the researcher eventually 'interprets' (Creswell, 1998; Guba and Lincoln, 1994). Social science questions therefore reveal different answers depending on both the nature of the questions and which paradigm the researcher is inclined to use to achieve his or her aims and objectives.

I first outline the questions and aims and review the assumptions I make in approaching these questions. Then I lay out the sources of data and the methods used to analyse the data set for each question. Table C.1 lists the research questions and their key aims, while Table C.2 provides an overview of the entire research design outlined in this chapter.

C.2 RESEARCH METHODOLOGY

The research questions listed earlier could be approached using any post-positivist, constructivist, interpretivist or phenomenological approach. The epistemological and ontological stance of the researcher is marked by the paradigm of post-positivism (specifically,

Table C.1 *Research questions and objectives*

Main question: How do social entrepreneurs perceive innovation broadly and under extreme conditions marked by institutional voids and resource scarcity?	
Sub-question	**Objective**
1. How do social entrepreneurs conceptualise innovation?	To investigate through exploratory and descriptive analysis what social entrepreneurs think about innovation and say they do, as opposed to what they 'really' do on the ground
2. How do they conceptualise innovation under institutional voids?	To determine how this perception and view of innovation is shaped when confronted by the contingency of institutional voids
3. How do they conceptualise innovation under resource scarcity?	To determine how this perception and view of innovation is shaped when confronted by the contingency of resource scarcity

critical realism) as outlined in Table C.3. In this post-positivist philosophy of analysis, whether qualitative or quantitative, I as the researcher am responsible for putting aside my biases and beliefs and seeing the world as it 'really' is (Trochim, 2005). However well I can achieve this and provide assurance to our respondents, I am unlikely to be perfectly unbiased or entirely free of error. Post-positivists believe that, although we can try to be objective, we can never fully achieve that. This is because our observations are affected by culture, worldviews and theory-laden perspectives. Therefore, the post-positivist relies on multiple measures and observations and uses these for triangulation across multiple error-prone sources (Trochim, 2005). Using different methods and sources of data provides for convergence and the triangulation of findings (Jick, 1979) over several fallible sources. As assumed within the critical realism paradigm, this achieves a greater robustness of results.

Table C.2 Overview of the research design

Main Research Question	Sub-Questions	Objective	Contribution	Conceptual Level of Analysis	Data Sources	Analysis Method	TRIANGULATION of DATA
How do social entrepreneurs conceptualise innovation broadly and specifically under extreme conditions marked by institutional voids and resource scarcity?	*How do social entrepreneurs conceptualise innovation?*	To investigate through exploratory and descriptive analysis what social entrepreneurs think about innovation and say they do as opposed to what they 'really' do on the ground.	Contributes to perceptions and key features of models of innovation relevant for management theory and policy.	Innovation as a belief system	*PHASE 1:* *Document analysis: 163* Innovation summaries from 2005 (23), 2006 (35), 2007 (59), 2011 (46)	Use Meta-Thematic Content Analysis to create initial template	
	How do they conceptualise innovation under institutional voids?	To determine how this perception and view on innovation is shaped when confronted by the contingency of institutional voids.	Contributes to the literature on how contextual conditions shape innovation.	Value chain of service or product	*PHASE 2:* *In-depth interviews: 31* Conducted at GSBI and DEA of social entrepreneurs, innovators, academics and investors as expert discussants (2011-12)	Apply template analysis to all data and revise 1st order codes	
	How do they conceptualise innovation under resource scarcity?	To determine how this perception and view on innovation is shaped when confronted by the contingency of resource scarcity.	Specifically advances theoretical models of innovation by bridging the literatures on innovation with institutional and resource theories.	Value chain of service or product	*PHASE 3:* *Participant observation and interviews: 50* During GSBI social entrepreneur boot camp and innovation lab (2012)	Iteratively improve template and reveal 2nd and 3rd order codes	
						Theory Development	

Multiple sources of qualitative data and retroductive analysis (Ragin and Amoroso 2010) helps triangulate findings.

Table C.3 *Components of the research process adopted for this study*

Research process	
Research philosophy or paradigm	Post-positivistic critical realism (not interpretivism)
Research approach	Iterative mix of induction and deduction: retroduction
Research strategy	Individual level 'cases'
Time horizon	Cross-sectional over two years
Data collection method	Secondary literature, archival documents, participant observation and interviews

Source: Adapted from Saunders, Lewis and Thornhill (2003).

The appropriateness of employing a qualitative research methodology derives from the nature of the social phenomena (Morgan and Smircich, 1980), in this case, how social entrepreneurs talk about innovation. According to Cohen and Manion (1980, p. 27), 'the purpose of the social science is to understand social reality as different people see it and to demonstrate how their views shape the action which they take within that reality'. The research objectives (Table C.1) call for an in-depth, detailed exploratory study, delving into the perception of innovation among social entrepreneurs.

A concept is a general expression of a particular phenomenon and is used to impose a coherent meaning on the world. Among social entrepreneurs, there is no coherent or agreed single meaning for 'innovation' in the current literature. As a social scientist, I recognise that the widely acclaimed but deep concept of innovation will be understood in relation to opinions, values, traditions, cultures and rules that cannot, unlike in the natural sciences, be precisely defined (Clarke, 2005). I therefore focus on social entrepreneurs' discourse around innovation. To reveal and analyse this talk and thinking, I use a qualitative descriptive approach that involves presenting the facts of the case in everyday language (Sandelowski, 2000). The orientations or logics displayed by informants are treated as socially constructed and not necessarily universally or materially 'objective'. Similar descriptive research on management and strategy practices (for instance Whittington, 1996) has used fieldwork, interviews and observations to create models of understanding and to generate theories and eventual paradigms. I explore the phenomenon of innovation among social entrepreneurs to help reveal patterns of differences and similarities and to broaden our understanding of theories. Consequently, I build propositions that stem from the findings in Chapters 2, 3, and 4 and to suggest models of innovation that reflect what innovation means to and among social entrepreneurs.

C.3 RESEARCH DESIGN

A research design is a characterisation of the research strategy that allows one to address specific research questions. I adopted a descriptive qualitative research design that allowed me to describe how social entrepreneurs think about innovation. This design was appropriate because of the relatively limited knowledge we have of such conceptualisations of innovation. I identified two social entrepreneurship-related programmes in Silicon Valley, California as my source of social entrepreneurs: The Global Social Benefit Institute (GSBI®) is part of Miller Center for Social Entrepreneurship at Santa Clara University and the Design for Extreme Affordability (DEA) programme is part of d.school (Hasso Plattner Institute of Design) at Stanford University. The former is a professional programme or workshop that seeks to accelerate growth for existing social entrepreneurs, while the latter is a university degree module that serves as sort of incubator for enrolled students. I used members, current and past, of these programmes to gain access to a diverse group of social entrepreneurs; they also provided textual sources (in the form of business plans) and the opportunity to carry out in-depth interviews and observations.

I was drawn to these programmes because several globally renowned social entrepreneurship cases, including Kiva, Whirlwind Wheelchair, Anudip, Toughstuff, Thrive, MIT OpenCourseWare,

Vision Spring, Jaipur / ReMotion Knee, Embrace and D-Light can be traced back to these two programmes. Initially, my reasons for going to California were logistical – having access to historical documents in the form of business plan summaries from multiple social entrepreneurs and an opportunity to meet with them in person. Both programmes have extensive networks spanning the whole social entrepreneurial community; participants originate from all over the world and focus on diverse markets, mainly emerging and developing markets, but also developed ones. I found that these well-networked programmes in California provided a concentrated and accessible way in which to collect extensive and diverse data within the span of time allowed for a DPhil or PhD. Consequently, I returned to California for another round of data collection, which I shall describe in more detail later. It did not seem either feasible or necessary to source my social entrepreneurs from among local people in the countries in which the social enterprises were being established, given the complexities involved in multiple and historical document access, the cost of extensive travel and time limitations.

Recall that the object of study is the concept of innovation, while the subjects of study are individual practitioners: primarily social entrepreneurs and experts who work with social entrepreneurs, such as academics, mentors and investors. Collectively, these types of informants, belonging to diverse geographical locations and sectors, serve as the source of data for this meta-analysis of social entrepreneurs' perceptions of innovation. Although the programmes are headquartered and convened in the West, there are contextual features that make these venues relevant and interesting to source data from, and I describe these contextual features in detail in Section C.3.2.

After exploratory fieldwork, negotiating access and the final accumulation of data, I decided to draw most of the data analysis and findings from the site which produced the most data – the GSBI programme. I made use of a smaller amount of rich data from the second site, using it to perform a final external validity and restricted generalisability test.

C.3.1 Research Phases

The research data collection spanned one year over the two research sites and is best described in three phases. From September to November 2011, I conducted fieldwork at the two sites, followed by a second round of fieldwork from August to September 2012, which concentrated more on one site. Phase 1 involved mostly archival document collection comprising business plan outlines. In Phase 2, I contacted social entrepreneurs and administrators, organisers and academics from the directories of the two programmes to create a purposive sample. Respondents were approached through email and personal referrals. Not all were available or accessible, due to relocation and 'research fatigue', but from these two sources, I was able to accrue thirty-one in-depth interviews in Phase 2 and subsequently another fifty in Phase 3 of the data collection, amounting to eighty-one interviews. Table C.4 shows how many participants were interviewed during Phases 2 and 3, as explained in more detail below.

C.3.2 Main Research Site

The main research site was the decade-old, well-known Global Social Benefit Institute hosted by Santa Clara University. (The programme is currently housed under the Miller Center for Social Entrepreneurship). The GSBI has been helping social entrepreneurs build sustainable, scalable organisations since 2003. By the time the research had commenced, the GSBI had trained '165 entrepreneurs who have collectively gone on to positively impact the lives of 74 million people' (GSBI, 2013). Ninety-five per cent of these are still in operation and 55 per cent are scaling.

The contextual features of this community or network of social entrepreneurs are depicted in Figure C.1. Broadly, the community is one in which social entrepreneurs are both globally networked and formally recognised. 'Globally networked' implies that these social entrepreneurs have broad global networks aware of GSBI-type Western-based programmes and the ability and means to apply to such programmes. The application process is both complicated and elongated, requiring

Table C.4 *Total number of interviews during Phases 2 and 3*

Phase 2	Interviews	Phase 3	Interviews	Interactions[a]	Total for each community
Site A: GSBI		**Site A: GSBI**			
Entrep (E)	12	Entrep (E)	16	7	Both interview and interaction = 5
Experts (F)	8	Experts (F))	10	3	Site A Phase 2 = 20
Site B: DEA		Mentors (M)	9	3	Site A Phase 3 = 39 + 16 − 5 = 50
Entrep (E)	10	Investors (I)	4	3	
Experts (F)	1				**Site A total = 70**
Sub-total	**31**	**Sub-total**	**39**	**16**	**Site B total = 11**

[a] Interaction means that a conversation among group members about a related issue was observed.

	Selected Research Sites	
Globally Networked	**1. Global Social Business Incubator** **2. Design for Extreme Affordability** Variation geographically & sector-wise; Quick access to diverse group; Conducive environment for sharing ideas; Western/developed programs; Focus on developing/EM but not limited; Well educated, English proficiency; 'Elite' representatives / role models; High ambition to scale	*Future Research*
Locally Networked	*Future Research*	*Future Research*
	Formally recognised	Not formally recognised

FIGURE C.I Contextual elements of research sites

candidates to complete several exercises that can help to shortlist applicants. Application to the programme is advertised through a social edge
platform, as well as through development agencies that work on the
ground in many countries around the globe. 'Formally recognised' means
that the applicants are labelled as social entrepreneurs by the programme
and awarded certificates when they complete it. The implication is that
some participants may not see themselves as social entrepreneurs, but
are recognised as social entrepreneurs because they have gone through
the rigorous application and training programme.

The advantages of studying this type of community include
quick access to a diverse group of social entrepreneurs who are geographically and sectorally dispersed. A substantial number of them
convene at one place at one time, at least once a year, and the learning
environment that brings them together encourages the sharing of ideas,
not only amongst themselves but also with researchers Although the
programme is headquartered and run in the West, the focus of most
projects is on developing and emerging market contexts, although this
is not a limitation – many developed market social entrepreneurs also
take part. The regional breakdown of GSBI alumni over the last decade
is 29 per cent in Africa, 21 per cent in India, 15 per cent in Latin America
and the Caribbean, 12 per cent in Asia and the South Pacific, 6 per cent
in Canada and the USA and 17 per cent worldwide.

All participating social entrepreneurs were well educated, many with higher degrees; they spoke English as a requirement for programme attendance. To a large degree, social entrepreneurs enjoy elite status and are role models. Again, as a requirement of the GSBI programme and the training provided by DEA, the participants are very ambitious about scaling up their products and services. By focusing on this group, I acknowledge that I bypassed social entrepreneurs in the 'locally networked' and/or 'not formally recognised' categories. These were based in local communities without access, means or (in some cases) the desire to be globally recognised or to have a global reach. While important, these categories of social entrepreneurs were better suited to an expanded, future study. This book concentrates on collecting data from social entrepreneurs who are globally networked and formally recognised.

C.4 DATA COLLECTION

Insights are revealed through three sets of data: (1) archival innovation summaries from business plans that cover specific questions on the nature of innovation; (2) semi-structured interviews and (3) participant observations at a boot camp. Most of the data came from GSBI; I therefore focused on findings from this one community. The stages of data collection in a crude sequence involved pilot interviews, document collection, in-depth interviews, observations and further interviews. For reliability and authenticity, I maintained meticulous records of the raw data, notes, transcriptions and phases of analysis.

C.4.1 Field Procedures

My credentials were as follows: I was a researcher from Oxford University collecting data for my PhD thesis. No direct commercialisation interests were involved; this research was intended to inform academic theory and practical knowledge in the field. Consequently, the information collected in this study has been used for the purpose of publishing a PhD dissertation as a book and academic papers.

Respondents with confidential information or anonymous sources were given the option to withhold such details from publication.

I hold my research accountable to general ethical values, including respect, integrity and (where requested by respondents) confidentiality. In particular, I have tried to ensure that my project did no harm to individuals or organisations. To confirm this, I received formal ethical approval from the Oxford University Inter-Departmental Research Ethics Committee (IDREC). In all circumstances, I made it clear to the respondents that the research discussions with me were entirely voluntary. They were advised that they could opt out of the research project at any time and could request anonymity or content omission as and when desired. I shared audio files and transcripts with several interviewees who requested them.

Phase 1/Year 1: Archival Business Plans and Application Forms (2006–2011): During my first field trip to the region in fall 2011, I was able to acquire innovation summary documents from the Global Social Business Incubator and to negotiate access for next year's boot camp, the latter activity contributing to Phase 3. I went through the archival documents and collected 163 application forms that included business plans and answers to structured questions on the nature, target and development of the innovation. Data from 2008 to 2010 was not available to me, as the GSBI offices in Santa Clara University had recently suffered a computer theft, losing the machines on which this data was held. Table C.5 shows the number

Table C.5 *Innovation summary documents*

Year	Number
2005	23
2006	35
2007	59
2011	46
Total	163

of innovation summaries by year of programme. The innovation summaries were drafted by applicants in response to the following questions posed by the programme:

1. *How is your approach innovative (better then alternatives)?*
2. *Describe the key innovation(s) of your organisation (e.g, business models, products or services, processes, value chain enhancements).*
3. *Explain the potential for these innovations to be deployed or replicated elsewhere.*
4. *Explain the potential for licensing these innovations.*
5. *Challenges and obstacles faced?*

Although the full application forms exceeded 400 pages, I concentrated on the section on innovation, as outlined by the questions listed earlier. These innovation summaries together amounted to 158 pages, or around 65,000 words, which were used in thematic analyses.

Phase 2/Years 1 and 2: Interviews (November 2011–September 2012): Of the different forms of interviews possible, i.e. open-ended, focused and structured or survey, I conducted semi-structured interviews. Semi-structured interviews provide structure to focus on the problem of investigation and are also flexible enough to reveal unexpected lines of enquiry (Grix, 2004). I already had an idea of the questions to focus on, but wanted to allow the respondent to reveal insights beyond my current radar. I therefore used an interview guide to conduct semi-structured interviews with social entrepreneurs and those who work with social entrepreneurs. The questionnaire and methodology were approved by the Research Ethics committee (CUREC) of the University of Oxford following the pilot study.

C.4.2 Pilot Interviews

I completed the pilot phase of a draft questionnaire with two social entrepreneurs and two experts contacted through my home institution. The sequence of questions and the questionnaire format were revised and two versions created. One version was for those entrepreneurs, who were directly involved in an innovation-related project; the other was for experts, including faculty members, mentors and investors who worked with social entrepreneurs but were not neces-sarily directly involved in a specific project. The questions were the same across the two versions, reworded to address the relevant respondent.

Although recorded, the pilot interviews were not transcribed and the data was not analysed extensively. Instead, the purpose of this activity was to better formulate questions and the interview guide. The wording and sequence of questions was revised in light of the pilot interviews. It was clear that respondents did not understand academic terms, such as 'value chain' or 'institutional voids', so questions were framed to avoid this scholarly language. Other ques-tions were merged or split. Questions on competencies were difficult for the respondents to answer, particularly on the spot. As this was a secondary focus of the research, such questions were not asked. Overall, the interview guide went through two iterations to make it agreeable to respondents while preserving the intent of the study.

Interviews during the pilot study lasted between thirty and ninety minutes, with an average time of one hour. Since the pilot interviews had indicated that an hour could be tiring for both the interviewer and the interviewee, I opted for face-to-face interviews, usually over coffee, in all cases. In two circumstances, this was not logistically possible, so were conducted through video-call.

C.4.3 Sampling

I used purposive sampling to identify the community or network of social entrepreneurs represented by the contextual features outlined in Figure C.1. Respondents were drawn from this community because they enabled exploration of a particular aspect of behaviour relevant to the research study. They did not need to be representative, from a statistical or probabilistic perspective, since the objective was to understand social processes (Mays and Pope, 1995). Purposive sam-pling allowed me to draw on a wide range of types of informants and to select key informants who were likely to divulge relevant and important knowledge. I approached not only social entrepreneurs but also people who worked with or understood social entrepreneurs, in particular, mentors, investors and programme tutors and organisers. Respondents were globally networked and formally recognised members of two Western communities or networks (GSBI and DEA) that sought to identify, build and nurture social entrepreneurs.

I approached as many of the respondents with available contact information as possible. Respondents agreed to answer questions based on their availability and willingness. In some cases, the respondents referred potential interviewees. If they matched the above contextual characteristics and programmes, they were approached for interviews. In Phase 2 of data collection, I identified twenty-four projects from the DEA programme. From these projects, forty-six individuals were contacted, resulting in eleven interviews. Of these, ten were face-to-face and one was conducted using Skype. The GSBI SCU programme included more than 150 alumni in their directory, but most were abroad. Incidentally, fifteen social entrepreneurship organisations attended the co-hosted GSBI-Tech Awards, to which I was also invited by Radha Basu, who was at the time Director of the Frugal Innovation Lab. Through these fifteen projects, I contacted thirty-two individuals and eventually gained twenty face-to-face interviews. These interviews were transcribed and used as part of the analysis. I describe the representativeness of these informants during Phase 2, indicating who they were, where they came from, which sector they worked in and the length of each interview in Table C.6.

Phase 3/Year 2: Participant Observation (11 August–24 August 2012): During the Phase 1 trip to the GSBI in 2011, I was invited to participate in and observe its annual workshop or boot camp. This was an opportunity to observe and collect face-to-face interviews from a large and diversified group of real social enterprise ventures. I returned to the GSBI research site A in late summer 2012 for its tenth anniversary programme.

Each year, the GSBI selects and 'admits' twenty enterprises from around the world that work in various sectors such as renewable energy, mobile services and economic empowerment. The actual

Table C.6 Respondent profiles for Phase 2

	Code	Site	Type	Solution	Sector	Interview (minutes)
1	A1E	A	SE and Expert	Education	Education	79
2	A2E	A	SE and Expert	IT jobs	Economic Development	81
3	A3E	A	SE	Transportation and banking	Economic Development	65
4	A4E	A	SE	Mobile pump regulator	Economic Development	108
5	A5E	A	SE	Mobile banking	Economic Development	84
6	A6E	A	SE	Foot pumps	Economic Development	41
7	A7E	A	SE	Off-grid lighting	Energy	66
8	A8E	A	SE	Educational media	Energy	19
9	A9E	A	SE	Clean water	Sanitation	55
10	A10E	A	SE	Clean water	Sanitation	29
11	A11E	A	SE	Female sanitary pads	Healthcare	41
12	A12E	A	SE and Expert	Eye hospital	Healthcare	43
13	A13F	A	Expert	N.A.	Researcher	64
14	A14F	A	Expert	N.A.	Professor and Organiser	97
15	A15F	A	Expert	N.A.	Mentor	29
16	A16F	A	Expert	N.A.	Professor	32
17	A17F	A	Expert	N.A.	Associate Dean	43
18	A18F	A	Expert	N.A.	Dean	65
19	A19F	A	Expert	N.A.	Professor	31
20	A20F	A	Expert	N.A.	Engineer	45
						1,117
						(19 hours)

Table C.6 (cont.)

	Code	Site	Type	Solution	Sector	Interview (minutes)
1	B1E	B	Entrep	Pepper grinder	Economic Development	63
2	B2E	B	Entrep	Foot pump	Agricultural Machinery	66
3	B3E	B	Entrep	Fertiliser pellet applicator	Agricultural Machinery	60
4	B4E	B	Entrep	Deep treadle pump	Agricultural Machinery	65
5	B5E	B	Entrep	Nasal interface	Healthcare	54
6	B6E	B	Entrep	Prosthetics	Healthcare	94
7	B7E	B	Entrep	Toilet	Sanitation	41
8	B8E	B	Entrep	Water storage	Sanitation	42
9	B9E	B	Entrep	Toilet	Sanitation	62
10	B10E	B	Entrep	Hand cleanser	Sanitation	74
11	B11F	B	Expert	N.A.	Professor and Organiser	75
						696 (12 hours)
					Total minutes	**1,813**
						(30 hours)

programme runs over an eight-month period from May to December, during which time the GSBI equips selected social enterprises to scale up their impact. Midway through August, everyone convenes for an in-residence, two-week boot camp to learn from each other and from venture capitalists (VCs), investment and foundation heads, technology leaders and business model experts who serve as mentors or trainers. This intense group programme provided an opportunity to explore interesting and relevant themes pertaining to the actual discussions social entrepreneurs have among themselves and with colleagues.

It was not possible to conduct the ethnographic technique of participant observation since I am not and could not disguise myself as a 'team member'. However, I was allowed to sit in on the whole process as an active and direct observer. I gained approval from the GSBI organisers to participate for observations and interviews, and was introduced to all of the participants as a 'researcher doing my PhD'. On further informed consent, I introduced myself to each person I was meeting for the first time as a visiting researcher working on understanding innovation as viewed and practiced by social entrepreneurs.

A social entrepreneur's typical day at this in-residence programme includes eight hours of classroom work led by presenters from business, academia and successful social enterprises. This is followed by two to three hours of evening work in which social entrepreneurs work together and with their mentors to develop organisational plans, business models, presentations and tactical plans. The programme culminated in all-day business plan presentations on 23 August, which were attended by hundreds of Silicon Valley notables.

I not only attended all of the working sessions, but also stayed with the cohort twenty-four hours a day over two weeks, as we were accommodated and provided with meals in the conference rooms. This privileged opportunity allowed me to observe and converse with the cohort both inside workshop activities and outside during leisure time. My main sources of information were observed conversations and face-to-face interviews. Seeing how the participants progressed through the activities and exercises of the boot camp provided an additional source of data and insights. My understanding of innovation was broadened as a result of the discovery process, through this mostly observatory and partly participatory experience.

The cohort was made up of ten women and ten men, operating in sixteen countries. Eight worked in sustainability (clean energy and environment), four in the area of economic development (agriculture, artisan products, culture, tourism and financial services), three on issues concerning infrastructure (ICT, technical assistance services, supply chain services and facilities development) and five in health and human needs (water, public health, education and housing development). Several other social entrepreneurs participated as workshop presenters or mentors. I was able to interview some of these.

In addition to field notes from my observations, I accumulated fifty interviews, which ranged from sporadic, brief interactions and conversations to in-depth interview sessions that lasted over an hour. The respondents were drawn from four categories: entrepreneurs, organisers or faculty members, mentors and investors. Several mentors were in fact investors, so I was not sure which category to place them in. I chose 'mentor' since that was the explicit role the programme organisers gave them, although they were 'on the lookout' for investment. I interviewed thirty-nine people and interacted with another eleven. Please see Table C.4 for a summary breakdown. Table C.7 provides a more detailed list of informants.

While interviews were one-on-one conversations with me, the researcher, interactions involved observations and listening in on conversations and discussions among participants on themes related to the research study. Although participants were not directly answering my questions, they were nevertheless answering them and I was listening, for which reason I considered them informants, for the sake of analysis.

To begin a conversation, I asked all fifty respondents four main questions extracted from the original interview guide that could be ideally asked and answered during coffee breaks, networking sessions

Table C.7 Respondent profiles for Phase 3 (all from site A)

	Code	Type	Solution	Sector	Engagement
1	22E	Entrep	Water filters	Water	Interview
2	35E	Entrep	School lighting	Education	Interview
3	51E	Entrep	Radio media	Education	Interaction and interview
4	13E	Entrep	Farm fertilisers	Agriculture	Interview
5	45E	Entrep	Agricultural insurance	Agriculture	Interview
6	7E	Entrep	Health clinics	Healthcare	Interaction
7	44E	Entrep	Eye hospital	Healthcare	Interview
8	14E	Entrep	Sanitary pads	Healthcare	Interview
9	11E	Entrep	Sanitary pads	Healthcare	Interview
10	3E	Entrep	Wheelchairs	Healthcare	Interaction
11	31E	Entrep	Solar lights	Energy	Interview
12	30E	Entrep	Organic fuel	Energy	Interaction
13	28E	Entrep	Solar lights	Energy	Interview
14	25E	Entrep	Solar lights	Energy	Interview
15	23E	Entrep	Solar lights	Energy	Interview
16	4E	Entrep	Rice husk power	Energy	Interview
17	46E	Entrep	Cookstoves	Energy	Interview
18	5E	Entrep	Solar lights	Energy	Interaction
19	43F	Entrep	Mobile charging	Economic Development	Interview
20	42E	Entrep	Micro-credit checks	Economic Development	Interaction

Table C.7 (cont.)

	Code	Type	Solution	Sector	Engagement
21	38F	Entrep	Mobile finance	Economic Development	Interview
22	6E	Entrep	Distribution network	Economic Development	Interaction
23	9I	Investor	N.A.		Interaction
24	50I	Investor	N.A.		Interview
25	48I	Investor	N.A.		Interaction
26	47I	Investor	N.A.		Interaction
27	27I	Investor	N.A.		Interview
28	17I	Investor	N.A.		Interview
29	10I	Investor	N.A.		Interview
30	49M	Mntr	N.A.		Interview
31	41M	Mntr	N.A.		Interaction and interview
32	37F	Mntr	N.A.		Interview
33	36M	Mntr	N.A.		Interview
34	33M	Mntr	N.A.		Interaction and interview
35	32M	Mntr	N.A.		Interview
36	2M	Mntr	N.A.		Interview
37	26M	Mntr	N.A.		Interaction
38	24M	Mntr	N.A.		Interview
39	19M	Mntr	N.A.		Interview
40	18M	Mntr	N.A.		Interview

41	8F	Organiser N.A.	Interview
42	53F	Organiser N.A.	Interaction and interview
43	34F	Organiser N.A.	Interview
44	29F	Organiser N.A.	Interview
45	21F	Organiser N.A.	Interaction and interview
46	20F	Organiser N.A.	Interview
47	1F	Organiser N.A.	Interview
48	16I	Organiser N.A.	Interaction
49	15F	Organiser N.A.	Interview
50	12F	Organiser N.A.	Interview

*E: Social Entrepreneur; F: Faculty or Staff Organiser; M: Mentor; I: Investor.

and walks between conference centre lodges. Depending on the availability of the respondent and his or her willingness to speak about a topic, I conducted further lengthy interview protocol-guided interviews. The starting interview questions were:

1. *In what way have you come across innovation?*
2. *What is your perception of it? Can you provide examples?*
3. *How could it be useful to you or others?*
4. *What lessons have you learned?*

Even though I, as the lead researcher, had been introduced by the GSBI organisers as a visiting researcher there to observe, interact and have discussions with the participants for this research study, I reintroduced myself to each person I met as 'a visiting researcher here to observe the GSBI workshop activities for my PhD research'. I then asked my four questions, more or less in the sequence above. If the narratives lasted for a long time, I explicitly asked if I could audio-record the conversation for research purposes. In this way, a few detailed conversations were audio-recorded, although most were not. In every case, I wrote out detailed notes and compared them with the actual transcripts (where available) for the sake of reflexivity. In qualitative research, one depends 'on one's interpretative resources to make sense of what the person is saying, but at the same time one is constantly checking one's own sense-making against what the person actually said' (Smith, Osborn and Smith, 2003, p. 72).

Most of these interviews were not audio-recorded because they were 'convenient' interviews carried out during breaks, sessions or group work. Getting formal consent for audio-recording during social breaks would have been considered somewhat rude and might also have made participants self-conscious and unable to share frank and impromptu insights immediately relevant to the context of the gathering. Detailed notes were quickly written down within an hour or so of the discussion for all one-on-one discussions, lectures and other observations. In all, 242 passages totalling 9,000 words were extracted for thematic analysis from the handwritten notes taken during this phase alone.

C.5 DATA ANALYSIS

Content analysis provides an objective assessment of written materials and can extract meaning from textual data. Thematic analysis is a type of content analysis that involves the identification of themes or major ideas in any set of textual documents. Template analysis, in particular, is a type of thematic analysis that follows an iterative approach to highlight themes and their associated patterns through the continuous development of a template.

In developing the category scheme, on the one hand, the criterion of reliability induces analysts to derive standard categories from theory that can be repeatedly used. On the other hand, the criterion of validity calls for analysts to inductively develop original categories that stem from the phenomenon (Druckman and Hopmann, 2002; Golafshani, 2003; Srnka and Koeszegi, 2007;). While some methods call for analysis to begin without any notions of a priori codes or areas of interest, this is seldom easy.

Researchers often review existing literature and then consciously choose to ignore it in the interest of developing purely grounded theory (Glaser and Strauss, 1967). For instance, Jay Weerawardena and Gillian Sullivan Mort (2006, p. 25) write, 'Having reviewed the literature and found it to be theoretically inadequate, I followed the recommendation of Stern (1994). I put the literature aside and turned to the field to focus on the phenomenon of social entrepreneurship to inductively derive a theoretical model from the phenomenon.' I personally find this conscious decision to 'put the literature aside' rather difficult in practice. As part of the process of reflexivity, I discovered that it was hard to adhere to, given my extensive reading of topic-related literature and various informal discussions before and during the selection of this project.

So, although I was motivated by inductive reasoning, 'in which you would collect data and develop theory as a result of your data analysis' (Saunders et al., 2007, p. 117), I opted for retroductive or abductive reasoning and coding (Ragin, 1994) and template analysis

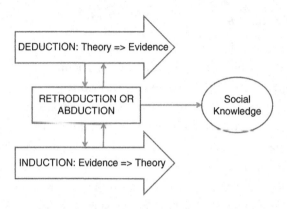

FIGURE C.2 Retroduction as an iterative combination of induction and deduction (adapted from Ragin and Amoroso, 2010, p. 60)

(King, 2004a; 2004b). In retroduction, as depicted in Figure C.2, I used an inductive–deductive procedure because it combined the advantages of achieving both reliability and validity. The different phases of this research design iteratively employed a back-and-forth process, using theory and inductive analysis to allow for a newly constructed or an extended theory. I began with categories identified from both literatures, as well as an initial data analysis, and iteratively adapted them to better address the research problem and match the themes gathered from the data. This approach acknowledges that prior knowledge of the theory partly determines what one looks for and appropriate rules are specified for data analysis.

An initial conceptual framework is developed after reviewing secondary literature and popular secondary cases. The conceptual framework helps to define the terms in relation to what we expect from the data. This conceptual framework is 'emergent' and is informed by each subsequent source of data. The data analysis follows an iterative process in which we move back and forth between an emerging thematic understanding of the data and the existing literature (Miles and Huberman, 1994). The accuracy of any method depends on analysing appropriate data that are representative of what is being researched and steps undertaken to prevent inaccurate or biased results. Eventually, this must be revisited iteratively, in light of the qualitative data, to develop models of innovation as perceived by social entrepreneurs. It is expected that this will evolve into a theoretical framework grounded in data, which future studies can set up in a way that is testable.

For analysis, Nigel King's (2004a; 2004b) template analysis acknowledges the awareness of a priori themes, in particular, as generated from a sample or subset of the data. These themes are construed as strongly relevant to the analysis, although they may be modified or dispensed should they prove not be useful or appropriate to the actual data examined (King, 2004a). This initial template is then applied to the whole data set and segments of data that appear to be of relevance to the research question(s) are highlighted and coded where they correspond to the a priori themes in the template. If a new theme is encountered, the initial template is revised in light of the new category. Once a final version of the template is defined and all transcripts have been coded to it, the template serves as a basis for the researcher's interpretation and illumination of the data set (King, 2004a).

C.5.1 Data Presentation

Although this has been covered in Chapters 2 and 3, I elaborate here how the raw data was analysed and the thematic codes were generated. The unit of analysis for research question 1 is the innovation concept; for questions 2 and 3, it is the value chain. The units of measurement are themes or ideas, regardless of phrases, sentences or words. These are extracted from archival textual documents, primary interviews and observation field notes. As explained earlier, data is analysed to identify thematic codes, as exemplified by supporting data extracts. For research question 1, I came up with twenty-five first-order codes and eight second-order codes; for research questions 2 and 3, I came up with thirty-two first-order and nine second-order codes.

The steps involved in the data coding were as follows. First, I categorised data snippets into several first-order codes. Second, I identified patterns and connections among the first-order codes to find common aspects that explained the variation and similarities across second-order codes. In the third and final stage of coding, I aggregated second-order codes into third-level abstractions that were reflected in the current theoretical literature. The steps in data presentation usually involve outlining first-order codes and then second-order codes, each supported by quotations from data snippets. However, in some instances, it made more sense to outline and describe the evidence around second-order codes and then first-order codes, following this with a discussion of third-level theoretical abstractions. Embedded within the empirical chapters are various tables that outline raw data to support the first-, second- and third-level codes and a breakdown of the number of passages that fall into the three levels of abstraction.

It may be noted that the categorisation structure presented does not comply with the MECE principle – i.e. mutually exclusive and collectively exhaustive. The categorisation of clauses is neither mutually exclusive (some clauses address more than one construct) nor collectively exhaustive (some clauses address no constructs; there may be important constructs not reflected in the clauses collated from data). Although MECE would present an optimum arrangement of information to be exhaustive and would not double count at any level of the hierarchy, it was not possible to adhere to it, since textual snippets often addressed multiple interrelated constructs. However these overlaps turned out to be useful, as they provided a way to cross-link themes that, in turn, helped to develop the models of innovation.

C.5.2 Validity and Reliability

Of the twelve strategies suggested by R. Burke Johnson (1997) to promote qualitative research validity (descriptive, interpretive and theoretical) and reliability, I use the following four strategies:

1. *Extended fieldwork:* The researcher should have adequate time to become thoroughly familiar with the context under scrutiny; likewise, the participants should become accustomed to having the researcher around (Mays and Pope, 1995). In quantitative research, credibility depends on instrument construction; while in qualitative research, the researcher is the instrument of both data collection and data interpretation, and because a qualitative strategy includes having personal contact with and getting close to the people and situation under study (Patton, 2015). For this reason, the two field trips made to the GSBI over two years were useful in gaining mutual familiarity and increasing trust. The first trip helped to gather interviews and archival documents but was conducted outside the time frame of the boot camp. The goal of the second trip was to observe and carry out interviews during the very intense boot camp. The first trip was particularly beneficial in gaining largely unrestricted access from the GSBI organisers and permission to meet with and approach not only organisers but all participating social entrepreneurs, mentors, investors and tutors.

2. *Data Triangulation:* Triangulation is defined as 'a validity procedure where researchers search for convergence among multiple and different sources of information to form themes or categories in a study' (Creswell and Miller, 2000, p. 126). I use the convergence of multiple types of data from within the main GSBI community and follow this up with a test of data convergence from other sites (Denzin, 1978). This triangulation technique allows me to cross-check and corroborate interpretations through multiple data sources. In my empirical chapters, I present data from the document analysis and interviews, both of which support the models presented.

3. *Peer Review:* The intent here is to have my own interpretations and conclusions reviewed by disinterested and therefore unbiased researchers who are not directly involved with the research (Barbour, 2001). The role of such peers is to be sceptical and to challenge me to validate findings through evidence from the raw data and trail of analytical procedures. I accomplished this by having my PhD supervisors go through the data, as well as by presenting the findings at several international and local conferences, such as the Academy of Management in Boston (2012), the Trans-Atlantic Doctoral Conference at the London Business School (2012) and the West Coast Research Symposium at the University of Southern California (2012).

4. *Reflexivity:* This is the researcher's process of continual self-awareness and critical self-reflection throughout the study. The intent is to avoid potential biases and predispositions, which may affect the research process and findings. I made myself aware of these in part through repeated supervisory meetings, peer reviews and conference presentations, as outlined above.

C.5.3 Generalisability Test

I acknowledge that qualitative studies do not aim to infer or generalise findings from a sample to a population. Generalisability in the statistical sense is neither the goal of this study nor even possible in the quantitative sense, since sampling is not randomised. However, generalisability is often a part of enhancing the theoretical validity of research findings (Johnson, 1997). As per Johnson, I argue that a rough generalisation to similar settings, people and time can be attempted. This process of generalising based on similarity is called naturalistic generalisation (Stake, 1990) and replication logic (Yin, 1994). For instance, experimental researchers without random samples use replication logic to generalise beyond the contexts of their own studies.

I attempted to investigate whether the findings from the GSBI might also apply to the DEA Stanford community, which is contextually similar in nature. Since the DEA-Stanford cohort fit into the same quadrant of contextual characteristics as the GSBI cohort (Figure C.1), the findings from the GSBI can be corroborated and partially generalised to other social entrepreneurs within the same quadrant. I made use of the rich narratives in eleven interviews from the DEA-Stanford to corroborate results and attain some degree of generalisability, albeit limited to the purposive sampling quadrant of those social entrepreneurs who are globally networked and formally recognised.

I believe that this process can be an exercise in corroboration, verification and limited generalisability for qualitative research. I would like to clarify, however, that the intent is not to generalise the coding scheme and models of innovation derived from the GSBI to all social entrepreneurs, but to suggest that the same themes might be found in samples that are very similar to the original sample (replication logic). This generalisability test has lent support to similar findings between the GSBI and DEA. Details supporting this have been left out here due to space limitations and have been reserved for possible future publication.

C.6 SUMMARY

As commonly practised in qualitative research, this study pursued a general analytic approach that analysed evidence to generate codes often based on the natural language of the interviewee or document. The codes were amalgamated, based on similarities and relevance, to develop sub-themes and then a progressively smaller number of overall themes. The empirical chapters report on these codes and themes in depth, along with the supporting data. The themes helped to generate theoretically linked dimensions and propositions. Finally, the themes, dimensions and propositions were integrated into coherent models of innovation, as perceived by social entrepreneurs. In the integrative chapter, I returned to the literature to compare the models with existing knowledge and to cases beyond those that were used empirically to develop the insights in this work. This practice conforms to the widely acclaimed guidelines of Kathleen M. Eisenhardt (1989) on relating emergent theory to extant literature to improve internal validity and generalisability at the theoretical level. We hope this appendix has exhibited the rigour with which the research that underpins this book was carried out. We also hope that it serves as a resource for colleagues to help extend this work in other directions and contexts.

To continue the discussion and for online resources, visit our book blog:
www.frugal-innovation.com

References

Abbott, A. (1988). *The system of professions: An essay in the division of expert labor.* Chicago: University of Chicago Press.

Abernathy, W. J. and Clark, K. B. (1985). Innovation: Mapping the winds of creative destruction. *Research Policy*, **14**(1): 3–22.

Abernathy, W. J. and Utterback, J. M. (1978). Patterns of industrial innovation. *Technology Review*, **80**(7): 40–47.

Abrahamson, E. (1991). Managerial fads and fashions: The diffusion and rejection of innovations. *The Academy of Management Review*, **16**(3): 586–612.

Aderhold, J. (2005). Gesellschaftsentwicklung am Tropf technischer Neuerungen. In J. Aderhold and R. John, eds., *Innovation. Sozialwissenschaftliche Perspektiven*, Constance: UVK.

Agarwal, B. (1983). Diffusion of rural innovations: Some analytical issues and the case of wood-burning stoves. *World Development*, **11**(4): 359–376.

Agarwal, N., Grottke, M., Mishra, S. and Brem, A. (2017). A systematic literature review of constraint-based innovations: State of the art and future perspectives. *IEEE Transactions on Engineering Management*, **64**(1): 3–15.

Agarwal, R., Echambadi, R. and Sarkar, M. (2002). The conditioning effect of time on firm survival: An industry life-cycle approach. *Academy of Management Journal*, **45**(5): 971–994.

Ahlstrom, D. (2010). Innovation and growth: How business contributes to society. *Academy of Management Perspectives*, **24**(3): 10–23.

Ahlstrom, D., Chen, S. J. and Yeh, K. S. (2010). Managing in ethnic Chinese communities: Culture, institutions and context. *Asia Pacific Journal of Management*, **27**(3): 341–354.

Ahlstrom, D., Dacin, M. T., Hitt, M. A., Levitas, E. and Svobodina, L. (2004). The institutional effects on strategic alliance partner selection in transition economies: China vs. Russia. *Organization Science*, **15**(2): 173–185.

Ajadi, S. and Bayen, M. (2017). *Building synergies: How mobile operators and start-ups can partner for impact in emerging markets.* London: GSMA. Available at: www.gsma.com/mobilefordevelopment/wp-content/uploads/2017/01/Building-Synergies_How-Mobile-Operators-and-Start-ups-Can-Partner-for-Impact-in-Emerging-Markets.pdf (last accessed 25 February 2018).

Aldrich, H. E. (1999; 2003). *Organizations evolving.* Thousand Oaks: Sage Publications.

Aldrich, H. E. and Fiol, M. (1994). Fools rush in? The institutional context of industry creation. *Academy of Management Review*, **19**(4): 645–670.

Altamirano, M. A. and van Beers, C. P. (2018). Frugal innovations in technological and institutional infrastructure: Impact of mobile phone technology on productivity, public service provision and inclusiveness. *The European Journal of Development Research*, 30(1): 84–107.

Altenburg, T. (2009). Building inclusive innovation systems in developing countries: Challenges for IS research. In C. Chaminade, K. Joseph, B. Lundvall and J. Vang, eds., *Handbook of innovation systems and developing countries.* Cheltenham: Edward Elgar, pp. 33–56.

Alvord, S. H., Brown, L. D. and Letts, C. W. (2004). Social entrepreneurship and societal transformation. *Journal of Applied Behavioral Science*, **40**(3): 260–282.

Amabile, T. M. (1988). A model of creativity and innovation in organizations. *Research in Organizational Behavior*, **10**(1): 123–167.

(1996). *Creativity in context.* Boulder: Westview Press.

Amit, R., Glosten, L. and Muller, E. (1990). Entrepreneurial ability, venture investments and risk sharing. *Management Science*, **36**(10): 1233–1246.

Anand, G. (2009). The Henry Ford of heart surgery. *The Wall Street Journal*, 25 November. Available at: http://online.wsj.com/news/articles/SB1258758928 87958111 (last accessed 15 January 2017).

Anderson, P. and Tushman, M. L. (1986). Technological discontinuities and organizational environments. *Administrative Science Quarterly*, 31(3): 439–465.

Anderson, R. (2007). *Thematic Content Analysis (TCA). Descriptive presentation of qualitative data.* Available at: http://rosemarieanderson.com/wp-content/uploads/2014/08/ThematicContentAnalysis.pdf (last accessed 8 December 2011).

Annala, L., Sarin, A. and Green, J. L. (2016). Co-production of frugal innovation: Case of low cost reverse osmosis water filters in India. *Journal of Cleaner Production*, 171(Supplement).

Antal, A. B. (2006). Reflections on the need for 'between times' and 'between places'. *Journal of Management Inquiry*, **15**(2): 154–166.

Aram, J. D., Lynn, L. H. and Mohan Reddy, N. (1996). Linking technology and institutions: The innovation community framework. *Research Policy*, **25**(1): 91–106.

Aravind Eye Care System. (2011). Available at: www.aravind.org (last accessed 15 January 2017).

Arend, R. J. (2013). A heart-mind-opportunity nexus: Distinguishing social entrepreneurship for entrepreneurs. *Academy of Management Review*, **38**(2): 313–315.

Arikan, A. M. and Barney, J. B. (2001). The resource-based view: Origins and implications. In M. A. Hitt, R. E. Freeman and J. S. Harrison, eds., *The Blackwell handbook of strategic management*. Oxford: Blackwell, pp. 124–188.

Armstrong, E. A. (2002). *Forging gay identities: Organizing sexuality in San Francisco, 1950–1994*. Chicago: University of Chicago Press.

Arrow, K. J. (1962). Economic welfare and the allocation of resources for invention. In R. Nelson, ed., *The rate and direction of inventive activity*. Princeton: Princeton University Press.

Artz, K. W. and Brush, T. H. (1999). Toward a contingent resource-based theory: The impact of information asymmetry on the value of capabilities in veterinary medicine. *Strategic Management Journal*, **20**(3): 223–250.

Astley, W. G. (1985). The two ecologies: Population and community perspectives on organizational evolution. *Administrative Science Quarterly*, **30**(2): 224–241.

Athreye, S. and Kapur, S. (2009). Introduction: The internationalization of Chinese and Indian firms – Trends, motivations and strategy. *Industrial and Corporate Change*, **18**(2): 209–221.

Austin, J. E. (2000). *The collaboration challenge: How nonprofits and business succeed through strategic alliances*. San Francisco: Jossey Bass Publishers.

Austin, J. E., Stevenson, H. and Wei Skillern, J. (2006). Social and commercial entrepreneurship: Same, different, or both? *Entrepreneurship Theory and Practice*, **30**(1): 1–22.

Bailey, B. P. and Horvitz, E. (2010). What's your idea? A case study of a grassroots innovation pipeline within a large software company. Proceedings of the SIGCHI Conference on Human Factors in Computing Systems. ACM, pp. 2065–2074.

Baker, T., Miner, A. S. and Eesley, D. T. (2003). Improvising firms: Bricolage, account giving and improvisational competencies in the founding process. *Research Policy*, **32**(2): 255–276.

Baker, T. and Nelson, R. E. (2005). Creating something from nothing: Resource construction through entrepreneurial bricolage. *Administrative Science Quarterly*, **50**(3): 329–366.

Bamford, C. E., Marsden, J. W. and West, G. P. (2008). Contrasting entrepreneurial economic development in emerging Latin American economies: Applications and extensions of resource-based theory. *Entrepreneurship Theory and Practice*, **32**(1): 15–36.

Barbour, R. S. (2001). Checklists for improving rigour in qualitative research: A case of the tail wagging the dog? *British Medical Journal*, 322(7294): 1115.

Barley, S. R. and Tolbert, P. S. (1997). Institutionalization and structuration: Studying the links between action and institution. *Organization Studies*, 18(1): 93–117.

Barlow, J. (2016). *Managing Innovation in Healthcare*. London: World Scientific Publishing Company.

Barney, J. B. (1991). Firm resources and sustained competitive advantage. *Journal of Management*, 17(1): 99–120.

Barré, R. (2001). The Agora model of innovation systems: S and T indicators for a democratic knowledge society. *Research Evolution*, 10(1): 13–18.

Basu, R. R., Banerjee, P. M. and Sweeny, E. G. (2013). Frugal innovation: Core competencies to address global sustainability. *Journal of Management for Global Sustainability*, 1(2): 63–82.

Bates, S. M. (2011). *The social innovation imperative: Create winning products, services and programs that solve society's most pressing challenges.* New York: McGraw-Hill Education.

Baud, I. (2016). Moving towards inclusive development? Recent views on inequalities, frugal innovations, urban geo-technologies, gender and hybrid governance. *The European Journal of Development Research*, 28(2): 119–129.

Baumol, W. J. (1990). Entrepreneurship: Productive, unproductive and destructive. *Journal of Political Economy*, 98(5): 893–921.

(2002). *The free-market innovation machine: Analysing the growth miracle of capitalism*. Princeton, NJ: Princeton University Press.

Bayliss, D. (2004). Ireland's creative development: Local authority strategies for culture-led development. *Regional Studies*, 38(7): 817.

Beard, D. W. and Dess, G. G. (1984). Dimensions of organizational task environments. *Administrative Science Quarterly*, 29(1): 52–73.

Begley, T. M., Khatri, N. and Tsang, E. W. K. (2010). Networks and cronyism: A social exchange analysis. *Asia Pacific Journal of Management*, 27(2): 279–295.

Bhandari, B. (2009). Frugal innovation. *Business Standard Magazine*. Available at: www.business-standard.com/india/news/frugal-innovation/360886/ (last accessed 15 January 2017).

Bhatti, Y. A. (2012). What is frugal, what is innovation? Towards a theory of frugal innovation. Academy of Management Annual Meeting, 3–7 August 2012, Boston. *Academy of Management Proceedings*, 2012:1 10794; Available from: http://dx.doi.org/10.2139/ssrn.2005910 (last accessed 10 December 2017).

(2013a). Review of *Reverse Innovation* by Govindarajan and Trimble (2012). *South Asian Journal of Global Business Research*, 1.

(2013b). *Jugaad* innovation: Think frugal, be flexible, generate breakthrough growth (2012). *South Asian Journal of Global Business Research*, **2**(2): 279–282.

(2014). Frugal innovation: Social entrepreneurs' perceptions of innovation under institutional voids, resource scarcity and affordability constraints. DPhil dissertation. Oxford University.

Bhatti, Y. and Prabhu, J. (2018). Frugal innovation and social innovation: Linked paths to achieving inclusion sustainably. In G. George, T. Baker, P. Tracey and H. Joshi, eds., *Handbook of inclusive innovation: The role of organizations, markets and communities in social innovation*. Cheltenham: Edward Elgar.

Bhatti, Y., Prime, M., Harris, M. et al. (2017a). The search for the holy grail: Frugal innovation in healthcare from developing countries for reverse innovation to developed countries. *BMJ Innovations*, **3**(4): 212–220.

Bhatti, Y., Taylor, A., Harris, M., et al. (2017b). Global lessons in frugal innovation to improve healthcare delivery in the United States. *Health Affairs*, **36**(11): 1912–1919.

Bhatti, Y., Khilji, S. and Basu, R., (2013). Frugal innovation. In S. Khilji and C. Rowley, eds., *Globalization, change and learning in South Asia*. Oxford: Chandos Publishing, pp. 123–146.

Bhatti, Y. and Ventresca, M. (2012). The emerging market for frugal innovation: Fad, fashion, or fit? *SSRN working paper*: http://ssrn.com/abstract=2005983.

(2013). How can 'frugal innovation' be conceptualized? *SSRN working paper*: http://ssrn.com/abstract=2203552.

Bhutto, B. and Vyas, V. (2017). Frugal innovation in emerging markets. *ISPIM Innovation Summit*, 10–13 December, Melbourne, Australia.

Bloodgood, J. M. (2000). Understanding a firm's culture before changing the business planning process. *Strategic Change*, **9**(4): 237–247.

Boeker, W. (1989). Strategic change: The effects of founding and history. *Academy of Management Journal*, **32**(3): 489–515.

Boland, R. J. and Collopy, F., eds. (2004). *Managing as designing*. Stanford: Stanford University Press.

Bold, C. (2011). *Branchless banking in Pakistan: A laboratory for innovation*. Available at: www.cgap.org (last accessed 15 January 2017).

Borins, S. (2000). Loose cannons and rule breakers, or enterprising leaders? Some evidence about innovative public managers. *Public Administration Review*, **60**(6): 498–507.

Boronat-Navarro, M., Camison-Zornoza, C., Lapiedra-Alcami, R. and Segarra-Cipres, M. (2004). A meta-analysis of innovation and organizational size. *Organization Studies*, **25**(3): 331–361.

Bornstein, D. (2004). *How to change the world: Social entrepreneurs and the power of new ideas*. Oxford: Oxford University Press.

Bornstein, D. and Davis, S. (2010). *Social entrepreneurship: What everyone needs to know*. Oxford: Oxford University Press.

Bosk, C. L. and Hilgartner, S. (1988). The rise and fall of social problems: A public arenas model. *American Journal of Sociology*, **94**: 53–78.

Bosma, N., Justo, R., Lepoutre, J. and Terjesen, S. (2013). Designing a global standardized methodology for measuring social entrepreneurship activity: The Global Entrepreneurship Monitor social entrepreneurship study. *Small Business Economics*, **40**(3): 693–714.

Bound, K. and Thornton, I. (2012). *Our frugal future: Lessons from India's innovation system*. London: NESTA.

Bower, J. L. and Christensen, C. M. (1995). Disruptive technologies: Catching the wave. *Harvard Business Review*, **73**(1): 43–53.

Boyatzis, R. E. (1998). *Transforming qualitative information: Thematic analysis and code development*. London: Sage.

Braun, V. and Clarke, V. (2006). Using thematic analysis in psychology. *Qualitative Research in Psychology*, 3(2): 77–101.

Braund, P. and Schwittay, A. (2006). The missing piece: Human-driven design and research in ICT and development. Paper presented at the *International Conference on Information and Communication Technologies for Development*, Berkeley, CA.

Brem, A. and Ivens, B. (2013). Do frugal and reverse innovation foster sustainability? Introduction of a conceptual framework. *Journal of Technology Management for Growing Economies*, 4(2): 31–50.

Brinckerhoff, P. (2000). *Social entrepreneurship: The art of mission-based venture development*. New York: John Wiley and Sons.

Brooks, A. (2008). *Social entrepreneurship*. Upper Saddle River: Pearson Prentice Hall.

Brown, T. (2008). Design thinking. *Harvard Business Review*, June, 85–92.

Brown, T. and Wyatt, J. (2010). Design thinking for social innovation. *Stanford Social Innovation Review*, 8(1), Winter: 30–35.

Bruland, K. and Mowery, D. C. (2005). Innovation through time. In J. Fagerberg, D. C. Mowery and R. E. Nelson, eds., *The Oxford handbook of innovation*. Oxford: Oxford University Press.

Bryman, A. and Bell, E. (2003). *Business research methods*. Oxford: Oxford University Press.

Burg, E., Podoynitsyna, K., Beck, L. and Lommelen, T. (2012). Directive deficiencies: How resource constraints direct opportunity identification in SMEs. *Journal of Product Innovation Management*, **29**(6): 1000–1011.

Butkevičiene, E. (2008). Social innovations in rural communities: Methodological framework and empirical evidence. *Social networks*. Available at: https://pdfs

.semanticscholar.org/68f7/584f42fa804ea759f4946bbabb8b38483705.pdf (last accessed 17 January 2017).

Cameron, H. (2011). Social entrepreneurs in the social innovation ecosystem. In A. Nicholls and A. Murdock, eds., *Social innovation: Blurring boundaries to reconfigure markets*. London: Palgrave Macmillan UK, pp. 199–220.

Campbell, J. L. (2004). *Institutional change and globalization*. Princeton: Princeton University Press.

Cappelli, P., Singh, H., Singh, J. and Useem, M. (2010). The India way: Lessons for the U.S. *Academy of Management Perspectives*, **24**(2): 6–24.

Caradonna, T. and Koch, J. (2006). Technologies and business models that work in developing countries. Paper presented at the *International Conference on Information and Communication Technologies for Development*, Berkeley, CA.

Carsrud, A. L., Meyskens, M., Reynolds, P. D., Robb-Post, C. and Stamp, J. A. (2010). Social ventures from a resource-based perspective: An exploratory study assessing global Ashoka Fellows. *Entrepreneurship Theory and Practice*, **34**(4): 661–680.

Carter, S. and Shaw, E. (2007). Social entrepreneurship: Theoretical antecedents and empirical analysis of entrepreneurial processes and outcomes. *Journal of Small Business and Enterprise Development*, **14**(3): 418–434.

Caulier-Grice, J., Davies, A., Patrick, R. and Norman, W. (2012). *Defining social innovation, social innovation overview: A deliverable of the project: The theoretical, empirical and policy foundations for building social innovation in Europe (TEPSIE)*, Vol. 7. Brussels: European Commission.

Cavalli, N. (2007). The symbolic dimension of innovation processes. *American Behavioral Scientist*, **50**(7): 958–969.

Chand, T. J., Chandan, M., Gupta, A. R., James, A., Koradia, R., Parmar, P., Patel, K., Patel, M., Patel, T. N., Patel, V. S., Prakash, P., Rohit, H., Sinha, D., Vivekanandan and other members of the Honey Bee Network (2003). Mobilizing grassroots' technological innovations and traditional knowledge, values and institutions: Articulating social and ethical capital. *Futures*, **35**(9): 975–987.

Chandy, R. and Prabhu, J. (2011). Innovation typologies. In Barry Bayus, ed., *Wiley International Encyclopedia of Marketing*. Hoboken, NJ: John Wiley and Sons.

Chao, E. (1999). The Maoist shaman and the madman: Ritual bricolage, failed ritual and failed ritual theory. *Cultural Anthropology*, **14**(4): 505–534.

Chen, M. J. and Miller, D. (2010). West meets East: Toward an ambicultural approach to management. *Academy of Management Perspectives*, **24**(4): 17–24.

Child, J. and Lu, Y. (1996). Institutional constraints on economic reform: The case of investment decisions in China. *Organization Science*, **7**: 60–67.

Christensen, C. M. (1997). *The innovator's dilemma: When new technologies cause great firms to fail.* Boston: Harvard Business School Press.

Christensen, C. M., Baumann, H., Ruggles, R. and Sadtler, T. M. (2006). Disruptive innovation for social change. *Harvard Business Review,* 84(12): 94.

Christensen, C. M. and Hart, S. L. (2002). The great leap: Driving innovation from the base of the pyramid. *Sloan Management Review,* 44(1): 51–56.

Chu, M. and Barley, L. (2013). Omidyar Network: Pioneering impact investment. *Harvard Business School Case,* 313–390.

Clark, K. B. and Henderson, R. M. (1990). Architectural innovation: The reconfiguration of existing product technologies and the failure of established firms. *Administrative Science Quarterly,* 35(1).

Clarke, V. (2005). We're all very liberal in our views: Students' talk about lesbian and gay parenting. *Lesbian and Gay Psychology Review,* 6(2): 15.

Clemens, E. S. (1997). *The people's lobby: Organizational innovation and the rise of interest group politics in the United States, 1890–1925.* Chicago: University of Chicago Press.

Cobb, J. A. and Davis, G. F. (2010). Resource dependence theory: Past and future. *Research in the Sociology of Organizations,* 28: 21–42.

Cohen, L. and Manion, L. (1980; 1994). *Research methods in education,* 2nd edn. Dover: Croom Helm; revised 4th edn., London: Routledge.

Collier, P. (2007). *The bottom billion: Why the poorest countries are failing and what can be done about it.* Oxford: Oxford University Press.

Collins, B. J., Hillman, A. J. and Withers, M. C. (2009). Resource dependence theory: A review. *Journal of Management,* 35(6): 1404–1427.

Cooperrider, D. I. and Pasmore, W. A. (1991). Global social change: A new agenda for social science? *Human Relations,* 44: 1037–1055.

Corbin, J. M. and Strauss, A. L. (1998). *Basics of qualitative research: Techniques and procedures for developing grounded theory.* Thousand Oaks: Sage Publications.

Corner, P. D. and Ho, M. (2010). How opportunities develop in social entrepreneurship. *Entrepreneurship Theory and Practice,* 34: 635–659.

Cornwell, B. (2007). The Protestant sect credit machine: Social capital and the rise of capitalism. *Journal of Classical Sociology,* 7(3): 267–290.

Cotten, M. N. and Lasprogata, G. A. (2003). Contemplating 'enterprise': The business and legal challenges of social entrepreneurship. *American Business Law Journal,* 41: 567–595.

Cozzens, S. and Sutz, J. (2012). *Innovation in informal settings: A research agenda.* Ottawa: IDRC.

Crabtree, J. (2012). More with less. *FT.com,* May 19. Available at: www.ft.com/content/d5612fac-960f-11e1-a6a0-00144feab49a (last accessed 23 July 2017).

Creswell, J. W. (1998). *Qualitative inquiry and research design: Choosing among five traditions*. Thousand Oaks: Sage Publications.

(2003). *Research design: Qualitative, quantitative and mixed method approaches*, 2nd edn. Thousand Oaks: Sage Publications.

Creswell, J. W. and Miller, D. L. (2000). Determining validity in qualitative inquiry. *Theory into Practice*, **39**(3): 124–131.

Dacin, M. T., Dacin, P. A. and Matear, M. (2010). Social entrepreneurship: Why we don't need a new theory and how we move forward from here. *Academy of Management Perspectives*, **24**(3): 37–57.

Dahl, D. W. and Moreau, C. P. (2005). Designing the solution: The impact of constraints on consumers' creativity. *Journal of Consumer Research*, **32**(1): 13–22.

Dahlman, C. and Utz, A. (2007). Promoting inclusive innovation in India. In M.A. Dutz, ed., *Unleashing India's innovation: Towards sustainable and inclusive growth*. Washington, DC: World Bank, pp. 105–128.

Daily Nation. (20 October 2011). *M-Pesa transactions surpass Western Union moves across the globe*. Available at: www.nation.co.ke/business/news/-/1006/1258864/-/4hyt6qz/-/index.html (last accessed 15 January 2017).

Damanpour, F. (1991). Organizational innovation: A meta-analysis of effects of determinants and moderators. *Academy of Management Journal*, **34**(3): 555–590.

Dart, R. (2004a). Being 'business-like' in a nonprofit organization: A grounded and inductive typology. *Nonprofit and Voluntary Sector Quarterly*, **33**(2): 290–310.

(2004b). The legitimacy of social enterprise. *Nonprofit Management and Leadership*, **14**: 411–424.

Darzi, A. (2017). The cheap innovations the NHS could take from sub-Saharan Africa *The Guardian*. 27 Oct. Available at: www.theguardian.com/healthcare-network/2017/oct/27/cheap-innovations-nhs-take-sub-saharan-africa (last accessed 2 January 2018).

Dean, T. J. and McMullen, J. S. (2007). Toward a theory of sustainable entrepreneurship: Reducing environmental degradation through entrepreneurial action. *Journal of Business Venturing*, **22**(1): 50–76.

Dedrick, J., Kraemer, K. L. and Linden, G. (2010). Who profits from innovation in global value chains? A study of the iPod and notebook PCs. *Industrial and Corporate Change*, **19**(1): 81–116.

Dees, J. G. (1996). *Social enterprise spectrum: Philanthropy to commerce*. Cambridge, MA: Harvard Business School Press.

(1998). Enterprising nonprofits. *Harvard Business Review*, **76**, Jan–Feb: 55–67.

(2011). Social ventures as learning laboratories. *Tennessee's Business*, **20**(1): 3–5.

Dees, G. and Anderson, B. B. (2006). Framing a theory of social entrepreneurship: Building on two schools of practice and thought. In *Research on social entrepreneurship: Understanding and contributing to an emerging field*. Association for Research on Non-profit Organizations and Voluntary Action (ARNOVA).

Dees, J. G., Emerson, J. and Economy, P. (2001). *Enterprising nonprofits: A toolkit for social entrepreneurs*. New York: John Wiley and Sons.

Defourny, J. and Nyssens, M. (2008). Social enterprise in Europe: Recent trends and developments. *Social Enterprise Journal*, **4**(3): 202–228.

Denrell, J., Fang, C. and Winter, S. G. (2003). The economics of strategic opportunity. *Strategic Management Journal*, **24**(10): 977–990.

Denzin, N. K. (1978). *The research act*, 2nd edn. New York: McGraw-Hill.

Denzin, N. K. and Lincoln, Y. S., eds. (2005). *The Sage handbook of qualitative research*, 3rd edn. Thousand Oaks: Sage Publications, Inc.

DePasse, J. W., Caldwell, A., Santorino, D., Bailey, E., Gudapakkam, S., Bangsberg, D. and Olson, K. R. (2016). Affordable medical technologies: Bringing value-based design into global health. *BMJ Innovations*, **2**(1): 4–7.

Desa, G. (2009a). Mobilizing resources in constrained environments: A study of technology social ventures. Doctoral dissertation, University of Washington.

(2009b). Social entrepreneurship: Snapshots of a research field in emergence. In K. Hockerts, J. Mair and J. Robinson, eds., *Values and opportunities in social entrepreneurship*. New York: Palgrave, pp. 6–30.

(2011). Resource mobilization in international social entrepreneurship: Bricolage as a mechanism of institutional transformation. *Entrepreneurship Theory and Practice*, **36**(4): 727–751.

Desa, G. and Koch, J. L. (2014). Scaling social impact: Building sustainable social ventures at the base-of-the-pyramid. *Journal of Social Entrepreneurship*, **5**(2): 146–174.

Desa, G. and Kotha, S. (2005). Ownership mission and environment: An exploratory analysis into the evolution of a technology social venture. In J. Mair, J. Robinson and K. Hockerts, eds., *Social entrepreneurship*. New York: Palgrave, pp. 155–179.

(2006). Technology social ventures and innovation: Understanding the innovation process at Benetech. In F. Perrini, ed., *The new social entrepreneurship: What awaits social entrepreneurial ventures*. Northampton: Edward Elgar.

Diamandis, P. and Kotler, S. (2012). *Abundance: The future is better than you think*. New York: Free Press.

DiDomenico, M., Haugh, H. and Tracey, P. (2010). Social bricolage: Theorizing social value creation in social enterprises. *Entrepreneurship Theory and Practice*, **34**: 681–703.

DiMaggio, P. J. (1988). Interest and agency in institutional theory. In L. G. Zucker, ed., *Institutional patterns and organizations: Culture and environment.* Cambridge: Ballinger, pp. 3–22.

DiMaggio, P. J. and Powell, W. W. (1983). The iron cage revisited: Institutional isomorphism and collective rationality in organizational fields. *American Sociological Review,* **48**: 147–160.

(1991). Introduction. In W. Powell and P. J. DiMaggio, eds., *The new institutionalism in organizational analysis.* Chicago: University of Chicago Press, pp. 1–38.

Donaldson, T. and Preston, L. E. (1999). Stakeholder management and organizational wealth. *Academy of Management Review,* **24**(4): 619–620.

Dorado, S. (2013). Small groups as context for institutional entrepreneurship: An exploration of the emergence of commercial microfinance in Bolivia. *Organization Studies,* **34**(4): 533–557.

Dorado, S. and Ventresca, M. J. (2013). Crescive entrepreneurship in complex social problems: Institutional conditions for entrepreneurial engagement. *Journal of Business Venturing,* **28**(1): 69–82.

Dosi, G. (1982). Technological paradigms and technological trajectories: A suggested interpretation of the determinants and directions of technical change. *Research Policy,* **11**(3): 147–162.

Douglas, M. (1986). *How institutions think.* London: Routledge.

Drazin, R. and Schoonhoven, C. B. (1996). Community, population and organization effects on innovation: A multilevel perspective. *The Academy of Management Journal* **39**(5): 1065–1083.

Druckman, D. and Hopmann, P. T. (2002). Content analysis. In V. Kremenyuk, ed., *International negotiations: Analysis, approaches.* San Francisco: Jossey Bass.

Dutton, J. E. (1993). Interpretations on automatic: A different view of strategic issue diagnosis. *Journal of Management Studies,* **30**: 339–357.

Dutz, M. A. (2007). *Unleashing India's innovation toward sustainable and inclusive growth.* Washington, DC: World Bank.

Easterly, W. R. (2006). *The white man's burden: Why the West's efforts to aid the rest have done so much ill and so little good.* New York: Penguin Group USA.

Eden, L., Hoskisson, R. E., Lau, C. M. and Wright, M. (2000). Strategy in emerging economies. *The Academy of Management Journal,* **43**(3): 249–267.

Edquist, C., Johnson, B. and Lundvall, B. Å. (2003). Economic development and the national system of innovation approach. *First Globelics Conference,* Rio de Janeiro November 3–6.

Eisenhardt, K. M. (1989). Building theories from case study research. *Academy of Management Review,* **14**: 532–550.

Emerson, J. and Twersky, F., eds. (1996). *New social entrepreneurs: The success, challenge and lessons of non-profit enterprise creation.* San Francisco: The Roberts Foundation.

Ernst and Young. (2011). *Innovating for the next three billion.* London: Ernst and Young.

Espeland, W. N. and Stevens, M. L. (1998). Commensuration as a social process. *Annual Review of Sociology:* 313–343.

Estrin, S., Mickiewicz, T. and Stephan, U. (2011). For benevolence and for self-interest: Social and commercial entrepreneurial activity across nations. *Economics working papers* 115, Centre for Comparative Economics, SSEES, UCL: London.

Etzkowitz, H. and Leydesdorff, L. (2000). The dynamics of innovation: From national systems and 'mode 2' to a triple helix of university-industry-government relations. *Research Policy*, **29**: 109–123.

European Bank for Reconstruction and Development (EBRD) (1998). *Transition report 1998.* London: EBRD.

European Commission. (2009). *Reinvent Europe through innovation: From a knowledge society to an innovation society. Recommendations by a business panel on future EU innovation policy.* Brussels: DG Enterprise and Industry, Special Business Panel. Available at: http://ec.europa.eu/DocsRoom/docu ments/11268/attachments/1/translations/en/renditions/native (last accessed 23 July 2017).

(2017). *Frugal innovation and the re-engineering of traditional techniques.* Brussels: Directorate-General for Research and Innovation, European Commission. Available at: https://publications.europa.eu/en/publication-detail/-/publication/ 20d6095a-2a44-11e7-ab65-01aa75ed71a1 (last accessed 01 August 2017).

Extreme. (2013). *Design for extreme affordability.* Available at: http://extreme .stanford.edu/ (last accessed 15 April 2013).

Fagerberg, J. (2005). Innovation: A guide to the literature. In J. Fagerberg, D. C. Mowery and R. E. Nelson, eds., *The Oxford handbook of innovation.* Oxford: Oxford University Press.

Farjoun, M., Ansell, C., and Boin, A. (2015). Pragmatism in organization studies: Meeting the challenges of a dynamic and complex world. *Organization Science*, 26(6): 1787–1804.

Farooq, R. and Farooq, R. (2017). A conceptual model of frugal innovation: Is environmental munificence a missing link? *International Journal of Innovation Science*, **9**(4), 320–334.

Fligstein, N. (1996). Markets as politics: A political-cultural approach to market institutions. *American Sociological Review*, 61: 656–673.

(1997). Social skills and institutional theory. *American Behavioral Scientist*, **40**: 397–405.

(2001). *The architecture of markets: An economic sociology of twenty-first-century capitalist societies*. Princeton: Princeton University Press.

Freiberg, K., Freiberg, J. and Dunston, D. (2012). *Nanovation: How a little car can teach the world to think big and act bold*. Nashville: Thomas Nelson Inc.

Foster, C. and Heeks, R. (2013). Conceptualising inclusive innovation: Modifying systems of innovation frameworks to understand diffusion of new technology to low-income consumers. *The European Journal of Development Research*, **25**(3): 333–355.

Foster, P. and Malhotra, P. (2008). Ultimate economy drive: The £1,300 car. *Telegraph*. London, 10 January 2008.

Freeman, C. (1995). The 'national system of innovation' in historical perspective. *Cambridge Journal of Economics*, **19**: 5–22.

Gair, C. (2005). *If the shoe fits: Non-profit or for-profit? The choice matters*. San Francisco: Roberts Enterprise Development Fund.

Garud, R. and Karnoe, P. (2003). Bricolage versus breakthrough: Distributed and embedded agency in technology entrepreneurship. *Research Policy*, **32**: 277–300.

Gassmann, O. and von Zedtwitz, M. (2003). Trends and determinants of managing virtual R and D teams. *R and D Management*, **33**(3): 243–262.

Gault, F., Muchie, M., Bell, M., Kahn, M. and Wamae, W. (2012). Building capacity to develop and use science, technology and innovation indicators for grassroots innovation. *African Journal of Science, Technology, Innovation and Development*, **4**(3): 22–31.

George, G. and Bock, A. J. (2011). The business model in practice and its implications for entrepreneurship research. *Entrepreneurship Theory and Practice*, **35**(1): 83–111.

George, G., McGahan, A. M. and Prabhu, J. (2012). Innovation for inclusive growth: Towards a theoretical framework and a research agenda. *Journal of Management Studies*, **49**(4): 661–683.

Gerometta, J., Haussermann, H. and Longo, G. (2005). Social innovation and civil society in urban governance: Strategies for an inclusive city. *Urban Studies*, **42**(11): 2007–2021.

Geroski, P. (2003). *The evolution of new markets*. Oxford: Oxford University Press.

Ghaziani, A. and Ventresca, M. (2005). Keywords and cultural change: Frame analysis of business model public talk, 1975–2000. *Sociological Forum*, **20**(4): 523–559.

Gibbert, M., Hoegl, M. and Mazursky, D. (2008). Financial constraints in innovation projects: When is less more? *Research Policy*, **37**(8): 1382–1391.

Gibbert, M., Hoegl, M. and Välikangas, L. (2007). In praise of resource constraints. *MIT Sloan Management Review*, **48**(3): 15–17.

Gibbons, M., Nowotny, H. and Scott, P. (2001). *Re-thinking science, knowledge and the public in the age of uncertainty*. London: Polity Press.

Giddens, A. (1984). *The constitution of society: Outline of the theory of structuration*. Berkeley: University of California Press.

Gioia, D. A. and Thomas, J. B. (1996). Identity, image, and issue interpretation: Sensemaking during strategic change in academia. *Administrative Science Quarterly*, 41(3): 370–403.

Girling, P., Harrison, R. T. and Mason, C. M. (2004). Financial bootstrapping and venture development in the software industry. *Entrepreneurship and Regional Development*, **16**: 307–333.

Glaser, B. G. and Strauss, A. L. (1967). *The discovery of grounded theory: Strategies for qualitative research*. Piscataway: Aldine Transaction Publishers, Rutgers University.

Godin, S. (1998). *The bootstrapper's bible: How to start and build a business with a great idea and (almost) no money*. Dover: Upstart Publishing.

Goffman, E. (1983). The interaction order: American Sociological Association, 1982 presidential address. *American Sociological Review*, **48**(1): 1–17.

Golafshani, N. (2003). Understanding reliability and validity in qualitative research. *The Qualitative Report*, 8(4): 597–607.

Goldenberg, J., Lehmann, D. R. and Mazursky, D. (2001). The idea itself and the circumstances of its emergence as predictors of new product success. *Management Science*, **47**(1): 69–84.

Goldsmith, S. (2010). *The power of social innovation: How civic entrepreneurs ignite community networks for good*. San Francisco: Jossey-Bass.

Goldstein, E. R. (2011). The anatomy of influence. *The Chronicle of Higher Education*.

Gonzalez, S., Martinelli, F., Moulaert, F. and Swyngedouw, E. (2005). Towards alternative model(s) of local innovation. *Urban Studies*, **42**(11): 1969–1990.

Govindarajan, V. and Ramamurti, R. (2011). Reverse innovation, emerging markets and global strategy. *Global Strategy Journal*, 1(3–4): 191–205.

  (2013). Delivering world-class health care, affordably. *Harvard Business Review*, **91**(11): 117.

Govindarajan, V. and Trimble, C. (2012). *Reverse innovation*. Cambridge: Harvard Business Review Press.

Grant, R. M. (1991). The resource-based theory of competitive advantage: Implications for strategy formulation. *California Management Review*, **33**(3): 114–135.

Green, K. (1992). Creating demand for biotechnology: Shaping technologies and markets. In R. Coombs, P. Saviotti and V. Walsh, eds., *Technological change and company strategies: Economic and sociological perspectives*. San Diego: Harcourt Brace Jovanovich, pp. 164–184.

Greenwood, R., Oliver, C., Sahlin, K. and Suddaby, R., eds. (2008). *Handbook of organizational institutionalism*. Oxford: Oxford University Press.

Grix, J. (2004). *The foundations of research*. New York: Palgrave.

GSBI. (2013). *Global social business incubator*. Available at: www.scu.edu/social benefit/entrepreneurship/gsbi/ (last accessed 15 January 2013).

Guba, E. G. and Lincoln, Y. S. (1994). Competing paradigms in qualitative research. In Norman K. Denzin and Yvonna S. Lincoln, eds., *Handbook of qualitative research*. Thousand Oaks: Sage Publications, pp. 105–107.

Guillén, M. F. (1994). *Models of management: Work, authority and organization in a comparative perspective*. Chicago: University of Chicago Press.

Gulati, R. and Nohria, N. (1996). Is slack good or bad for innovation? *Academy of Management Journal*, **39**(5): 1245–1264.

Gundry, L. K., Kickul, S. C., Griffiths, M. D. and J. R., Bacq. (2011). Creating social change out of nothing: The role of entrepreneurial bricolage in social entrepreneurs' catalytic innovations. In G. Lumpkin and J. A. Katz, eds., *Advances in entrepreneurship, firm emergence and growth*. Bingley: Emerald Group Publishing, pp. 1–24.

Gupta, A. (1998). Rewarding local communities for conserving biodiversity: The case of the honey bee. In *Protection of Global Biodiversity: Converging Strategies*, pp. 180–189.

Gupta, A. and Wang, H. (2009). *Getting China and India right: Strategies for leveraging the world's fastest-growing economies for global advantage*. Hoboken: John Wiley and Sons.

Hall, R. (1992). The strategic analysis of intangible resources. *Strategic Management Journal*, **13**(2): 135–144.

Halme, M., Lindeman, S. and Linna, P. (2012). Innovation for inclusive business: Intrapreneurial bricolage in multinational corporations. *Journal of Management Studies*, **49**(4): 743–784.

Hamalainen, T. J. and Heiskala, R. (2007). *Social innovations, institutional change and economic performance*. Helsinki: SITRA.

Hang, C. C., Chen, J. and Subramian, A. M. (2010). Developing disruptive products for emerging economies: Lessons from Asian cases. *Research-Technology Management*, **53**(4): 21–26.

Hanna, N. K. (2011). Grassroots innovation for the information society. In *Transforming government and building the information society*. New York: Springer, pp. 199–226.

Hansen, M. T. and Birkinshaw, J. (2007). The innovation value chain. *Harvard Business Review*, **85**(6): 121.

Haque, U. (2011). *The new capitalist manifesto: Building a disruptively better business*. Cambridge: HBS.

Hargadon, H. and Sutton, R. (1997). Technology brokering and innovation in a product development firm. *Administrative Science Quarterly*, **42**(4): 716–749.

Hargrave, T. J. and Van de Ven, A. H. (2006). A collective action model of institutional innovation. *The Academy of Management Review*, **31**(4): 864–888.

Harris, M., Bhatti, Y. and Darzi, A. (2016). Innovations in health care delivery: Does the country of origin matter in health care innovation diffusion? *Journal of the American Medical Association*, **315**(11): 1103–1104.

Harris, M., Marti, J., Watt, H., Bhatti, Y., Macinko, J. and Darzi, A. (2017). Explicit bias towards high-income country research: A randomized, blinded, crossover experiment in English clinicians. *Health Affairs*, 36(11).

Hart, S. L. and London, T. (2004). Reinventing strategies for emerging markets: Beyond the transnational model. *Journal of International Business Studies*, **35**(5): 350–370.

Hart, S. L. and Prahalad, C. (2002). The fortune at the bottom of the pyramid. *Strategy+Business*, **26**: 54–67.

Hartigan, P. (2006). It's about people, not profits. *Business Strategy Review*, **17**: 42–45.

Hartigan, P. and Elkington, J. (2008). *The power of unreasonable people: How social entrepreneurs create markets that change the world*. Boston: Harvard Business School Press.

Hartley, J. (2004). Case study research. In C. Cassell and G. Symon, eds., *Essential guide to qualitative methods in organizational research*. London: Sage Publications, pp. 323–333.

Haugh, H. (2005). A research agenda for social entrepreneurship. *Social Enterprise Journal*, **1**: 1–12.

Heimer, C. A. (2001). Solving the problem of trust. *Trust in society*, **2**: 40–89.

Helfat, C. E. and Lieberman, M. B. (2002). The birth of capabilities: Market entry and the importance of pre-history. *Industrial and Corporate Change*, **11**(4): 725–760.

Helfat, C. E. and Peteraf, M. A. (2003). The dynamic resource-based view: Capability lifecycles. *Strategic management journal*, **24**(10): 997–1010.

Henderson, R. (1993). Underinvestment and incompetence as responses to radical innovation: Evidence from the photolithographic alignment equipment industry. *The RAND Journal of Economics*, **24**(2): 248–270.

Hess, D., Breyman, S., Campbell, N. and Martin, B. (2007). Science, technology and social movements. In E. Hackett, O. Amsterdamska, M. Lynch and J. Wajcman, eds., *New handbook of science and technology studies*. Cambridge, MA: The MIT Press, pp. 473–498.

Hesseldahl, P. (2013). *Frugal solutions: A manual.* Denmark: Universe Foundation.

Hessels, J. and Terjesen, S. (2010). Resource dependency and institutional theory perspectives on direct and indirect export choices. *Small Business Economics*, **34**(2): 203–220.

Hinings, C. R., Meyer, A. D. and Tsui, A. S. (1993). Configurational approaches to organizational analysis. *Academy of Management Journal*, **36**(6): 1175–1195.

Hinings, C. R. and Reay, T. (2009). Managing the rivalry of competing institutional logics. *Organization Studies*, **30**: 629–652.

Hirsch, P. M. and Levin, D. Z. (1999). Umbrella advocates versus validity police: A life-cycle model. *Organization Science*, **10**(2): 199–212.

Hockerts, K. (2006). Entrepreneurial opportunity in social purpose business ventures. In K. Hockerts, J. Mair and J. Robinson, eds., *Social entrepreneurship*. London: Palgrave Macmillan, pp. 142–154.

Hoffman, A. J. and Ventresca, M. J. (2002). *Organizations, policy and the natural environment: Institutional and strategic perspectives*. Stanford: Stanford University Press.

Hoogendoorn, B., Pennings, E. and Thurik, R. (2010). *What do we know about social entrepreneurship: An analysis of empirical research*. Amsterdam: ERIM.

Hossain, M. (2016). Frugal innovation: A systematic literature review. April 21. SSRN working paper, https://ssrn.com/abstract=2768254.

  (2017). Mapping the frugal innovation phenomenon. *Technology in Society*, 51: 199–208.

Hossain, M., Simula, H. and Halme, M. (2016). Can frugal go global? Diffusion patterns of frugal innovations. *Technology in Society*, **46**, 132–139.

Howaldt, J. and Schwarz, M. (2010). *Social innovation: Concepts, research fields and international trends*. Aachen: IMA/ZLW.

Howell, R., van Beers, C. and Doorn, N. (2018). Value capture and value creation: The role of information technology in business models for frugal innovations in Africa. *Technological Forecasting and Social Change*, **131**: 227–239.

Hsieh, H. F. and Shannon, S. E. (2005). Three approaches to qualitative content analysis. *Qualitative Health Research*, **15**(9): 1277–1288.

Hsu, D. H. (2008). Technology-based entrepreneurship. In Scott Shane, ed., *Blackwell handbook on technology and innovation management*. Oxford: Blackwell Publishing, pp. 367–388.

Hsu, D. H. and Lim, K. (2006). *Knowledge bridging by biotechnology start-ups.* Available at: https://myweb.rollins.edu/tlairson/pek/bioknowbridge.pdf (last accessed 23 July 2017).

Hughes, T. P. (1983). *Networks of power: Electrification in Western society, 1880–1930.* Baltimore: Johns Hopkins University Press.

Huybrechts, B. and Nicholls, A. (2013). The role of legitimacy in social enterprise-corporate collaboration. *Social Enterprise Journal*, **9**(2): 130–146.

Hyvarinen, A., Keskinen, M. and Varis, O. (2016). Potential and pitfalls of frugal innovation in the water sector: Insights from Tanzania to global value chains. *Sustainability*, **8** (888).

Immelt, J. R., Govindarajan, V. and Trimble, C. (2009). How GE is disrupting itself. *Harvard Business Review*, **87**(10): 56–65.

Jacobsson, S. and Johnson, A. (2000). The diffusion of renewable energy technology: An analytical framework and key issues for research. *Energy Policy*, **28**: 625–640.

Jain, A. and Verloop, J. (2012). Repositioning grassroots innovation in India's S and T policy: From divider to provider. *Current Science*, **103**(3): 282–285.

Jankowski, J., Moris, F. and Perolle, P. (2008). Advancing measures of innovation in the United States. *Journal of Technology Transfer*, **33**: 123–130.

Jiang, Y., Peng, M. W. and Wang, D. Y. L. (2008). An institution-based view of international business strategy: A focus on emerging economies. *Journal of International Business Studies*, **39**(5): 920–936.

Jick, T. (1979). Mixing qualitative and quantitative methods: Triangulation in action. *Administrative Science Quarterly*, **24**: 602–611.

Johannisson, B. and Olaison, L. (2007). The moment of truth: Reconstructing entrepreneurship and social capital in the eye of the storm. *Review of Social Economy*, **LXV**: 55–78.

John F. Kennedy Space Center. (2008). *Frequently asked questions.* Available at: www.nasa.gov/centers/kennedy/about/information/shuttle_faq.html#10 (last accessed 14 January 2017).

John, S. and Thakkar, K. (2012). Frugal engineering is fine, but not *jugaad*, says Anand Mahindra. *India Times, 12 April.* Available at: http://articles .economictimes.indiatimes.com/2012-04-12/news/31331403_1_r-d-facility-chrysler-s-r-d-r-d-centre (last accessed 14 January 2017).

Johnson, R. B. (1997). Examining the validity structure of qualitative research. *Education*, **118**(2): 282–292.

Kahneman, D. and Tversky, A. (1979). Prospect theory: An analysis of decision under risk. *Econometrica: Journal of the Econometric Society*, 263–291.

Kaplinsky, R. and Morris, M. (2001). *A handbook for value chain research.* New York: IDRC.

Katila, R. and Shane, S. (2005). When does lack of resources make new firms innovative? *Academy of Management Journal*, **48**(5): 814–829.

Kay, J. (2011). *Obliquity: Why our goals are best achieved indirectly.* New York: Profile Books.

Kay, L. (2011). The effect of inducement prizes on innovation: Evidence from the Ansari XPrize and the Northrop Grumman Lunar Lander Challenge. *R and D Management*, **41**(4): 360–377.

Keller, S. and Price, C. (2011). *Beyond performance: How great organizations build ultimate competitive advantage.* New York: Wiley.

Kerlin, J. A. (2011). Considering context: Social innovation in comparative perspective. In A. Nicholls and A. Murdock, eds., *Social innovation.* London: Palgrave Macmillan UK, pp. 66–88.

Kesselring, A. (2009). Social innovation in private companies: An exploratory empirical study. In S. Roth, ed., *Non-technological and non-economic innovations: Contributions to a theory of robust innovation.* Bern: Peter Lang, p. 147.

Keown, O. P., Parston, G., Patel, H., Rennie, F., Saoud, F., Al Kuwari, H. and Darzi, A. (2014). Lessons from eight countries on diffusing innovation in health care. *Health Affairs*, 33(9), 1516–1522.

Khan, R. (2016). How frugal innovation promotes social sustainability. *Sustainability*, 8(10), 1034.

Khanna, T. and Palepu, K. (1997). Why focused strategies may be wrong for emerging markets. *Harvard Business Review*, July–August: 41–51.

Khanna, T. and Palepu, K. G. (2006). Emerging giants: Building world-class companies in developing countries. *Harvard Business Review*, **84**(10): 60–72.

King, N. (1998). Template analysis. In C. Cassell and G. Symon, eds., *Qualitative methods and analysis in organizational research.* London: Sage Publications.

(2004a). *Template analysis: What is template analysis?* University of Huddersfield. Available at: www-old.hud.ac.uk/hhs/research/template-analysis (last accessed 23 July 2017).

(2004b). Using templates in the thematic analysis of text. In C. Cassell and G. Symon, eds., *Essential guide to qualitative methods in organizational research.* London: Sage Publications.

(2012). *Template analysis.* Available at: http://hhs.hud.ac.uk/w2/research/template_analysis/ (last accessed 14 January 2017).

King, B. G. and Pearce, N. A. (2010). The contentiousness of markets: Politics, social movements and institutional change in markets. *Annual Review of Sociology*, **36**: 249–267.

Knorr Cetina, K. (1995). Laboratory studies: The cultural approach to the study of science. In S. Jasanoff, ed., *Handbook of science and technology studies*. Los Angeles: Bielefeld University Library.

Kodithuwakku, S. S. and Rosa, P. (2002). The entrepreneurial process and economic success in a constrained environment. *Journal of Business Venturing*, **17**(5): 431–465.

Knorringa, P., Peša, I., Leliveld, A. and Van Beers, C. (2016). Frugal innovation and development: Aides or adversaries? *The European Journal of Development Research*, 28(2): 143–153.

Kramer, M. R. (2011). Creating shared value. *Harvard Business Review*, **89**(1/2): 62–77.

Kuriyan, R., Ray, I. and Toyama, K. (2006). Integrating social development and financial sustainability: The challenges of rural kiosks in Kerala. Paper presented at the *International Conference on Information and Communication Technologies for Development*, Berkeley, CA.

Lamont, M. and Molnar, V. (2002). The study of boundaries in the social sciences. *Annual Review of Sociology*, 167–195.

Lanzara, G. F. (1998). Self-destructive processes in institution building and some modest countervailing mechanisms. *European Journal of Political Research*, **33**(1): 1–39.

Latour, B. and Woolgar, S. (1986). *Laboratory life: The construction of scientific facts*, 2nd edn. Princeton: Princeton University Press.

Latour, S. (1978). Determinations of participant and observer satisfaction with adversary and inquisitorial modes of adjudication. *Journal of Personality and Social Psychology*, **36**(12): 1531.

Law, J. and Callon, M. (1988). Engineering and sociology in a military aircraft project: A network analysis of technological change. *Social Problems*, **35**(3): 284–297.

Law, K. S., Wong, C. and Mobley, W. H. (1998). Toward a taxonomy of multidimensional constructs. *Academy of Management Review*, **23**(4): 741–755.

Lawrence, P. R. and Lorsch, J. W. (1967). *Organization and environment: Management differentiation and integration*. Boston: Harvard Business School Press.

Lawrence, T., Phillips, N. and Tracey, P. (2012). From the guest editors: Educating social entrepreneurs and social innovators. *Academy of Management Learning and Education*, **11**(3): 319–323.

Leadbeater, C. (2014). *The frugal innovator: Creating change on a shoestring budget.* New York: Springer.

Lee, K. and Sherer, P. D. (2002). Institutional change in large law firms: A resource dependency and institutional perspective. *Academy of Management Journal*, **45**(1): 102–119.

Leliveld, A. and Knorringa, P. (2018). Frugal innovation and development research. *The European Journal of Development Research*, **30**(1): 1–16.

Leonard-Barton, D. (1988). Implementation characteristics of organizational innovations: Limits and opportunities for management strategies. *Communication Research*, **15**: 603–631.

Letty', B., Shezi, Z. and Mudhara, M. (2012). Grassroots innovation as a mechanism for smallholder development in South Africa: Can impact be measured? *African Journal of Science, Technology, Innovation and Development*, **4**(3): 32–60.

Lévi-Strauss, C. (1967). *The savage mind.* Chicago: University of Chicago Press.

Lewin, A. Y., Weigelt, C. B. and Emery, J. D. (2004). Adaptation and selection in strategy and change. In M. S. Poole and A. H. Van de Ven, eds., *Handbook of organizational change and innovation.* Oxford: Oxford University Press, pp. 108–160.

Leydesdorff, L. (2005). The triple helix model and the study of knowledge-based innovation systems. *International Journal of Contemporary Sociology*, **42**(1): 12–27.

Lincoln, Y. S. and Guba, E. G. (1985). *Naturalistic inquiry.* London: Sage Publications.

Little, D. (2008). The professions as an object of study. *Understanding Society.* Available at: www.understandingsociety.blogspot.co.uk/2008/06/professions-as-object-of-study.html (last accessed 15 January 2017).

Liu, Y. (2011). High-tech ventures' innovation and influences of institutional voids: A comparative study of two high-tech parks in China. *Journal of Chinese Entrepreneurship*, **3**(2): 112–133.

Liu, Y., Woywode, M. and Xing, Y. (2012). Technology start-up innovation and the role of Guanxi: An explorative study in China from an institutional perspective. *Prometheus*, **30**(2): 211–229.

Lounsbury, M. and Crumley, E. T. (2007). New practice creation: An institutional perspective on innovation. *Organization Studies*, **28**(7): 993–1012.

Lounsbury, M., Ocasio, W. and Thornton, P. H. (2012). *The institutional logics perspective: A new approach to culture, structure and process.* Oxford: Oxford University Press.

Lounsbury, M. and Ventresca, M. (2002). Social structure and organizations revisited. In M. Lounsbury and M. Ventresca, eds., *Research in the sociology of organizations.* Emerald Group Publishing Limited, Vol. 19: 3–36.

Lounsbury, M., Ventresca, M. and Hirsch, P. M. (2003). Social movements, field frames and industry emergence: A cultural–political perspective on US recycling. *Socio-Economic Review*, 1(1): 71.

Louridas, P. (1999). Design as bricolage: Anthropology meets design thinking. *Design Studies*, 20(6): 517–535.

Loveridge, R. (2006). Developing institutions – 'Crony capitalism' and national capabilities: A European perspective. *Asian Business and Management*, 5(1): 113–136.

Low, M. B. and Abrahamson, E. (1997). Movements, bandwagons and clones: Industry evolution and the entrepreneurial process. *Journal of Business Venturing*, 12(6): 435–457.

Lundvall, B. A., ed. (1992). *National systems of innovation: Towards a theory of innovation and interactive learning*. London: Pinter.

Lyon, F. (2012). Social innovation, co-operation and competition: Inter-organizational relations for social enterprises in the delivery of public services. In A. Nicholls and A. Murdock, eds., *Social innovation*. London: Palgrave Macmillan, pp. 139–161.

MacMillan, I. C. and Starr, J. A. (1990). Resource cooptation via social contracting: Resource acquisition strategies for new ventures. *Strategic Management Journal*, 11: 79–92.

Mahoney, J. T. and Michael, S. C. (2005). A subjectivist theory of entrepreneurship. In S. A. Alvarez, R. Agarwal and O. Sorenson, eds., *Handbook of entrepreneurship*. Boston: Kluwer, pp. 33–53.

Mair, J., Battilana, J. and Cardenas, J. (2012). Organizing for society: A typology of social entrepreneuring models. *Journal of Business Ethics*, 111(3): 353–373.

Mair, J. and Martí, I. (2006). Social entrepreneurship research: A source of explanation, prediction and delight. *Journal of World Business*, 41(1): 36–44.

(2007). Entrepreneurship for social impact: Encouraging market access in rural Bangladesh. *Corporate Governance*, 7(4): 493–501.

(2009). Entrepreneurship in and around institutional voids: A case study from Bangladesh. *Journal of Business Venturing*, 24(5): 419–435.

Mair, J., Martí, I. and Ventresca, M. J. (2012). Building inclusive markets in rural Bangladesh: How intermediaries work institutional voids. *Academy of Management Journal*, 55(4): 819–850.

Mair, J. and Noboa, E. (2006). Social entrepreneurship: How intentions to create a social venture are formed. In J. Mair, J. Robinson and K. Hockerts, eds., *Social entrepreneurship*. New York: Palgrave, pp. 57–85.

Mair, J., Robinson, J. and Hockerts, K. (2006). *Social entrepreneurship*. New York: Palgrave.

Mair, J. and Seelos, C. (2007). Profitable business models and market creation in the context of deep poverty: A strategic view. *The Academy of Management Perspectives*, **21**(4): 49–63.

Makadok, R. (2001). Toward a synthesis of the resource based and dynamic-capability views of rent creation. *Strategic Management Journal*, **22**: 387–401.

Marinova, D. and Phillimore, J. (2003). Models of innovation. In L. V. Shavinina, ed., *The international handbook on innovation*. Oxford: Elsevier Science, pp. 44–53.

Martin, R. L. and Osberg, S. (2007). Social entrepreneurship: The case for definition. *Stanford Social Innovation Review*, **5**(2): 28–39.

(2015). *Getting beyond better: How social entrepreneurship works*. Boston: Harvard Business Review Press.

Maxwell, J. A. (2005). *Qualitative research design: An integrative approach*, 2nd edn. Thousand Oaks: Sage Publications.

Mayer, C. (2011). *Voices from Oxford: Rector interviews Colin Mayer*. Video. Available at: www.voicesfromoxford.org/video/Colin-Mayer-Final-Export/76 (last accessed 27 February 2018).

Maylor, H. and Blackmon, K. (2005). *Researching business and management*. London: Palgrave Macmillan.

Mays, N. and Pope, C. (1995). Rigour and qualitative research. *British Medical Journal*, **311**(6997): 109.

McLean, M. and Peredo, A. M. (2006). Social entrepreneurship: A critical review of the concept. *Journal of World Business*, **41**: 56–65.

McMullen, J. S. (2011). Delineating the domain of development entrepreneurship: A market-based approach to facilitating inclusive economic growth. *Entrepreneurship: Theory and Practice*, **35**(1): 185–193.

McMullen, J. S. and Shepherd, D. A. (2006). Entrepreneurial action and the role of uncertainty in the theory of the entrepreneur. *Academy of Management Review*, **31**(1): 131–152.

Mehta, Pavithra K. and Shenoy, S. (2011). *Infinite vision: How Aravind became the world's greatest business case for compassion*. San Francisco: Berrett-Koehler.

Mensch, G. (1979). *Stalemate in technology: Innovations overcome the depression*. New York: Ballinger.

Meyer, J. W. (1983). Organizational environments: Ritual and rationality. In J. Meyer and R. Scott, eds. (with the assistance of Brian Rowan and Terrance E. Deal), *Organizational environments: Ritual and rationality*. Thousand Oaks: Sage Publications.

Meyer, J. W. and Rowan, B. (1977). Institutionalized organizations: Formal structure as myth and ceremony. *American Journal of Sociology*, **83**(2): 340.

Michael, M. (1996). *Constructing identities: The social, the nonhuman and change*. Thousand Oaks: Sage Publications.

Miles, M. B. and Huberman, A. M. (1994). *Qualitative data analysis: An expanded sourcebook*, 2nd edn. Thousand Oaks: Sage Publications.

Miller, T., Grimes, M., McMullen, J. and Vogus, T. (2012). Venturing for others with heart and head: How compassion encourages social entrepreneurship. *Academy of Management Review*, **37**(4): 616–640.

Miner, A. S., Bassof, P. and Moorman, C. (2001). Organizational improvisation and learning: A field study. *Administrative Science Quarterly*, **46**: 304–337.

Minks, M. L. (2011). Social innovation: New solutions to social problems. Master of Arts Thesis, Georgetown University, Washington, DC.

Moertl, P. and Mumford, M. D. (2003). Cases of social innovation: Lessons from two innovations in the 20th century. *Creativity Research Journal*, **15**(2–3): 261–266.

Monaghan, A. (2009). Conceptual niche management of grassroots innovation for sustainability: The case of body disposal practices in the UK. *Technological Forecasting and Social Change*, **76**(8): 1026–1043.

Moore, K. (2011). The best way to innovation? An important lesson from India. *Forbes*, 24 May. Available at: www.forbes.com/sites/karlmoore/2011/05/24/the-best-way-to-innovation-an-important-lesson-from-india (last accessed 15 January 2017).

Morgan, G. and Smircich, L. (1980). The case for qualitative research. *Academy of Management Review*, **5**(4): 491–500.

Mowery, D. and Rosenberg, N. (1979). The influence of market demand upon innovation: A critical review of some recent empirical studies. *Research Policy*, **8**(2): 102–153.

Mulgan, G. (2006). The process of social innovation. *Innovations: Technology, Governance, Globalization*, **1**(2): 145–162.

Mulgan, G., Ali, R., Halkett, R. and Sanders, B. (2007a). In and out of sync: The challenge of growing social innovations. Research report. NESTA, London. Available at: www.nesta.org.uk/sites/default/files/in_and_out_of_sync.pdf (last accessed 23 July 2017).

Mulgan, G., Tucker, S., Ali, R. and Sanders, B. (2007b). *Social innovation: What it is, why it matters and how it can be accelerated*. Oxford: Skoll Centre for Social Entrepreneurship. Available at: https://youngfoundation.org/wp-content/uploads/2012/10/Social-Innovation-what-it-is-why-it-matters-how-it-can-be-accelerated-March-2007.pdf (last accessed 23 July 2017).

Murray, R., Caulier-Grice, J. and Mulgan, G. (2010). *Open book of social innovation*. London: The Young Foundation. Available at: http://youngfoundation

.org/wp-content/uploads/2012/10/The-Open-Book-of-Social-Innovationg.pdf (last accessed 15 January 2017).

Nair, C. (2008). Frugal engineering: Ghosn has it wrong? Available at: http://chandranrn.blogspot.com/2008/05/frugal-engineering-ghosn-has-it-wrong.html (last accessed 15 January 2017).

Nakata, C. (2012). From the special issue editor: Creating new products and services for and with the base of the pyramid. *Journal of Product Innovation Management*, **29**(1): 3–5.

Neuendorf, K. A. (2002). *The content analysis guidebook*. Thousand Oaks: Sage Publications.

Nicholls, A. (2006a). Social entrepreneurship. In S. Carter and D. Evans-Jones, eds., *Enterprise and small business: Principles, practice and policy*, 2nd edn. London: Prentice Hall, pp. 220–242.

Nicholls, A., ed. (2006b). *Social entrepreneurship: New models of sustainable social change*. Oxford: Oxford University Press.

Nicholls, A. and Murdock, A., eds. (2011). *Social innovation: Blurring boundaries to reconfigure markets*. London: Palgrave Macmillan.

Nielsen, K. B. and Wilhite, H. (2015). The rise and fall of the 'people's car': Middle-class aspirations, status and mobile symbolism in 'New India'. *Contemporary South Asia*, **23**(4): 371–387.

Nijhof, A., Fisscher, O. and Looise, J. K. (2002). Inclusive innovation: A research project on the inclusion of social responsibility. *Corporate Social Responsibility and Environmental Management*, 9(2): 83–90.

Nobel Prize. (2006). Homepage. Available at: www.nobelprize.org/nobel_prizes/peace/laureates/2006 (last accessed 14 Jan 2017).

North, D. C. (1990). *Institutions, institutional change and economic performance*. Cambridge: Cambridge University Press.

Novogratz, J. (2010). *The blue sweater: Bridging the gap between rich and poor in an interconnected world*. Emmaus: Rodale Books.

Ocasio, W. and Thornton, P. H. (2008). Institutional logics. In R. Greenwood, R. Oliver, K. Sahlin and R. Suddaby, eds., *The SAGE handbook of organizational institutionalism*. London: Sage Publications, pp. 99–129.

O'Leary, Z. (2004). *The essential guide to doing research*. London: Sage Publications.

Oliver, C. (1997). Sustainable competitive advantage: Combining institutional and resource-based views. *Strategic Management Journal*, **18**(9): 697–713.

Osborn, M., Smith, J. A. and Smith, J. (2003). *Interpretative phenomenological analysis. Qualitative psychology: A practical guide to research methods*. Thousand Oaks: Sage Publications, pp. 51–80.

Paananen, M. (2012). I'll find it where I can: Exploring the role of resource and financial constraints in search behaviour among innovators. *Industry and Innovation*, **19**(1): 63–84.

Pansera, M. (2013). Frugality, grassroots and inclusiveness: New challenges for mainstream innovation theories. *African Journal of Science, Technology, Innovation and Development*, 5(6): 469–478.

Pansera, M. and Sarkar, S. (2016). Crafting sustainable development solutions: Frugal innovations of grassroots entrepreneurs. *Sustainability*, 8(1): 51.

Patton, M. Q. (2015). *Qualitative research & evaluation methods: Integrating theory and practice*, 4th edn. Thousand Oaks: Sage Publications.

Peng, M. W. (2003). Institutional transitions and strategic choices. *Academy of Management Review*, **28**(2): 275–296.

Penrose, E. (1959; 1995). *The theory of the growth of the firm*. Oxford: Oxford University Press.

Perrini, F. and Vurro, C. (2006). Social entrepreneurship: Innovation and social change across theory and practice. In J. Mair, J. Robinson and K. Hockerts, eds., *Social entrepreneurship*. New York: Palgrave, pp. 57–85.

Peteraf, M. A. (1993). The cornerstones of competitive advantage: A resource-based view. *Strategic Management Journal*, **14**(3): 179–191.

Peterson, M. F. (1995). Leading Cuban-American entrepreneurs: The process of developing motives, abilities and resources. *Human Relations*, **48**: 1193–1216.

Petrick, I. J. and Juntiwasarakij, S. (2011). The rise of the rest: Hotbeds of innovation in emerging markets. *Research-Technology Management*, **54**(4): 24–29.

Pfeffer, J. and Salancik, G. R. (1978). *The external control of organizations: A resource dependence perspective*. New York: Harper & Row.

Phills, J., Deiglmeier, K. and Miller, D. (2008). Rediscovering social innovation. *Stanford Social Innovation Review*, 6(4): 34–43.

Pisano, G., Shuen, A. and Teece, D. J. (1997). Dynamic capabilities and strategic management. *Strategic Management Journal*, **18**(7): 509–533.

Pisoni, A., Michelini, L. and Martignoni, G. (2018). Frugal approach to innovation: State of the art and future perspectives. *Journal of Cleaner Production*, 171: 107–126.

Pol, E. and Ville, S. (2009). Social innovation: Buzz word or enduring term? *The Journal of Socio-Economics*, **38**(6): 878–885.

Polak, P. (2008). *Out of poverty: What works when traditional approaches fail*. Oakland: Berrett-Koehler Publishers.

Poole, M. S. and Van de Ven, A. H. (1988). Paradoxical requirements for a theory of change. In K. Cameron and R. Quinn, eds., *Paradox and transformation: Towards a theory of change in organization and management*. Cambridge: Ballinger, pp. 19–63.

(1989). Using paradox to build management and organization theories. *Academy of Management Review*, **14**: 562–578.

eds. (2004). *Handbook of organizational change and innovation*. Oxford: Oxford University Press.

Porter, M. E. (1990). The competitive advantage of nations. *Harvard Business Review*, **68**(2): 73–93.

(1995). The competitive advantage of the inner city. *Long Range Planning*, **28**: 132.

(1998). *Competitive advantage: Creating and sustaining superior performance*, 2nd edn. New York: Free Press.

Porter, M. E. and Kramer, M. R. (1999). Philanthropy's new agenda: Creating value. *Harvard Business Review*, **77**(6): 121–131.

Porup, J. M. (2015). This 3D-printed stethoscope costs $5, outperforms $200 competitors. *Motherboard*, 21 August. Available at: http://motherboard.vice.com/read/this-3d-printed-stethoscope-head-costs-5-outperforms-200-competitors (last accessed 02 January 2018).

Pot, F. W. and Vaas, F. (2008). Social innovation, the new challenge for Europe. *International Journal of Productivity and Performance Management*, **57**(7): 468–473.

Prabhu, J. (2017). Frugal innovation: Doing more with less for more. *Philosophical Transactions of the Royal Society*, **375**(2095): 20160372.

Prabhu, J., Tracey, P. and Hassan, M. (2017). Marketing to the poor: An institutional model of exchange in emerging markets. *AMS Review*, 1–22.

Prahalad, C. K. (2005). *Fortune at the bottom of pyramid: Eradicating poverty through profits*. Philadelphia: Wharton School Publishing.

(2006). The innovation sandbox. *Strategy + Business*, **44**, Autumn.

Prahalad, C. K. and Hammond, A. (2002). Serving the world's poor, profitably. *Harvard Business Review*, **80**(9): 48–59.

Prahalad, C. K. and Mashelkar, R. A. (2010). Innovation's Holy Grail. *Harvard Business Review*, **88**(7–8): 132–141.

Prime, M. (2018). Frugal innovation for healthcare: Strategies and tools for the identification and evaluation of frugal and reverse innovations in healthcare. Unpublished PhD dissertation, Imperial College of London.

Prime, M., Attaelmanan, I., Imbuldeniya, A., Harris, M., Darzi, A. and Bhatti, Y. (2018). From Malawi to Middlesex: The case of the Arbutus Drill Cover System as an example of the cost saving potential of frugal innovations for the UK NHS. *BMJ Innovations*, **4**: 103–110.

Prime, M., Bhatti, Y. and Harris, M. (2017). Frugal and reverse innovation in surgery. In A. Park and R. Price, eds., *Global surgery: The essentials*. Springer, pp. 193–206.

Prime, M., Bhatti, Y., Harris, M. and Darzi, A. (2016a). African healthcare innovation: An untapped resource? Special issue on Learning from African Innovations. *World Hospitals and Health Services Journal*, **52**(3).

(2016b). Frugal innovations for healthcare: A toolkit for innovators. Academy of Management Annual Meeting, 5–9 August 2016, Anaheim, CA. *Academy of Management Proceedings*, 2016:1, 12622. doi:10.5465/AMBPP.2016.12622abstract.

Puffer, S. M., Boisot, M. and McCarthy, D. J. (2010). Entrepreneurship in Russia and China: The impact of formal institutional voids. *Entrepreneurship Theory and Practice*, **34**: 441–467.

Punch, K. F. (2005). *Introduction to social research: Quantitative and qualitative approaches*, 2nd edn. London: Sage Publications.

Radjou, N. and Prabhu, J. (2015). *Frugal innovation: How to do more with less*. London: The Economist and Profile Books.

Radjou, N., Prabhu, J. and Ahuja, S. (2012). *Jugaad innovation: Think frugal, be flexible, generate breakthrough growth*. San Francisco: Jossey-Bass.

Ragin, C. (1994). *Constructing social research: The unity and diversity of method*. Thousand Oaks: Sage Publications.

Ragin, C. C. and Amoroso, L. M. (2010). *Constructing social research: The unity and diversity of method*. Thousand Oaks: Sage Publications.

Rao, B. C. (2013). How disruptive is frugal? *Technology in Society*, **35**(1): 65–73.

Rao, H. (1998). Caveat emptor: The construction of non-profit consumer watchdog organizations. *American Journal of Sociology*, **103**: 912–961.

(2009). *Market rebels: How activists make or break radical innovations*. Princeton: Princeton University Press.

Rao, H. and Drazin, R. (2002). Overcoming resource constraints on product innovation by recruiting talent from rivals: A study of the mutual fund industry, 1986–94. *The Academy of Management Journal*, **45**(3): 491–507.

Rao, H., Morrill, C. and Zald, M. N. (2000). Power plays: How social movements and collective action create new organizational forms. *Research in Organizational Behavior*, **22**: 237–282.

Rappa, M. (1987). The structure of technological revolutions: An empirical study of the development of III–V compound semiconductor technology. Unpublished doctoral dissertation, Carlson School of Management, University of Minnesota, Minneapolis.

Ray, G., Barney, J. B. and Muhanna, W. A. (2004) Capabilities, business processes, and competitive advantage: Choosing the dependent variable in empirical tests of the resource-based view. *Strategic Management Journal*, 25(1): 23–37.

Ray, P. K. and Ray, S. (2010). Resource-constrained innovation for emerging economies: The case of the Indian telecommunications industry. *IEEE Transactions on Engineering Management*, **57**(1): 144–156.

Rennings, K. (2000). Redefining innovation: Eco-innovation research and the contribution from ecological economics. *Ecological Economics*, **32**(2): 319–332.

Robinson, J. (2006). Navigating social and institutional barriers to markets: How social entrepreneurs identify and evaluate opportunities. In J. Mair, J. Robinson and K. Hockerts, eds., *Social Entrepreneurship*. New York: Palgrave, pp. 95–120.

Rogers, E. M. (2003). *Diffusion of innovations*, 5th edn. New York: Free Press.

Roper, S., Du, J. and Love, J. H. (2008). Modelling the innovation value chain. *Research Policy*, **37**(6–7): 961–977.

Rosenberg, N. (1976). *Perspectives on technology*. Cambridge: Cambridge University Press.

Ross, T., Mitchell, V. A. and May, A. J. (2012). Bottom-up grassroots innovation in transport: Motivations, barriers and enablers. *Transportation Planning and Technology*, **35**(4): 469–489.

Roth, S. (2009). Introduction: Towards a theory of robust innovation. In S. Roth, ed., *Non-technological and non-economic innovations: Contributions to a theory of robust innovation*. Oxford: Peter Lang Publishing.

Rowe, P. G. (1991). *Design thinking*. Cambridge: The MIT Press.

Rubin, H. (2007). Aravind Eye Hospital: The perfect vision of Dr V. *FAST Company*, 19 December Available at: www.fastcompany.com/42111/perfect-vision-dr-v (last accessed 23 July 2017).

Rucht, D. (1999). The transnationalization of social movements: Trends, causes, problems. In H. K. Donatella della Porta and D. Rucht, eds., *Social movements in a globalizing world*. London: MacMillan Press, pp. 206–222.

Sachs, J. (2006). *The end of poverty: Economic possibilities for our time*. New York: Penguin Group USA.

Sambandaraska, D. (2010). Telco to help rural majority access banking services. *Bangkok Post*, 5 May.

Sandelowski, M. (2000). Focus on research methods: Whatever happened to qualitative description? *Research in Nursing and Health*, **23**(4): 334–340.

Sandelowski, M. and Leeman, J. (2012). Writing usable qualitative health research findings. *Qualitative Health Research*, 22(10): 1404–1413.

Sarasvathy, S. D. (2001). Causation and effectuation: Toward a theoretical shift from economic inevitability to entrepreneurial contingency. *Academy of Management Review*, **26**(2): 243–263.

(2006). Markets in human hope. In D. K. Sarasvathy, ed., *Effectuation: Elements of entrepreneurial expertise*. Charlottesville.

Sarkar, M. B. (2011). Moving forward by going in reverse: Emerging trends in global innovation and knowledge strategies. *Global Strategy Journal*, 1(3–4): 237–242.

Sarmah, P. K. (2010). Rickshaw Bank: Empowering the poor through asset ownership (Innovations case narrative: Rickshaw Bank). *Innovations: Technology, Governance, Globalization*, 5(1): 35–55.

Saunders, M., Lewis, P. and Thornhill, A. (2007). *Research methods for business students*, 4th edn. London: Prentice Hall.

Schneiberg, M. and Lounsbury, M. (2008). Social movements and institutional analysis. In R. Greenwood, C. Oliver, S. Sahlin-Andersson and R. Suddaby, eds., *Handbook of organizational institutionalism*. Sage Publications, pp. 648–670.

Schoonhoven, C. B. and Romanelli, E. (2001). Emergent themes and the next wave of entrepreneurship research. In C. B. Schoonhoven and E. Romanelli, eds., *The entrepreneurship dynamic: Origins of entrepreneurship and the evolution of industries*. Stanford: Stanford University Press, pp. 383–408.

Schumacher, E. F. (1974). *Small is beautiful: Economics as if people mattered.* London: Abacus.

Schumpeter J. (1934a). *The theory of economic development: An inquiry into profits, capital, credit, interest and the business cycle.* Cambridge: Harvard University Press.

(1934b). *Capitalism, socialism and democracy.* New York: Harper & Row.

Scotchmer, S. (2005). *Innovation and incentives.* Cambridge: MIT Press.

Scott, W. R. (1995). *Institutions and organizations: Foundations for organizational science.* London: Sage Publications.

(2001). *Institutions and organizations*, 2nd edn. Thousand Oaks: Sage Publications.

(2008). Approaching adulthood: The maturing of institutional theory. *Theory and Society*, 37(5): 427–442.

Sen, A. K., Last, A. G. M. and Quirk, R. (1986). Prediction and economic theory. *Proceedings of the Royal Society of London*, 407(1832): 3–23.

Seelos, C. and Mair, J. (2005). Social entrepreneurship: Creating new business models to serve the poor. *Business Horizons*, 48(3): 241–246.

Seyfang, G. and Smith, A. (2007). Grassroots innovations for sustainable development: Towards a new research and policy agenda. *Environmental Politics*, 16(4): 584–603.

Shane, S. (2000). Prior knowledge and the discovery of entrepreneurial opportunities. *Organization Science*, 11(4): 448–469.

(2003). *A general theory of entrepreneurship: The individual opportunity nexus.* Cheltenham: Edward Elgar.

Shane, S. and Stuart, T. (2002). Organizational endowments and the performance of university start-ups. *Management Science*, 48(1): 154–170.

Shane, S. and Venkataraman, S. (2000). The promise of entrepreneurship as a field of research. *Academy of Management Review*, **25**: 217–226.

(2003). Guest editors' introduction to the special issue on technology entrepreneurship. *Research Policy*, **32**(2): 181–184.

Sharma, A. and Iyer, G. R. (2012). Resource-constrained product development: Implications for green marketing and green supply chains. *Industrial Marketing Management*, **41**(4): 599–608.

Silicon India. (2010). Frugal innovation to accelerate financial growth in India. Available at: www.siliconindia.com/shownews/Frugal_innovation_to_acceler ate_financial_growth_in_India-nid-68373-cid-3.html (last accessed 15 January 2017).

Singh, S. K., Gambhir, A., Sotiropoulos, A. and Duckworth, S. (2012). *Frugal innovation by social entrepreneurs in India*. UK: Serco Institute.

Smith, A. (1904). *An inquiry into the nature and causes of the wealth of nations*. E. Cannan, ed., 5th edn. London: Methuen and Co.

(2007). Translating sustainabilities between green niches and socio-technical regimes. *Technology Analysis and Strategic Management*, **19**(4): 427–450.

Smith, A., Fressoli, M. and Thomas, H. (2014). Grassroots innovation movements: Challenges and contributions. *Journal of Cleaner Production*, **63**: 114–124.

Snow, D. and Benford, R.(1992). Master frames and cycles of protest. In A. Morris and C. Mueller, eds., *Frontiers in social movement theory*. New Haven: Yale University Press, pp. 133–155.

Soete, L. (2007). From industrial to innovation policy. *Journal of Industrial Competition and Trade*, **7**: 273–284.

(2008). Science, technology and development: Emerging concepts and visions. Working Paper No. 001. United Nations University, Maastricht Economic and Social Research and Training Centre on Innovation and Technology.

Soni, P. and Krishnan, R. T. (2014). Frugal innovation: Aligning theory, practice, and public policy. *Journal of Indian Business Research*, **6**(1): 29–47.

SpaceX. (2018). Website. Available at: www.spacex.com/falcon-heavy (last accessed 27 February 2018).

Srnka, K. J. and Koeszegi, S. T. (2007). From words to numbers: How to transform qualitative data into meaningful quantitative results. *Schmalenbach Business Review (SBR)*, **59**(1): 29–57.

Stiglitz, J. (2015). *The great divide*. London: Penguin UK.

Stake, R. E. (1990). Situational context as influence on evaluation design and use. *Studies in Educational Evaluation*, **16**: 231–246.

Star, S. L. (2010). This is not a boundary object: Reflections on the origin of a concept. *Science, Technology and Human Values*, **35**(5): 601–617.

Stark, D. (1996). Recombinant property in East European capitalism. *American Journal of Sociology*, **101**(4): 993–1027.

State Bank of Pakistan. (2011). New microfinance strategic framework to promote financial inclusion in Pakistan. Available at: www.sbp.org.pk/press/2011/Framework-02-Nov-11.pdf (last accessed 15 January 2017).

State Bank of Pakistan. (2017). Statistics on scheduled banks in Pakistan. Available at: www.sbp.org.pk/publications/schedule_banks/Jun-2017/Title.pdf (last accessed 15 December 2017).

Stemler, S. (2001). An overview of content analysis. *Practical Assessment, Research and Evaluation*, 7(17). Available at: PAREonline.net/getvn.asp?v=7 andn=17 (last accessed 15 January 2017).

Stern, P. N. (1994). Grounded theory methodology: Its uses and processes. In B. Glaser, ed., *More grounded theory methodology: A reader*. Mill Valley: Sociology Press, pp. 116–126.

Stewart, R. (1972). *The reality of organizations: A guide for managers*. London: Macmillan.

Stiglitz, J. E. (2001). *Joseph Stiglitz and the World Bank: The rebel within*. London: Anthem Press.

Strang, D. and Soule, S. A. (1998). Diffusion in organizations and social movements: From hybrid corn to poison pills. *Annual Review of Sociology*, **24**: 265–290.

Streeck, J. and Mehus, S. (2005). Microethnography: The study of practices. In K. Fitch and R. Sanders, eds., *Handbook of language and social interaction*. Psychology Press, pp. 381–404.

Subramanian, E. and Tongia, R. (2006). Information and communications technology for development (ICT4D): A design challenge? Paper presented at the *International Conference on Information and Communication Technologies for Development*, Berkeley, CA.

Suchman, M. (1995). Managing legitimacy: Strategic and institutional approaches. *Academy of Management Review*, **20**(3): 571–611.

Suddaby, R. (2006). From the editors: What grounded theory is not. *Academy of Management Journal*, **49**(4): 633–642.

Taylor-Powell, E. and Renner, M. (2003). Analysing qualitative data. University of Wisconsin-Cooperative Extension. Available at: https://learningstore.uwex.edu/assets/pdfs/g3658-12.pdf (last accessed 18 January 2017).

Thompson, J. (2002). The world of the social entrepreneur. *International Journal of Public Sector Management*, **15**: 412–431.

Thompson, J. D. (1967). *Organization in action*. Chicago: McGraw-Hill.

Thun, E. (2006). *Changing lanes in China: Foreign direct investment, local governments and auto sector development*. Cambridge: Cambridge University Press.

Tiwari, R. and Herstatt, C. (2012). Assessing India's lead market potential for cost-effective innovations. *Journal of Indian Business Research*, **4**(2): 97–115.

(2012b). Frugal innovation: A global networks' perspective. *Die Unternehmung*, 66(3): 245–274.

Tiwari, R., Kalogerakis, K. and Herstatt, C. (2016). Frugal innovations in the mirror of scholarly discourse: Tracing theoretical basis and antecedents. In *R&D Management Conference*, Cambridge, UK.

Tolbert, P. S. (1990). Review of the book, *The system of professions: An essay on the division of labor*. *Administrative Science Quarterly*, **35**(2): 410–413.

Topol, E. J. (2011). Medicine needs frugal innovation. Technology Review. Cambridge, MA: MIT Press.

Tooley, M. (1990). Causation: Reductionism versus realism. *Philosophy and Phenomenological Research*, 50: 215–236.

(2016). *The patient will see you now: The future of medicine is in your hands*. Basic Books.

Tracey, P. and Jarvis, O. (2007). Toward a theory of social venture franchising. *Entrepreneurship Theory and Practice*, **31**(5): 667–685.

Tracey, P. and Phillips, N. (2011). Entrepreneurship in emerging markets. *Management International Review*, **51**(1): 23–39.

Tracey, P. and Stott, N. (2017). Social innovation: A window on alternative ways of organizing and innovating. *Innovation – Organization & Management*, 19(1): 51–60.

Trochim, W. M. (2005). *Research methods: The concise knowledge base*. Atomic Dog Publishing.

Tse, E., Jullens, J. and Russo, B. (2012). China's mid-market innovators. *Strategy +Business*, **67**. Booz Allen and Co.

Tushman, M. L., Anderson, P. C. and O'Reilly, C. (1996). Technology cycles, innovation streams and ambidextrous organizations: Organization renewal through innovation streams and strategic change. In P. Anderson and M. Tushman, eds., *Managing strategic innovation and change*. Oxford: Oxford University Press, pp. 3–23.

Utterback, J. (1994). *Mastering the dynamics of innovation*. Cambridge, MA: Harvard Business School Press.

Vaismoradi, M., Turunen, H. and Bondas, T. (2013). Content analysis and thematic analysis: Implications for conducting a qualitative descriptive study. *Nursing & Health Sciences*, 15(3): 398–405.

Van Agtmael, A. (2007). *The emerging markets century: How a new breed of world-class companies is overtaking the world*. New York: Simon and Schuster.

Van de Ven, A. H. (1986). Central problems in the management of innovation. *Management Science*, **32**(5): 590–607.

Van de Ven, A. H., Ganco, M. and Hinings, C. R. (2013). Returning to the frontier of contingency theory of organizational and institutional designs. *Academy of Management Annals*, **7**(1): 393–440.

Virgin Galactic. (2012). Website. Available at: www.virgingalactic.com/human-spaceflight/our-vehicles (last accessed 23 July 2017).

Von Hippel, E. (1986). Lead users: A source of novel product concepts. *Management Science*, 791–805.

(1988). *The sources of innovation*. Oxford: Oxford University Press.

(2005). *Democratizing innovation*. Cambridge: MIT Press Books.

Von Hippel, E. and von Krogh, G. (2003). Special issue on open source software development. *Research Policy*, **32**: 1149.

Wadge, H., Bhatti, Y., Carter, A., Harris, M., Parston, G. and Darzi, A. (2016). *Brazil's family health strategy: Using community health care workers to provide primary care*. New York: The Commonwealth Fund.

Walker, W. (2000). Entrapment in large technology systems: Institutional commitment and power relations. *Research Policy*, **29**: 833–846.

Wallace, S. L. (1999). Social entrepreneurship: The role of social purpose enterprises in facilitating community economic development. *Journal of Developmental Entrepreneurship*, **4**(2): 153.

Warren, D. M. (1990). *Using indigenous knowledge in agricultural development*. Washington, DC: World Bank.

Weber, K., Heinze, K. L. and DeSoucey, M. (2008). Forage for thought: Mobilizing codes in the movement for grass-fed meat and dairy products. *Administrative Science Quarterly*, **53**(3): 529–567.

Weber, R. P. (1990). *Basic content analysis*. Newbury Park: Sage Publications.

Weerawardena, J. and Mort, G. S. (2006). Investigating social entrepreneurship: A multidimensional model. *Journal of World Business*, **41**(1): 21–35.

Weick, K. E. (1993). Organization redesign as improvisation. In G. Huber and W. Glick, eds., *Organizational change and redesign*. Oxford: Oxford University Press, pp. 346–382.

Weinberg, A. S., Pellow, D. N. and Schnaiberg, A. (2000). *Urban recycling and the search for sustainable community development*. Princeton: Princeton University Press.

Weiss, M., Gibbert, M. and Hoegl, M. (2011). Making virtue of necessity: The role of team climate for innovation in resource-constrained innovation projects. *Journal of Product Innovation Management*, **S1**: 196–207.

Wernerfelt, B. (1984). A resource-based view of the firm. *Strategic Management Journal*, 5(2): 171–180.

Westhead, P. and Storey, D. J. (1997). Financial constraints on the growth of high technology small firms in the United Kingdom. *Applied Financial Economics*, 7(2): 197–201.

Weyrauch, T. and Herstatt, C. (2017). What is frugal innovation? Three defining criteria. *Journal of Frugal Innovation*, 2(1): 1.

Whittington, R. (1996). Strategy as practice. *Long Range Planning*, 29(5): 731–735.

Wikipedia. (2011). Design thinking. Available at: http://en.wikipedia.org/wiki/Design_thinking (last accessed 15 January 2017).

Winterhalter, S., Zeschky, M. B., Neumann, L. and Gassmann, O. (2017). Business models for frugal innovation in emerging markets: The case of the medical device and laboratory equipment industry. *Technovation*, 66: 3–13.

Woodward, D. (2011). Plain and simple. Director Magazine, London. Available at: www.director.co.uk/ONLINE/2011/08_11_frugal-innovation.html (last accessed 01 December 2011).

Woodward, J. (1965). *Industrial organization: Theory and practice*. Oxford: Oxford University Press.

Woolridge, A. (2010). The world turned upside down: A special report on innovation in emerging markets. *The Economist*, 15 April. Available at: www.economist.com/node/15879369 (last accessed 15 January 2017).

(2011). *Masters of management: How the business gurus and their ideas have changed the world – For better and for worse*. New York: Harper Collins.

Yin, R. K. (1994). *Case study research: Design and methods*, 2nd edn. Thousand Oaks: Sage Publications.

Yunus, M. (2007). *Creating a world without poverty: Social business and the future of capitalism*. New York: Public Affairs.

Zahra, S. A., Gedajlovic, E., Neubaum, D. O. and Shulman, J. M. (2009). A typology of social entrepreneurs: Motives, search processes and ethical challenges. *Journal of Business Venturing*, 24(5): 519–532.

Zahra, S. A., Rawhouser, H. N., Bhawe, N., Neubaum, D. O. and Hayton, J. C. (2008). Globalization of social entrepreneurship opportunities. *Strategic Entrepreneurship Journal*, 2(2): 117–131.

Zanello, G., Fu, X., Mohnen, P. and Ventresca, M. (2016). The creation and diffusion of innovation in developing countries: A systematic literature review. *Journal of Economic Surveys*, 30(5): 884–912.

Zedtwitz, M., Corsi, S., Søberg, P. V. and Frega, R. (2015). A typology of reverse innovation. *Journal of Product Innovation Management*, 32(1): 12–28.

Zeng, M. and Williamson, P. J. (2007). *Dragons at your door: How Chinese cost innovation is disrupting global competition.* Cambridge, MA: Harvard Business School Press.

Zeschky, M., Widenmayer, B. and Gassmann, O. (2011). Frugal innovation in emerging markets. *Research-Technology Management,* 54(4): 38–45.

(2014). Organising for reverse innovation in Western MNCs: The role of frugal product innovation capabilities. *International Journal of Technology Management,* 64(2–4): 255–275.

Zeschky, M. B., Winterhalter, S. and Gassmann, O. (2014). From cost to frugal and reverse innovation: Mapping the field and implications for global competitiveness. *Research-Technology Management,* 57(4): 20–27.

Bibliography

We list here works on frugal innovation chronologically based on our search conducted in January 2018. While we have cited more than half of these in the text, we detail here extensively, though not exhaustively, many others. We do so in order to acknowledge the growing community dedicated to a decade of scholarship in frugal innovation (2008–2018). This bibliography should also serve as a resource for those setting out to review and conduct research and on this topic and keep up the momentum for knowledge generation and application.

2018

1. Altamirano, M. A. & van Beers, C. P. (2018). Frugal innovations in technological and institutional infrastructure: Impact of mobile phone technology on productivity, public service provision and inclusiveness. *The European Journal of Development Research*, 30(1): 84–107.
2. Bhaduri, S., Sinha, K. M. & Knorringa, P. (2018). Frugality and cross-sectoral policy-making for food security. *NJAS-Wageningen Journal of Life Sciences*, 84: 72–79. Available at www.sciencedirect.com/science/article/pii/S1573521417300131.
3. Chavali, A. & Ramji, R., eds. (2018). *Frugal Innovation in Bioengineering for the Detection of Infectious Diseases*. New York: Springer.
4. da Costa Nogami, V. K., Vieira, F. G. D. & Veloso, A. R. (2018). Concept of innovation in low-income market. *Revista Brasileira de Gestão de Negócios*, 20(1): 127–149.
5. Devi, W. P. & Kumar, H. (2018). Frugal innovations and actor–network theory: A case of bamboo shoots processing in Manipur, India. *The European Journal of Development Research*, 30(1): 66–83.
6. Howell, R., van Beers, C. & Doorn, N. (2018). Value capture and value creation: The role of information technology in business models for frugal innovations in Africa. *Technological Forecasting and Social Change*, 131: 227–239. Available at www.sciencedirect.com/science/article/pii/S0040162517313161.
7. Konrad, K. & Wangler, L. U. (2018). Tailor-made technology: The stretch of frugal innovation in the truck industry. *Procedia Manufacturing*, 19: 10–17. Available at www.sciencedirect.com/science/article/pii/S2351978918300039.

8. Leliveld, A. & Knorringa, P. (2018). Frugal innovation and development research. *The European Journal of Development Research*, 30(1): 1–16.

9. Meagher, K. (2018). Cannibalizing the informal economy: Frugal innovation and economic inclusion in Africa. *The European Journal of Development Research*, 30(1): 17–33.

10. Peša, I. (2018). The developmental potential of frugal innovation among mobile money agents in Kitwe, Zambia. *The European Journal of Development Research*, 30(1): 49–65.

11. Prime, M. (2018). Frugal Innovation for Healthcare: Strategies and tools for the identification and evaluation of frugal and reverse innovations in healthcare. Unpublished PhD dissertation, Imperial College of London.

12. Prime, M., Attaelmanan, I., Imbuldeniya, A., Harris, M., Darzi, A. & Bhatti, Y. (2018). From Malawi to Middlesex: The case of the Arbutus Drill Cover System as an example of the cost saving potential of frugal innovations for the UK NHS. *BMJ Innovations*, 4: 103–110. doi: https://dx.doi.org/10.1136/bmjinnov-2017-000233.

13. Pisoni, A., Michelini, L. & Martignoni, G. (2018). Frugal approach to innovation: State of the art and future perspectives. *Journal of Cleaner Production*, 171: 107–126. Available at www.sciencedirect.com/science/article/pii/S0959652617322606.

14. Rosca, E., Reedy, J. & Bendul, J. C. (2018). Does frugal innovation enable sustainable development? *The European Journal of Development Research*, 30(1): 136–157.

15. Vossenberg, S. (2018). Frugal innovation through a gender lens: Towards an analytical framework. *The European Journal of Development Research*, 30(1): 34–48.

2017

16. Ackers, H. L., Ackers-Johnson, J., Chatwin, J. & Tyler, N. (2017). *Healthcare, frugal innovation, and professional voluntarism: A cost-benefit analysis.* London: Springer.

17. Agarwal, N., Grottke, M., Mishra, S. & Brem, A. (2017). A systematic literature review of constraint-based innovations: State of the art and future perspectives. *IEEE Transactions on Engineering Management*, 64(1): 3–15. Available at http://ieeexplore.ieee.org/document/7782762/.

18. Bhatti, Y., Prime, M., Harris, M., et al. (2017a). The search for the Holy Grail: Frugal innovation in healthcare from developing countries for reverse innovation to developed countries. *BMJ Innovations*, 3(4). Available at http://innovations.bmj.com/cgi/content/abstract/bmjinnov-2016-000186.

19. Bhatti, Y., Taylor, A., Harris, M., et al. (2017b). Global lessons in frugal innovation to improve healthcare delivery in the United States. *Health Affairs*, 36(11): 1912–1919. Available at www.healthaffairs.org/doi/abs/10.1377/hlthaff.2017.0480.

20. Bianchi, C., Bianco, M., Ardanche, M. & Schenck, M. (2017). Healthcare frugal innovation: A solving problem rationale under scarcity conditions. *Technology in Society*, 51: 74 80. Available at www.sciencedirect.com/science/article/pii/S0160791X15300452.

21. Bhutto, B. & Vyas, V. (2017). Frugal innovation in emerging markets. ISPIM Innovation Summit, 10–13 December, Melbourne, Australia.

22. European Commission. (2017). *Frugal innovation and the re-engineering of traditional techniques.* Brussels: Directorate-General for Research and Innovation, European Commission. Available at: https://publications.europa.eu/en/publication-detail/-/publication/20d6095a-2a44–11e7-ab65–01aa75ed71a1.

23. Farooq, R. & Farooq, R. (2017). A conceptual model of frugal innovation: Is environmental munificence a missing link? *International Journal of Innovation Science*, 9(4): 320–334. Available at www.emeraldinsight.com/doi/abs/10.1108/IJIS-08-2017-0076.

24. Harris, M., Bhatti, Y., Prime, M., et al. (2017). Low-cost innovation in healthcare: What you find depends on where you look. *Journal of the Royal Society of Medicine* (November). doi: https://doi.org/10.1177/0141076817738501.

25. Hossain, M. (2017). Mapping the frugal innovation phenomenon. *Technology in Society*, 51: 199–208. Available at www.sciencedirect.com/science/article/pii/S0160791X16301609.

26. Mazieri, M. R., Vils, L. & de Queiroz, M. J. (2017). Frugal innovation beyond emerging countries: The key role of developed countries. *Revista Gestão & Tecnologia*, 17(4): 232–257. Available at http://revistagt.fpl.emnuvens.com.br/get/article/view/1280.

27. Prabhu, J. (2017). Frugal innovation: Doing more with less for more. *Philosophical Transactions of the Royal Society*, 375(2095): 20160372. Available at http://rsta.royalsocietypublishing.org/content/375/2095/20160372.

28. Prabhu, J., Tracey, P. & Hassan, M. (2017). Marketing to the poor: An institutional model of exchange in emerging markets. *AMS Review*, 7(3–4): 101–122. doi: https://doi.org/10.1007/s13162–017–0100–0.

29. Prime, M., Bhatti, Y. & Harris, M. (2017). Frugal and reverse innovation in surgery. In Adrian Park and Ray Price (eds.), *Global Surgery: The Essentials*. London: Springer, pp. 193–206.

30. Weyrauch, T. & Herstatt, C. (2017). What is frugal innovation? Three defining criteria. *Journal of Frugal Innovation*, 2(1): 1. Available at https://link.springer.com/article/10.1186/s40669–016–0005-y.

31. Winterhalter, S., Zeschky, M. B., Neumann, L. & Gassmann, O. (2017). Business models for frugal innovation in emerging markets: The case of the medical device and laboratory equipment industry. *Technovation*, 66: 3–13. Available at www.sciencedirect.com/science/article/pii/S016649721730531X.

32. Woo, A. & Hew, T. K. F. (2017). A review of frugal innovation with practical implications for educators. Proceedings of the 2nd International Conference on Education and Development (*ICED*): 54–60. Available at www.dpi-proceed ings.com/index.php/dtssehs/article/view/15106.

2016

33. Agarwal, N. (2016). *Innovation landscape in developed and developing markets: A conceptual and empirical study on technology convergence and low cost innovations* (Vol. 21). Bamberg: University of Bamberg Press.

34. Altmann, P. & Engberg, R. (2016). Frugal innovation and knowledge transferability. *Research-Technology Management*, 59(1): 48–55. Available at www .tandfonline.com/doi/abs/10.1080/08956308.2016.1117323.

35. Annala, L., Sarin, A. & Green, J. L. (2016). Co-production of frugal innovation: Case of low cost reverse osmosis water filters in India. *Journal of Cleaner Production*, 171(Supplement). Available at www.sciencedirect.com/science/ article/pii/S0959652616309532.

36. Baud, I. (2016). Moving towards inclusive development? Recent views on inequalities, frugal innovations, urban geo-technologies, gender and hybrid governance. *The European Journal of Development Research*, 28(2): 119–129. Available at https://link.springer.com/article/10.1057%2Fejdr .2016.1.

37. Belkadi, F., Buergin, J., Gupta, R. K., et al. (2016). Co-definition of product structure and production network for frugal innovation perspectives: Towards a modular-based approach. *Procedia CIRP*, 50: 589–594. Available at www .sciencedirect.com/science/article/pii/S2212827116304000.

38. Bencsik, A., Renata, M. & Toth, Z. (2016). Cheap and clever-symbiosis of frugal innovation and knowledge management. *Problems & Perspectives in Management*, 14(1): 85–88. Available at http://bit.ly/2DFJqhT.

39. Colledani, M., Silipo, L., Yemane, A., et al. (2016). Technology-based product-services for supporting frugal innovation. *Procedia CIRP*, 47: 126–131. Available at www.sciencedirect.com/science/article/pii/S2212827116300634.

40. DePasse, J. W., Caldwell, A., Santorino, D., Bailey, E., Gudapakkam, S., Bangsberg, D. & Olson, K. R. (2016). Affordable medical technologies: Bringing value-based design into global health. *BMJ Innovations*, (2): 1. doi: http://dx .doi.org/10.1136/bmjinnov-2015-000069.

41. Khan, R. (2016). How frugal innovation promotes social sustainability. *Sustainability*, 8(10): 1034. Available at www.mdpi.com/2071-1050/8/10/1034.

42. Knorringa, P., Peša, I., Leliveld, A. & Van Beers, C. (2016). Frugal innovation and development: Aides or adversaries? *The European Journal of Development Research*, 28(2): 143–153. Available at https://link.springer.com/article/10.1057/ejdr.2016.3.

43. Hossain, M., Simula, H. & Halme, M. (2016). Can frugal go global? Diffusion patterns of frugal innovations. *Technology in Society*, 46: 132–139.

44. Hyvarinen, A., Keskinen, M. & Varis, O. (2016). Potential and pitfalls of frugal innovation in the water sector: Insights from Tanzania to global value chains. *Sustainability*, 8(888). Available at www.mdpi.com/2071-1050/8/9/888/htm.

45. Le Bas, C. (2016). Frugal innovation, sustainable innovation, reverse innovation: why do they look alike? Why are they different? *Journal of Innovation Economics and Management*, 3: 9–26.

46. Lehner, A. C. & Gausemeier, J. (2016). A pattern-based approach to the development of frugal innovations. *Technology Innovation Management Review*, 6(3): 13–21. Available at http://timreview.ca/sites/default/files/Issue_PDF/TIMReview_March2016.pdf#page=13.

47. Levänen, J., Hossain, M., Lyytinen, T., Hyvärinen, A., Numminen, S. & Halme, M. (2015). Implications of frugal innovations on sustainable development: Evaluating water and energy innovations. *Sustainability*, 8(1): 4. Available at www.mdpi.com/2071-1050/8/1/4/htm.

48. Mourtzis, D., Vlachou, E., Boli, N., Gravias, L. & Giannoulis, C. (2016). Manufacturing networks design through smart decision making towards frugal innovation. *Procedia CIRP*, 50: 354–359. Available at www.sciencedirect.com/science/article/pii/S2212827116304061.

49. Mourtzis, D., Vlachou, E., Giannoulis, C., Siganakis, E. & Zogopoulos, V. (2016). Applications for frugal product customization and design of manufacturing networks. *Procedia CIRP*, 52: 228–233. Available at www.sciencedirect.com/science/article/pii/S2212827116308058.

50. Pansera, M. & Sarkar, S. (2016). Crafting sustainable development solutions: Frugal innovations of grassroots entrepreneurs. *Sustainability*, 8(1): 51. Available at www.mdpi.com/2071-1050/8/1/51.

51. Prime, M., Bhatti, Y., Harris, M. & Darzi, A. (2016a). African healthcare innovation: An untapped resource? *World Hospitals and Health Services Journal. Special issue on Learning from African Innovations*, 52(3). Available at www.ihf-fih.org/resources/admindoc/1/medium_1_admindoc_1610.jpg.

52. Prime, M., Bhatti, Y., Harris, M. & Darzi, A. (2016b). Frugal innovations for healthcare: A toolkit for innovators. *Academy of Management Annual*

Meeting, 5–9 August 2016, Anaheim. Academy of Management Proceedings, 2016:1 12622. doi: https://doi.org/10.5465/AMBPP.2016.12622abstract.

53. Rosca, E., Arnold, M. & Bendul, J. C. (2016). Business models for sustainable innovation – An empirical analysis of frugal products and services. *Journal of Cleaner Production*, 162(Supplement). Available at www.sciencedirect.com/science/article/pii/S0959652616002122.

54. Shivdas, A. & Chandrasekhar, J. (2016). Sustainability through frugal innovations: An application of Indian spiritual wisdom. *Prabandhan: Indian Journal of Management*, 9(5): 7–23. Available at http://52.172.159.94/index.php/pijom/article/view/92567.

55. Tiwari, R., Kalogerakis, K. & Herstatt, C. (2016). Frugal innovations in the mirror of scholarly discourse: Tracing theoretical basis and antecedents. R&D Management Conference, Cambridge, UK.

56. Tran, V. T. & Ravaud, P. (2016). Frugal innovation in medicine for low resource settings. *BMC Medicine*, 14(1): 102. Available at https://bmcmedicine.biomedcentral.com/articles/10.1186/s12916–016–0651–1.

2015

57. Hartley, J. (2015). New development: Eight-and-a-half propositions to stimulate frugal innovation. *Public Money & Management*, 34(3): 227–232. Available at www.tandfonline.com/doi/full/10.1080/09540962.2014.908034.

58. Nielsen, K. B. & Wilhite, H. (2015). The rise and fall of the 'people's car': Middle-class aspirations, status and mobile symbolism in 'New India'. *Contemporary South Asia*, 23(4): 371–387. Available at www.tandfonline.com/doi/abs/10.1080/09584935.2015.1090951.

59. Radjou, N. & Prabhu, J. (2015). *Frugal innovation: How to do more with less.* London: The Economist and Profile Books.

60. Rai, A. S. (2015). The affect of Jugaad: Frugal innovation and postcolonial practice in India's mobile phone ecology. *Environment and Planning D: Society and Space*, 33(6): 985–1002. Available at http://journals.sagepub.com/doi/10.1177/0263775815598155.

61. Ramdorai, A. & Herstatt, C. (2015). *Frugal innovation in healthcare: How targeting low-income markets leads to disruptive innovation.* London: Springer.

62. Simula, H., Hossain, M. & Halme, M. (2015). Frugal and reverse innovations – Quo Vadis? *Current Science*, 109(5): 1–6. Available at http://bit.ly/2BvMSdu.

63. Soni, P. & Krishnan, R. T. (2014). Frugal innovation: Aligning theory, practice, and public policy. *Journal of Indian Business Research*, 6(1): 29–47. Available at www.emeraldinsight.com/doi/abs/10.1108/JIBR-03-2013-0025.

64. Sturgess, G. (2015). Frugal innovation: Beyond the concepts of 'public' and 'private'. In W. Wanna, H. A. Lee and S. Yates (eds.), *Managing under austerity, delivering under pressure: Performance and productivity in public service.* Canberra: Australian National University Press, pp. 183–194. Available at www.oapen.org/download?type=document&docid=588796.

2014

65. Barclay, C. (2014). Using frugal innovations to support cybercrime legislations in small developing states: Introducing the cyber-legislation development and implementation process model (CyberLeg-DPM). *Information Technology for Development,* 20(2): 165–195. Available at www.tandfonline.com/doi/abs/10.1080/02681102.2013.841630.

66. Bhatti, Y. (2014). Frugal innovation: Social entrepreneurs' perceptions of innovation under institutional voids, resource scarcity and affordability constraints. DPhil dissertation, Oxford University.

67. Leadbeater, C. (2014). *The frugal innovator: Creating change on a shoestring budget.* New York: Springer.

68. Mandal, S. (2014). Frugal innovations for global health – Perspectives for students. *IEEE Pulse,* 5(1): 11–13. Available at http://lifesciences.embs.org/wp-content/uploads/sites/53/2014/02/06725763.pdf.

69. Mani, G., Annadurai, K. & Danasekaran, R. (2014). Frugal innovations: The future of affordable health care. *Asian Journal of Pharmaceutical Research and Health Care,* 6(2): 1–2. Available at www.jprhc.in/index.php/ajprhc/article/download/158/126.

70. Ojha, A. K. (2014). MNCs in India: Focus on frugal innovation. *Journal of Indian Business Research,* 6(1): 4–28. Available at www.emeraldinsight.com/doi/abs/10.1108/JIBR-12-2012-0123.

71. Prathap, G. (2014). The myth of frugal innovation in India. *Current Science,* 106(3): 374–377. Available at http://ir.niist.res.in:8080/xmlui/handle/123456789/1479.

72. Zeschky, M., Widenmayer, B. & Gassmann, O. (2014). Organising for reverse innovation in Western MNCs: The role of frugal product innovation capabilities. *International Journal of Technology Management,* 64(2–4): 255–275. Available at www.inderscienceonline.com/doi/abs/10.1504/IJTM.2014.059948.

73. Zeschky, M. B., Winterhalter, S. & Gassmann, O. (2014). From cost to frugal and reverse innovation: Mapping the field and implications for global competitiveness. *Research-Technology Management,* 57(4): 20–27. Available at www.tandfonline.com/doi/abs/10.5437/08956308X5704235.

2013

74. Agarwal, N. & Brem, A. (2012). Frugal and reverse innovation: Literature overview and case study insights from a German MNC in India and China. *2012 18th International ICE Conference on Engineering, Technology and Innovation (ICE)*: 1–11. IEEE. Available at http://ieeexplore.ieee.org/document/6297683/.

75. Basu, R. R., Banerjee, P. M. & Sweeny, E. G. (2013). Frugal innovation: Core competencies to address global sustainability. *Journal of Management for Global Sustainability*, 1(2): 63–82.

76. Bhatti, Y., Khilji, S. & Basu, R., (2013). Frugal innovation. In S. Khilji and C. Rowley (eds.), *Globalization, change and learning in South Asia*. Oxford: Chandos Publishing, pp. 123–146.

77. Bhatti, Y. & Ventresca, M. (2013). How can 'frugal innovation' be conceptualized? SSRN: http://ssrn.com/abstract=2203552.

78. Brem, A. & Ivens, B. (2013). Do frugal and reverse innovation foster sustainability? Introduction of a conceptual framework. *Journal of Technology Management for Growing Economies*, 4(2): 31–50. Available at www.tmgejournal.com/abstract.php?id=302.

79. Cunha, M. P., Rego, A., Oliveira, P., Rosado, P. & Habib, N. (2013). Product innovation in resource-poor environments: Three research streams. *Journal of Product Innovation Management*, 31(2): 202–210. Available at http://onlinelibrary.wiley.com/doi/10.1111/jpim.12090/abstract.

80. Hesseldahl, P. (2013). *Frugal solutions: A manual*. Roskilde, Denmark: The Danish Universe Foundation.

81. Howitt, P., Darzi, A., Yang, G. Z., et al. (2012). Technologies for global health. *Lancet*, 380: 507–535. Available at www.thelancet.com/journals/lancet/article/PIIS0140-6736(12)61127-1/abstract.

82. Kahle, H. N., Dubiel, A., Ernst, H. & Prabhu, J. (2013). The democratizing effects of frugal innovation: Implications for inclusive growth and state-building. *Journal of Indian Business Research*, 5(4): 220–234. Available at www.emeraldinsight.com/doi/abs/10.1108/JIBR-01-2013-0008.

83. Pansera, M. (2013). Frugality, grassroots and inclusiveness: New challenges for mainstream innovation theories. *African Journal of Science, Technology, Innovation and Development*, 5(6): 469–478. Available at www.tandfonline.com/doi/abs/10.1080/20421338.2013.820445.

84. Rao, B. C. (2013). How disruptive is frugal? *Technology in Society*, 35(1): 65–73. Available at www.sciencedirect.com/science/article/pii/S0160791X13000134.

2012

85. van Beers, C., Leliveld, A. & Knorringa, P. (2012) Frugal innovation in Africa: Tracking Unilever's washing-powder sachets. In J.-B. Gewald, A. Leliveld and I. Peša (eds.), *Transforming innovations in Africa: Explorative studies on appropriation in African societies*. Leiden: Brill, pp. 59–77.

86. Bhatti, Y. 2012. What is frugal, what is innovation? Towards a theory of frugal innovation. *Academy of Management Annual Meeting*, 3–7, Boston. Academy of Management Proceedings, 2012:1 10794. Available at http://dx.doi.org/10.2139/ssrn.2005910.

87. Bhatti, Y. & Ventresca, M. (2012). The emerging market for frugal innovation: Fad, fashion, or fit? *SSRN*: http://ssrn.com/abstract=2005983.

88. Freiberg, K., Freiberg, J. & Dunston, D. (2012). *Nanovation: How a little car can teach the world to think big and act bold*. Nashville, TN: Thomas Nelson.

89. John, S. & Thakkar, K. (2012). Frugal engineering is fine, but not jugaad, says Anand Mahindra. *India Times*, 12 April. Available at http://articles.economictimes.indiatimes.com/2012–04–12/news/31331403_1_r-d-facility-chrysler-s-r-d-r-d-centre.

90. Mukerjee, K. (2012). Frugal innovation: The key to penetrating emerging markets. *Ivey Business Journal*, 76(4): 1. Available at http://iveybusinessjournal.com/publication/frugal-innovation-the-key-to-penetrating-emerging-markets/.

91. Nocera, D. G. (2012). Can we progress from solipsistic science to frugal innovation? *Daedalus*, 141(3): 45–52. Available at www.mitpressjournals.org/doi/abs/10.1162/DAED_a_00160.

92. Radjou, N., Prabhu, J. & Ahuja, S. (2012). *Jugaad innovation: Think frugal, be flexible, generate breakthrough growth*. San Francisco: Jossey-Bass.

93. Singh, R., Gupta, V. & Mondal, A. (2012). Jugaad – From 'making do' and 'quick fix' to an innovative, sustainable and low-cost survival strategy at the bottom of the pyramid. *International Journal of Rural Management*, 8(1–2): 87–105. Available at http://journals.sagepub.com/doi/abs/10.1177/0973005212461995.

94. Singh, S. K., Gambhir, A., Sotiropoulos, A. & Duckworth, S. (2012). *Frugal innovation by social entrepreneurs in India*. London: Serco Institute.

95. Tiwari, R. & Herstatt, C. (2012). Frugal innovation: A global networks' perspective. *Die Unternehmung*, 66(3): 245–274. Available at http://bit.ly/2prS3K0.

96. Bound, K. & Thornton, I. (2012). *Our frugal future: Lessons from India's innovation system*. London: NESTA.

2011

97. Petrick, I. J., and Juntiwasarakij, S. (2011). The rise of the rest: Hotbeds of innovation in emerging markets. *Research-Technology Management*, 54(4): 24–29.

98. Topol, E. J. (2011). *Medicine needs frugal innovation: Technology review*. Cambridge, MA: MIT Press.

99. Woodward, D. (2011). Plain and simple. Director Magazine, *London*. Available at www.director.co.uk/ONLINE/2011/08_11_frugal-innovation.html.

100. Zeschky, M., Widenmayer, B. & Gassmann, O. (2011). Frugal innovation in emerging markets. *Research-Technology Management*, 54(4): 38–45. Available at www.tandfonline.com/doi/abs/10.5437/08956308X5404007.

2010

101. Silicon India. (2010). Frugal innovation to accelerate financial growth in India. Available at ww.siliconindia.com/shownews/Frugal_innovation_to_acceler ate_financial_growth_in_India-nid-68373-cid-3.html.

102. Woolridge, A. (2010). The world turned upside down: A special report on innovation in emerging markets. *The Economist*, 15 April. Available at www.economist.com/node/15879369.

2009

103. Bhandari, B. (2009). Frugal innovation. *Business Standard Magazine*. Available at www.business-standard.com/india/news/frugal-innovation/360886/.

104. Gupta, A. & Wang, H. (2009). *Getting China and India right: Strategies for leveraging the world's fastest-growing economies for global advantage*. Hoboken, NJ: John Wiley and Sons.

2008

105. Nair, C. (2008). Frugal engineering: Ghosn has it wrong? Available at http://chandranrn.blogspot.com/2008/05/frugal-engineering-ghosn-has-it-wrong.html.

Index

Printed in the United States
by Baker & Taylor Publisher Services